Outdoors
with **Kids**

· ·

New York City

100 FUN PLACES TO EXPLORE IN AND AROUND THE CITY

CHERYL AND WILLIAM DE JONG-LAMBERT

Appalachian Mountain Club Books
Boston, Massachusetts

AMC is a nonprofit organization, and sales of AMC Books fund our mission of protecting the Northeast outdoors. If you appreciate our efforts and would like to become a member or make a donation to AMC, visit outdoors.org, call 800-372-1758, or contact us at Appalachian Mountain Club, 5 Joy Street, Boston, MA 02108.

outdoors.org/publications/books

Library of Congress Cataloging-in-Publication Data
de Jong-Lambert, Cheryl.
    Outdoors with kids New York city : 100 fun places to explore in and around the city / Cheryl and William de Jong-Lambert.
        p. cm.
    Includes index.
    ISBN 978-1-934028-59-9 (alk. paper)
    1. Outdoor recreation—New York (State)—New York—Guidebooks. 2. Family recreation—New York (State)—New York—Guidebooks. 3. New York (N.Y.)—Guidebooks.
I. de Jong-Lambert, William. II. Title.
    GV191.42.N7J66 2012
    796.5097471--dc23
                                        2011049762

10 9 8 7 6 5 4 3 2 1   12 13 14 15 16

· ·

To Squeaks and Bugs.

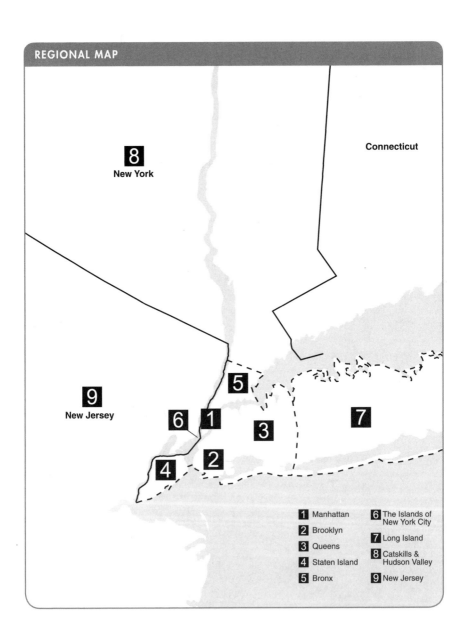

CONTENTS

· ·

THE "10 BEST" LISTS

. . . .

AT-A-GLANCE TRIP PLANNER

# Trip	Page	Best for Ages	Fee	Public Transit	Dog Friendly	Stroller Friendly
MANHATTAN						
1. Central Park (West)	16	All		🚌	🐕	👶
2. Central Park (South)	19	All	$	🚌	🐕	👶
3. Central Park (East)	22	All		🚌	🐕	👶
4. Central Park (North)	25	All		🚌	🐕	👶
5. Central Park (Central)	27	All		🚌	🐕	👶
6. Manhattan Waterfront Greenway (North)	30	5–8		🚌	🐕	👶
7. Manhattan Waterfront Greenway (South)	32	5–8		🚌	🐕	👶
8. Fort Tryon Park	34	All		🚌	🐕	👶
9. Inwood Hill Park	36	5–8		🚌	🐕	👶
10. Riverbank State Park	38	All		🚌		👶
11. Morningside Park	40	All		🚌	🐕	👶
12. Highbridge Park	43	5–8		🚌	🐕	
13. Swindler Cove Park	45	All		🚌		👶
14. East River Esplanade (67th to 125th)	47	9–12		🚌	🐕	👶
15. John Jay Park and Pool	49	5–8		🚌		👶
16. Carl Schurz Park and Gracie Mansion	51	All		🚌	🐕	👶
17. General Grant National Memorial	53	All		🚌		👶
18. Riverside Park (North)	55	0–4		🚌	🐕	👶
19. Riverside Park (South)	57	All		🚌	🐕	👶
20. Pier 84	59	5–8		🚌	🐕	👶
21. High Line	61	All		🚌		👶
22. Pier 96: Downtown Boathouse	63	9–12		🚌		
23. Battery Park	65	All		🚌	🐕	👶
24. Battery Park City Esplanade	67	All		🚌	🐕	👶

Hike / Walk	Bike	Swim / Paddle	Play-ground	Camp	Trip Highlights
✓	✓		✓		Designated outdoor classroom space
✓	✓		✓		The largest playground in the park
✓	✓		✓		Cherry blossom trees bloom here in spring
✓	✓	Swim	✓		Swimming in the park's only pool
✓	✓	Paddle	✓		Arthur Ross Pinetum's collection of evergreens
✓	✓		✓		Famous lighthouse near popular bikeway
✓	✓		✓		Artwork along the Hudson River shoreline
✓			✓		Carefully cultivated gardens
✓	✓	Paddle	✓		One of few places in the city to see a salt marsh
✓		Swim	✓		Rooftop playgrounds and merry-go-round
✓	✓		✓		Rugged cliffs and gentle lawns
✓	✓	Swim	✓		Excellent mountain biking
✓					Areas designed to attract wild animals
✓	✓				View of the Queens–Brooklyn skyline
✓	✓	Swim	✓		Rock-climbing playground epuipment
✓	✓		✓		Animal-themed art in Catbird Playground
✓			✓		Wide, flat paving stones
✓	✓		✓		Excellent sledding hill
✓	✓	Paddle	✓		Four playgrounds between beautiful gardens
✓	✓		✓		Free catch-and-release fishing
✓					Elevated park, wildflowers
		Paddle			Skyline views from a kayak
✓	✓		✓		Strolling around the fortress
✓	✓		✓		A chain of small parks and harbors

Hike/Walk	Bike	Swim/Paddle	Playground	Camp	Trip Highlights
Walk					Ice skating in winter
Walk		Swim	Playground		Wading in the fountain
Walk	Bike	Swim	Playground		Picnic tables along shaded paths
Walk	Bike		Playground		Beautiful gardens and themed playgrounds
Walk	Bike		Playground		Waterpark with wading pool and fountains
					Sailing aboard a sloop
Walk	Bike	Paddle	Playground		Swing Village's variety of swing sets
Walk	Bike		Playground		Multiple lakes and landscapes
Walk	Bike		Playground		Trails and a nature center
Walk					"Whispering" benches
Walk					Great hikes and views
Walk					Open areas for kite flying
Walk	Bike		Playground		Bustling sports fields
Walk	Bike			Camp	Hiking around abandoned hangars
Walk	Bike			Camp	Camping near former runways
Walk					An abundance of animals at the salt marsh
Walk	Bike	Swim	Playground		One of the largest swim facilities in the U.S.
Walk	Bike				Outdoor museum space for art exhibits
Walk	Bike		Playground		Playgrounds on your way to fishing area
Walk	Bike		Playground		Mountain-biking and horseback-riding trails
Walk	Bike	Paddle	Playground		Paddle boats on the city's largest lake
Walk					Strolling along garden paths
Walk	Bike		Playground		Historic tree grove
Walk	Bike	Swim			Views of the bay from the fort's top level
Walk					Forested trail around Windmill Pond
Walk					Maize maze in early fall
Walk					Bird houses and bat sanctuaries
Walk					Garden and pond views

Hike Walk	Bike	Swim Paddle	Play- ground	Camp	Trip Highlights
Walk					Maze accompanied by medieval castle
Walk	Bike		Playground		Impressive oaks around the lake
Walk	Bike	Paddle	Playground		Bridge across waterfalls
Walk	Bike	Paddle	Playground		Views of restored landscape from hilltop
Walk					Kid-friendly trails from nature center
Walk					Hike up mountain made from debris
Walk					Strolling around an outdoor museum
Walk	Bike				Hidden pond home to ducks
Walk					Wetlands creatures in many types of habitats
Walk					Trees dating to the American Revolution
Walk		Swim Paddle	Playground		Hillocks overlooking Long Island Sound
Walk		Swim Paddle	Playground		Tidal pools holding crabs and baby fish
Walk	Bike		Playground		Flat bike paths
Walk					Mansion museum with sundial on grounds
Walk	Bike	Swim	Playground		Easy bike trails
Walk		Swim	Playground		Hiking on woodsy trails
Walk					Stables at the trailhead
Walk					Exotic tree garden around the monument
Walk					Island walk with terrific views
Walk	Bike		Playground		Biking by a castle
Walk	Bike		Playground		Picnic in Lighthouse Park
Walk	Bike		Playground		Salt marsh and wetland areas
Walk	Bike	Swim Paddle	Playground		Boardwalk over the dunes
Walk	Bike	Swim Paddle		Camp	Rare Sunken Forest

# Trip	Page	Best for Ages	Fee	Public Transit	Dog Friendly	Stroller Friendly
77. Heckscher State Park	190	All	$		🐕	
78. Governor Alfred E. Smith/Sunken Meadow State Park	192	All	$		🐕	
79. Vanderbilt Museum	195	5–8	$			

CATSKILLS AND HUDSON VALLEY

# Trip	Page	Best for Ages	Fee	Public Transit	Dog Friendly	Stroller Friendly
80. Rockefeller State Park Preserve	198	5–8	$		🐕	🍼
81. Harriman State Park: Lake Sebago	200	5–8	$			
82. Clarence Fahenstock Memorial State Park: Pelton Pond	202	All	$		🐕	
83. Olana State Historic Site	205	5–8	$		🐕	
84. Walkway Over the Hudson	207	9–12		🚌	🐕	🍼
85. Taconic State Park: Rudd Pond	209	All	$			
86. Copake Falls Area and Bash Bish Falls	211	All	$		🐕	🍼
87. Bear Mountain State Park: Hessian Lake	215	All	$		🐕	🍼
88. Bear Mountain State Park: Appalachian Trail	217	9–12	$		🐕	
89. Kaaterskill Falls	219	9–12			🐕	
90. North-South Lake: Catskill Mountain House	221	All	$		🐕	🍼
91. Minnewaska State Park	223	5–8				

NEW JERSEY

# Trip	Page	Best for Ages	Fee	Public Transit	Dog Friendly	Stroller Friendly
92. Van Campens Glen	226	9–12				
93. Dunnfield Creek Natural Area	228	5–8				
94. Rattlesnake Swamp Trail	230	9–12			🐕	
95. Double Trouble State Park	233	5–8			🐕	🍼
96. Island Beach State Park	235	All	$			🍼
97. Allaire State Park	237	All	$			🍼
98. Delaware and Raritan Canal State Park	239	All			🐕	🍼
99. Washington Crossing State Park	241	All	$		🐕	
100. Grounds For Sculpture	243	5–8	$	🚌		🍼

Hike / Walk	Bike	Swim / Paddle	Play-ground	Camp	Trip Highlights
🚶	🚴	swim+paddle	🛝		Swimming or paddling in bay surf
🚶	🚴	swim+paddle	🛝		Glacier-formed bluffs
🚶					Marine museum with its animal specimens
🚶					Fishing at Swan Lake
🚶		swim	🛝	⛺	Swimming area in largest lake in the park
🚶	🚴	swim+paddle		⛺	Boat rentals at the beach
🚶					Beautiful view of the house from garden path
🚶	🚴				Longest elevated pedestrian park in the world
🚶		swim+paddle	🛝	⛺	Ice fishing near the campsites
🚶	🚴			⛺	Highest single-drop waterfall in MA
🚶	🚴	swim+paddle	🛝		Standing on boulders overlooking the lake
🚶		swim+paddle	🛝		Trailside Zoo and merry-go-round
🚶					Amazing cascade
🚶	🚴	swim+paddle	🛝	⛺	Short hike to breathtaking mountain ridge views
🚶	🚴	swim	🛝		Waterfall on your way to the beach
🚶				⛺	Riverside camping
🚶		paddle		⛺	Hike in a hemlock ravine
🚶		swim+paddle			Sightings of bears and rattlesnakes
🚶	🚴				Cranberry bog trails near historical village
🚶	🚴	swim			Ocean beach and bay trails
🚶	🚴	paddle	🛝	⛺	Horseback-riding, hiking, and biking trails
🚶	🚴	paddle			Flat walk along the canal
🚶	🚴			⛺	Walking along the Delaware River
🚶					Peacocks wandering around the art space

PREFACE

Gotham is known by many names and at different points in our life in New York City, some names have seemed more appropriate than others. However, "Emerald Empire" is the one that endures and we find most fitting now that we're parents. Fortunately, so many aspects of daily life facilitate getting outdoors to explore the city's green spaces with great frequency and for long periods. In this, the similarities between life in New York City and that in a rural village are manifold.

Indeed, working on *Outdoors with Kids New York City* crystallized the ways in which living in small towns and villages as Peace Corps teachers influenced our approach to the book's two central themes. Much as we weren't volunteers together—Cheryl was back from Guinea-Bissau before William went to Poland then Madagascar—this shared background has shaped how we view and do everything, including how we experience the outdoors and how we share it with our children.

Our years in the Peace Corps were lived largely out of doors, and walking was our primary mode of transportation—no matter the weather. In Africa, we shopped in open-air markets and cooked, ate, and socialized outdoors. Even the schools where we taught had nominal walls and felt more outside than inside. Poland, where we later lived during our son, Riley's, first year, likewise enjoys a robust farm-market culture and has a rich mountain-hiking tradition that is still very much a part of the national identity. In each place, we also witnessed parents taking babies and older children practically everywhere. Combine all this with a volunteer's relaxed attitude toward time, and we see a direct impact on our typical weekend agenda today: a massive urban hike followed by a long stay in a spot until we feel the place has been fully absorbed.

New York City is incredible for this, and in many ways it is an extension of village life. As apartment dwellers, our weekend chores are limited: We don't have a lawn to mow, a driveway to shovel, a car to maintain, or many rooms to dust and vacuum. In our view, the lack of a yard comes with the bonus of extra family time outdoors. All kids need to spend a good deal of time outside every day, and for us that means daily trips together to parks and playgrounds. Our building does not have a playroom, so we take Riley and our daughter, Halina, outside in rain and snow as well.

The lack of a car also adds greatly to the amount of time we spend outside with the kids. We walk to get the subway for school, to visit friends, to see local points of interest, and, of course, to run errands. We view household errands as opportunities to get Riley and Halina outside. When they were babies, we organized outdoor excursions around the places we needed to shop, and now that they're older—ages 8 and 5—we organize shopping around the destinations we want to see.

Living on the grid of Manhattan's streets, we quickly realized just how much walking and scootering kids can do. Twenty north–south blocks add up to a mile in our area, and any given errand may involve a walk of ten blocks or more. Return home, and we've walked at least a mile. With the kids conditioned in this way, we reinstituted our pre-parenthood practice of heading to a farther subway stop, rather than to one that's close by. In short order, Riley, then Halina, could do a straight 6-mile trip on scooters—taking in the splendor of the Hudson River from the Greenway bike path—and go the same distance on foot with a few breaks along the way.

Those breaks, whether a respite on a longer walk or the end point of a journey, are fundamental for getting city kids to know and appreciate the outdoors. We both grew up in suburban neighborhoods with great woods to explore, and deep therein, we extrapolated so much about the natural world and the sheer force of nature itself. At first blush, the city may seem anathema to this type of learning—the buildings, the cars, the noise—but a full exploration of the parks, shorelines, and rivers (even certain traffic islands) offers urban children the opportunity to see and glean as much as we did in New Jersey and Virginia, and then some.

A large and growing number of destinations feature excellent informational signs about flora, fauna, geologic foundations, and human history. The city's children also have the chance to see the birth of a park or outdoor space. Neither of us experienced this in our growing childhood communities; indeed, we watched the reverse. The five boroughs, however, as discussed in the Introduction and described throughout this book, teem with stunning examples of nature reclaiming its place on the land.

Where better to nurture a lifelong love of the outdoors?

ACKNOWLEDGMENTS

We are forever grateful to Nancy Forsyth, a publishing legend at Pearson and beyond, for taking the time to connect Cheryl and Heather Stephenson on an entirely different book project, *Our Bodies, Ourselves: Pregnancy and Birth*, back in November 2006. In equally large measure, we thank Heather, now publisher at the Appalachian Mountain Club, for embracing us as co-authors a little more than four years later when the concept for this amazing series, *Outdoors with Kids*, was developed and ready to launch.

In Kimberly Duncan-Mooney, AMC Books editor, we have someone from whom we couldn't have asked for more grace, flexibility, good humor, and positive energy at the helm of such a large and personal undertaking. Together with Athena Lakri, AMC production manager; Ellen Duffer, AMC Books editorial intern; and Chandra Asar, AMC Books production intern, Kimberly has kept this project on track in a way that has allowed us to fully explore and enjoy the research and the writing. We extend our deepest appreciation for this, as our children, Riley and Halina, now hold a trove of great family memories and personal impressions that will no doubt influence them in the years and decades to come. Thanks as well to Stefanie Brochu, director of AMC's Youth Opportunities Program; to Aaron Gorban, AMC's director of outdoor leadership training; and to AMC's Great Kids, Great Outdoors blogger Kristen Laine.

We are most fortunate that the children's grandparents, Nana Merle, Nana Beth, and Opi-din, joined us on several adventures and shared the excitement of this project throughout. The image of Nana Merle linked to Uncle Raine on inner tubes on the Delaware River will live eternally in our hearts and minds, and while we may never know where that one overgrown trail leads at Rudd Pond, we love that Nana Beth and Opi-din were willing to explore it with us. We are moved that so many others jumped on trips as well: Aunt LaLa, Uncle Eric, and the de Jong gang—Christine, Darren, Evan, and Sarah; Uncle George; Weerst, Andrew, Lauren, and Jason Bergamasco; Guapa! and Mike Hagan; Super Patton, Ginger, Megan, and Tripp Davis, along with Davis Watts; and David Gordon.

We also have many wonderful hosts to thank for their keen interest and kind hospitality during our travels outside New York City: Mr. and Mrs. Kochey and Christy Smetana, whose home in Sparta, New Jersey, is always a welcome retreat; Doreen and Melissa Masset, the sisters who run the Inn of the Hawke in Lambertville, New Jersey; the helpful staff at the Overlook Lodge in Bear Mountain, New York; Bonnie Schroader and her family at Brookside Campgrounds in Catskill, New York; Cathy Reinard and her family at the KOA campground in Copake, New York; Nancy Melius and docent Laura Bartholomew at the Oheka Castle in Huntington, New York; Jill Barnett at the Land's End Motel in Sayville, New York; and Lois and Richard Nicotra, owners of the Staten Island Hilton. Each of you, your local knowledge of our various trips was invaluable. In addition we thank Paula Rivera at Hertz for her flexible help with all the travel we packed into the summer of 2011.

Two AMC lodges—Mohican Outdoor Center and the Fire Island Cabin— fell within the geographic parameters of our book (within a two-hour drive north, south, east, or west of New York City). We loved our stays at both and came away with profound appreciation for the spirit and volunteer effort it takes to make such places run so smoothly—or simply exist at all. David and Kathy Scranton, AMC volunteers who have written about trails near Mohican, shaped the northwest New Jersey section of this book, and we thank Anita Barberis, Reva Golden, Marie Tanner, Cathy Calderon, Susan MacDonald, Dale Bailey, and many others at Fire Island whose memories and insights added richness to that trip and those pages.

We received additional content guidance from the aforementioned Aunt LaLa and Nana Merle, who could set up shop as New Jersey tour guides; Melissa Burdick Harmon, a hiker and travel writer who was a font of knowledge about must-do trips in and around the city; and Alison Lynch and Wendy Gibson at the New York State Office of Parks, Recreation and Historic Preservation, and Larry Ambrosino of SINY (Staten Island New York), who made insightful recommendations for the table of contents. We are also grateful to our neighbors—Susan, Randy, Sophia, and Eleanor—for sharing their local travel stories and photographs with us, and to Cathy Clarke for taking our author photograph.

To Cheryl's Mount Sinai Medical Center colleagues—Ann Marie Gothard, Carrie Gottlieb, and Marilyn Balamaci—extra-special thanks for your understanding and support as this project took on a life of its own.

Most of all, we are indebted to Halina and Riley for being the game and hardy children that they are. Your zeal, passions, interests, strong opinions, eagle eyes, connections, and humor enriched this book, as they do our everyday lives. We are so proud to be your parents.

INTRODUCTION

We have often been surprised by the common assumption that if you live in New York City, you don't get outdoors much. We feel like we're outside all the time. As much as we love our apartment, urban living pulls us outside with great frequency (see the Preface).

Many factors lie behind the confusion, however. You enter the city environment with different expectations than you bring to the "traditional" outdoors. In the latter, you will plan to follow blazed trails up mountains and around lakes to see stunning vistas, camp in the wild, and "rough it" a bit. To outsiders, the former brings to mind theaters, concerts, restaurants, the opera, museums—and maybe a quick detour into Central Park for a little recreation.

But the urban geography and outdoor spaces of New York City create their own kind of wilderness, which you and your kids will love. To that end, we have selected, from an abundance of possibilities, the geographic, historical, modern-day, and natural-world details that we hope will encourage you—parents and caregivers who read this book—to discover a park, green space, or hike in another neighborhood or borough. Children always love a trip to the local playground or park, but in our experience, they are invigorated and more inquisitive when you venture someplace new.

To appreciate the borough sections of this book, keep in mind that two forces are currently shaping the urban geography of New York City: the conversion of roads for pedestrians and bikers and the reclamation of former industrial space for transformation into sites for outdoor activity (see page ix for our "10 Best" list).

Thanks to the first, walking long distances has become easier and safer, and this makes trips in the city all the more enjoyable. Also admirable are the motives behind traffic-reduction efforts. Walking promotes health, and by reducing exhaust emissions, it helps protect the environment, historical landmarks, and, again, health. In addition, in many places street parking is limited or impossible to find, and parking garages can be expensive. Overall, cars are not a good option.

The second force—the reclamation of former industrial space, and the subsequent rescue of New York's ecosystem at large—is often thanks to the initiative and energy of local neighborhood organizations. Volunteers across the city have both raised money and contributed physical labor to create parklands or restore parks that had languished for many years. Private donors have also stepped in to fund innovative ideas such as the High Line, a linear park on a former elevated subway track (Trip 21).

In addition to discovering that New York City is becoming ever greener, you may have to rethink how you interpret space. Many spaces will feel smaller than they actually are. For example, if you walk through Gantry Plaza State Park (Trip 43) exactly as we have described it (hike west from the subway station, out onto all the piers, and around Piers Park) you will have walked over a mile. You will probably notice that it doesn't feel that far, but that's not just because the land is flat. The cacophony of details—the antique Pepsi-Cola sign in the middle distance, gantries hovering above, landmark buildings across the East River—distract you from thinking about the distance you're traveling.

Visiting destinations in the Catskills, Hudson Valley, and Long Island will put the city sites and recent developments in context with the larger history of the Empire State. Before the West was settled, New York State, cut through by the mighty Hudson River, occupied a place in the American imagination that lingers today. Kaaterskill Falls (Trip 89) and Olana State Historic Site (Trip 83) take you back to a time when a young nation was coming into its own. Not to be outdone, the trips in New Jersey provide convincing proof that the Garden State could also be called the "the great woods and beautiful mountains" state.

A few final points, or rather names, that represent distinct eras in the development of parks and green spaces in New York City: Frederick Law Olmsted and Calvert Vaux were legendary nineteenth-century architects and landscape designers who developed Central Park (Trips 1–5), Prospect Park (Trip 32), and many others in the city and around the nation. Robert Moses, the still-controversial urban planner, held multiple powerful state and city government positions from 1924 to 1968. He is responsible for greatly expanding the state park system, and to the city, he added 658 playgrounds, 10 giant pools, and numerous parks. He also created 13 bridges and hundreds of miles of highway, and, in the process, destroyed some pristine lands and cherished neighborhoods.

As for the final names—Mayor Michael Bloomberg and city Parks Commissioner Adrian Benepe—we can only speak from the present. Since Bloomberg took office in 2002 and appointed Benepe, the city has become greener, cleaner, more accessible, and friendlier to pedestrians and cyclists. We notice it, and we're glad. Welcome to the Big Apple.

HOW TO USE THIS BOOK

With 100 destinations to choose from, you may wonder how to decide where to go. The regional map at the front of this book and the locator maps at the beginning of each section will help you narrow down the trips by location, and the At-a-Glance Trip Planner that follows the table of contents will provide more information to guide you toward a decision. The four 10 Best lists might also influence your selections. Is everyone up for an urban hike, or are you more in the mood to see how nature is taking over a tract of land within the city?

If your children are old enough, involve them in the selection process. Do they love water play? Do they want to look for birds? Do they want to try an oar at boating? It can also help to connect the city to people and places they know. Did your daughter have a teacher who lived in Queens? Does your son love to walk over the Brooklyn Bridge? Are they interested in learning more about these boroughs? When kids have a say in the trip they are taking, they will be more vested in the excursion and everyone will have a much better time.

Once you settle on a destination and turn to a trip in this book, you'll find a series of icons that indicate whether the destination is accessible via public transportation; is stroller friendly; offers hiking, bicycling, swimming, or paddling; has a playground or camping facilities; or charges fees. An icon also indicates the ages for which the activities there are best suited.

The trip overview (in italic type) summarizes the main activities or points of interest that children will enjoy at the destination. Information on the basics follows: address, hours of operation, fees, contact information, bathrooms, water/snacks, and available maps. The recommendations are based on our perceptions.

The directions explain how to reach the destination by public transportation and, for a few trips, by car. Throughout the city, public parking is limited in availability and duration, so driving is discouraged for most destinations. As discussed in the Introduction, New York City has also made great strides in becoming accessible to pedestrians and cyclists, and, in some areas, less accessible for cars.

If you do drive, the directions section also includes Global Positioning System (GPS) coordinates. When you enter the coordinates into your GPS device, it will provide driving directions. Whether or not you own a GPS device, it is wise to consult an atlas, and no matter how you travel, it is always helpful to have a city street map with bus and subway information.

The maps that accompany some of the trips will help you arrive with the lay of the land in mind. For those destinations without maps, websites and other information about where to find maps are included in the bolded section at the start of each description. Hours, fees, and other details are all subject to change, so be sure to check websites or call the locations before heading out.

At the end of each trip overview, the Remember section does one of two things. In some cases, it provides insights that can help you sidestep potential glitches on the trip. In others, it alerts you to sights or experiences that are worth the extra effort to pursue.

Every trip includes a Plan B section, which gives ideas for nearby activities in case the original plan does not work out. Plan B should never be seen as a failure. Sometimes the weather doesn't cooperate, other times a long hike or day away from home isn't in the cards for a cranky child. Keep in mind that you're trying to share and foster a love of the outdoors with your kids, not make them go on a march.

You can find food and beverages virtually anywhere in New York City, which is handy if you like ad hoc picnics. The widespread availability of goods also extends to critical supplies such as wipes, diapers, sunblock, and sippy cups. For the few places that don't have a number of viable restaurants, delis, cafés, or shops near the destination, a Where to Eat Nearby section offers tips, or recommendations that you pack your own provisions.

All of the trips in this book have some sort of "payoff," from swimming and kayaking to carousels and destination playgrounds that have interesting themes and equipment. Some payoffs, such as kayaking on the Hudson River (see Trip 22), are the focus of the trip, while others are a layover on, or the end point of, a longer journey.

There are other payoffs to taking children outdoors, of course: payoffs in family time, in children's growing confidence and skills, in their increased comfort in the outdoors and connection to the natural world. Those are part of every destination.

STEWARDSHIP AND CONSERVATION

Frequent, unstructured outdoor play can increase children's health, school performance, self-esteem, and feelings of connection to nature. Kids who feel connected to nature today are likely to be tomorrow's conservation leaders. The Appalachian Mountain Club (AMC) is committed to helping kids build strong connections to the outdoor world, including its protection. When you bring young people outdoors, you should teach them to take care of the natural resources around them.

The first step in raising a conservation-conscious child takes place when that child falls in love with a special place. Foster a sense of fun at the outdoor destinations you visit, and then go one step further: Teach your children the Leave No Trace guidelines (see below). Join volunteer groups and participate in park cleanups, or sign up for a naturalist-led walk to explore the plants, animals, rocks, trees, and waterways.

AMC's regional chapters are a great resource. Join AMC for access to the chapters' family committees, which offer programs to get kids outdoors and teach conservation strategies. Suitable for adults and children of varying ages, these programs can be close to home or farther afield, and they include hiking, paddling, apple picking, winter weekends, exploring conservation areas and parks, and more.

LEAVE NO TRACE

The Appalachian Mountain Club (AMC) is a national educational partner of Leave No Trace, a nonprofit organization dedicated to promoting and inspiring responsible outdoor rec- reation through education, research, and partnerships. The Leave No Trace program seeks to develop wild land ethics—ways in which people think and act in the outdoors to minimize their impact on the areas they visit and to protect our natural resources for future enjoyment. Leave No Trace unites four federal land management agencies—the U.S. Forest Service, National Park Service, Bureau of Land Management, and U.S. Fish and Wildlife Service—with manufacturers, outdoor retailers, user groups, educators, organizations such as AMC, and individuals.

The Leave No Trace ethic is guided by these seven principles:

1. **Plan Ahead and Prepare.** Know the terrain and any regulations applicable to the area you're planning to visit, and be prepared for extreme weather or other emergencies. This will enhance your enjoyment and ensure that you've chosen an appropriate destination. Small groups have less impact on resources and on the experiences of other backcountry visitors.

2. **Travel and Camp on Durable Surfaces.** Travel and camp on established trails and campsites, rock, gravel, dry grasses, or snow. Good campsites are found, not made. Camp at least 200 feet from lakes and streams, and focus activities on areas where vegetation is absent. In pristine areas, disperse use to prevent the creation of campsites and trails.

3. **Dispose of Waste Properly.** Pack it in, pack it out. Inspect your camp for trash or food scraps. Deposit solid human waste in catholes dug 6 to 8 inches deep, at least 200 feet from water, camps, and trails. Pack out toilet paper and hygiene products. To wash yourself or your dishes, carry water 200 feet from streams or lakes and use small amounts of biodegradable soap. Scatter strained dishwater.

4. **Leave What You Find.** Cultural or historical artifacts, as well as natural objects such as plants and rocks, should be left as found.

5. **Minimize Campfire Impacts.** Cook on a stove. Use established fire rings, fire pans, or mound fires. If you build a campfire, keep it small and use dead sticks found on the ground.

6. **Respect Wildlife.** Observe wildlife from a distance. Feeding animals alters their natural behavior. Protect wildlife from your food by storing rations and trash securely.

7. **Be Considerate of Other Visitors.** Be courteous, respect the quality of other visitors' backcountry experience, and let nature's sounds prevail.

AMC is a national provider of the Leave No Trace Master Educator course. AMC offers this 5-day course, designed especially for outdoor professionals and land managers, as well as the shorter 2-day Leave No Trace Trainer course at locations throughout the Northeast.

For Leave No Trace information and materials, contact the Leave No Trace Center for Outdoor Ethics, P.O. Box 997, Boulder, CO 80306. Phone: 800-332-4100 or 302-442-8222; fax: 303-442-8217; web: lnt.org. For a schedule of AMC Leave No Trace courses, see outdoors.org/education/lnt.

Getting Started

Creating a lifetime connection to the outdoors starts with sharing fun experiences. Getting your kids outside doesn't need to be difficult—focus on enjoyment and exploration, one hike, day at the beach, bike ride, or winter walk at a time.

GETTING OUTSIDE NEAR HOME

A great way to get started is to get outdoors in your backyard or neighborhood. Whether it's walking to a local park or climbing trees in your yard, make time to play in nature and reap the benefits. Here are some ideas for projects and activities you can do close to home and in all types of weather.

In Your Neighborhood

- Build Fairy Houses: Construct tiny "homes" from sticks, twigs, leaves, rocks, and other natural materials. (Don't use living plants.)
- Feed the Birds: Set up a bird feeder (you can make a simple one by spreading peanut butter on a pinecone). See which types of birds come; have the kids keep a log of their visits.
- Plant Something: Start small with a flowerpot or window box. Or plant a vegetable garden, a flower garden, a butterfly garden, an herb garden, or a tree.
- Follow a Map: Devise a local treasure hunt, or try orienteering or geocaching (see page 42).
- Take the Inside Outside: Bring out your kids' traditionally indoor toys and set up a play space outside. Getting out of a routine can be entertaining.
- Embrace the Dark: Go on a night walk and gaze at the moon and stars. The world will feel different and bigger.
- Camp at Home: Set up a tent in the backyard if possible, or in the living room! Let the kids invite friends over, take turns telling stories, and make s'mores (the marshmallows can be "raw").

In a Park

- Have a Picnic: Have your kids help you plan a picnic and enjoy eating together at your favorite park.
- Celebrate Outdoors: Plan birthday parties, family visits, or holiday traditions that involve getting outside.
- Volunteer: Many parks have volunteer organizations that plant flowers, donate toys for the sandbox, and hold events. If your local park doesn't have such an organization, consider starting your own.

Through the Seasons

- During spring, look for signs of life in streams, ponds, puddles, or vernal pools. Local nature centers often make note of the seasonal vernal pools and organize events around salamander crossings.
- When it's raining, head out with umbrellas or put kids in bathing suits and let them run around and splash in puddles.
- During fall, try leafy crafts: Have kids collect leaves they like and iron them between sheets of wax paper to make a bookmark or window decoration. Or make a leaf sailboat from fallen pinecones, sticks, or pieces of bark. A leaf can be the sail, a stick the mast, and a pinecone or piece of bark the boat body.
- In winter, go sledding, look for animal tracks, build a snow fort, or make snow sculptures.

GROWING UP IN THE OUTDOORS

As parents or caregivers, we learn quickly that children have different needs at different ages. That's true of children in the outdoors as well. Remember, your enthusiasm is contagious. If you show excitement for the outdoors, your children will become excited too.

Babies, Toddlers, and Preschoolers (up to age 4)

With very small children, your primary goal is to create a positive association with being outdoors.

- It's surprisingly easy to bring babies on many outdoor excursions. Babies are easily carried and their needs are relatively simple: Keep them fed, warm, and dry. Nursing moms shouldn't hesitate about getting outside with their babies. No need to pack food for a baby who's nursing!
- Once children begin walking, you may cover less distance than with babies. Small children love repetition and engage with nature on a micro level. Young explorers may count every wildflower or try to jump over every rock on a trail, or want to turn around after half a mile or half an hour. Children at this age respond well to simple games, songs, and storytelling.
- Small children have a limited understanding of time, distance, and danger, and require constant supervision, especially near water and on steep terrain.

Young Children (ages 5 to 8)

Young children want to do everything you do and they'll try hard to keep up. This makes them great company outdoors.

- Children these ages are eager to learn new skills and information. Simple lessons work well.

- Young children are easily distracted or discouraged, but are also readily engaged and are easily motivated by clear goals and imaginative games. Offer encouragement and support for their efforts.
- Children at this stage still need you to set boundaries and safety guidelines. They're old enough, though, that you can share your reasoning with them. You can also start asking children to carry their own backpack.
- Inviting a friend along on an outdoor adventure lets children share the experience with someone their own age—and often makes your job easier.
- Young children may be able to join in child-focused group activities in the outdoors, but may not have long enough attention spans to join mixed-age groups.

Older Children (9 to 12)

Older children can take on more trip responsibilities and may enjoy testing their limits in outdoor activities. They may also focus more on peer relationships.

- Being outdoors offers parents the chance to engage their children with lessons about nature, history, weather, or any number of topics.
- Enlist older children in trip planning and decision-making; reading maps and assisting in navigation; and carrying personal gear.
- Leave electronic devices behind or turn them off. Talking on a phone, texting, or playing an electronic game is distracting and noisy.
- Children at this age often want to bring friends along on outings, but may be more reluctant to try something new in front of their peers or to follow safety guidelines.
- Some preteens will be ready to join organized mixed-age groups and educational activities.

TRIP PLANNING

When you're heading farther than the local park, you will want to map out your day and activity ahead of time. Just be prepared for changes.

Choose Your Goals

For most outdoor adventures, shorter is better with young children. Consider your child's pace and stamina when selecting destinations and routes.

- Think about payoffs: Hike to a waterfall or bicycle to a beach with public swimming.
- For cycling, plan trips that are not as hilly as adult trips and that minimize traffic and maximize children's safety. Bike paths are often fun for families, but can be busy; when kids are just learning to ride, you may be better off heading to a park or reservation with bike trails.

Before You Go

- Check the weather forecast. Be prepared for changes in the weather conditions.
- Leave a trip plan with someone you trust before you head out.
- Check directions, available parking, and facility hours.
- Always remember to check subway and bus schedules in advance. Visit mta.info or call 511 to learn about delays and track closures.

Once You're There

- Go over your route with children. Give them trail names when hiking and talk about stopping points and turnaround times. Tell children to always stop at a trail junction. Remind them that the group must stay together. Consider designating a "lead"—the person who will be at the front of the group—and a "sweep"—the person who stays at the back of the group to ensure that everyone stays together.
- Make a contingency plan for if you get separated, and make sure children understand it.
- Find the bathroom. Each trip description in this book gives information on where bathrooms are located.

Schedules and Routines

- Keep children's schedules and routines in mind. If your daughter eats lunch every day at 11:30 A.M. but you're holding out for the picnic tables at the end of the trail, no one is going to have fun. If your son usually has a nap right after lunch and you're starting a hike at that time, you're asking for a meltdown.
- Flexibility is important, too. If kids are having a blast climbing on rocks, there's no need to make them stop just because it's lunchtime.

Sharing the Outdoors with Others

- Inviting other children can make a big difference in fun and motivation.
- Having other adults along on a trip can give you extra sets of eyes—and arms. But be careful that socializing does not take your attention away from children. This is especially important with small children.
- Sharing outdoor activities with more than one family is a good way for single parents to get children outdoors.
- Grandparents and older adults also can be great additions to outings.

Fees, Deals, and Discounts

Many of the destinations in this guide are free or have a minimal cost. Some ask for voluntary donations. The following tips can help you save money while getting outdoors.

- Becoming a member of the Appalachian Mountain Club links you to a local chapter that organizes outings and offers discounts on everything from guidebooks and maps to Family Adventure Camps. Visit outdoors.org for more information about deals, discounts, and events.
- An annual membership to the Wildlife Conservation Society (wcs.org) is a worthwhile investment for days when you want to be outdoors but don't have the time to map out a new destination. The membership provides unlimited access to the Bronx Zoo, Central Park Zoo, Prospect Park Zoo, Queens Zoo, and the New York Aquarium at Coney Island.
- Consider purchasing an annual Empire Passport for $65 if you plan to visit New York State parks.

CLOTHING AND GEAR

Good-fitting, well-functioning clothes and equipment—from rain jackets and backpacks to hiking boots—can mean the difference between a good time and a miserable one. But you don't need to spend a lot of money; you can often find well-made snowsuits, synthetic long underwear, and life jackets for children at thrift stores or gear swaps. You also don't need all of the items listed below for every type of outing. For a day in the park, a fleece jacket, sturdy shoes, and long pants may do the trick.

Outdoor Clothing Basics
- Put kids in long-sleeved shirts and long pants for increased sun protection or to keep bugs away from tender skin.
- Lightweight and easily packed, hats offer quick warmth, shade children from sun, and protect from wind and cold.
- Teach kids to wear clothes that are quick-drying and retain warmth even when wet. That means steering clear of jeans, sweats, and cotton shirts; instead, choose wicking synthetics, fleeces, wools, and quick-drying nylons.
- Dress children in layers. Light wicking layers go under heavier layers, which are under warm outer layers and wind protection. Adding or removing layers keeps kids from being soaked with sweat or rain, and from becoming too hot or too cold.

Footwear
- Choose appropriate footwear. For hiking, wear closed-toe shoes with good ankle support. For biking, wear closed-toe shoes, not sandals or flip-flops. For paddling, pick closed-toe shoes that can get wet repeatedly and dry quickly. For snowshoeing, choose thick snow boots or hiking boots that hold their shape under snowshoe straps or buckles.

- Synthetic liner socks under wool socks offer the most warmth and blister protection when hiking, skiing, or snowshoeing. If you need smaller sizes that outdoor manufacturers don't make, kids' nylon dress socks work decently as liners.

Helmets

- Helmets are a must for bicycling, including riding in trailers and in bike seats. Fit is important for safety; the helmet should sit level on a child's head and fit securely with the strap fastened.
- Babies may not have the neck strength to wear a helmet until after age 1.
- Although it may be tempting to buy a used helmet at a yard sale, you may have trouble assessing its condition and whether it meets current safety standards. New helmets are relatively inexpensive (about $10 at discount stores) and worth the investment.

Dressing for Summer

- Sun hats protect children from intense sun. Look for lightweight hats with wide brims or visors long enough to shade a child's entire face. "Safari" hats with removable neck protection also work well, as do bandannas.
- Protect children's eyes with sunglasses, especially if you're traveling on water or over open landscapes. Expect to lose a few pairs along the way.

Dressing for Winter

- Don't overdress your children for winter. When active, people generate heat quickly. Dress in layers and remove a layer as necessary.
- One-piece snowsuits work best for younger children. Older children should practice the same layering system as adults. A common mistake: putting a child in a too-heavy winter coat when hiking, snowshoeing, or cross-country skiing.
- Balaclavas are great winter hats for kids because they cover both head and neck, leaving just an opening for the face.
- Keep toes warm—invest in a pair of wool or fleece socks.
- Mittens keep small hands warmer than gloves, so unless children need to use their fingers, mittens are best in winter. Wool socks can double as mittens.
- Remember sunglasses when out on the snow.
- Attach plastic bags over hands or mittens and socks or shoes to protect against rain or to add warmth in cold conditions.

Snowshoes and Skis

- Select snowshoes by weight, and look for ones that are easy for children to put on and take off.
- Waxless skis are the best choice for children who are learning the basics of cross-country skiing.
- Many Nordic centers and downhill ski resorts rent snowshoes and cross-country ski equipment for children.

Dressing for Wind or Rain

- Getting wet is often a safety risk, so be sure children have rain gear that is waterproof, not just water resistant. For extended trips, rain pants are a good addition to a rain jacket. Ponchos aren't recommended because they don't cover enough of the body and are useless in wind. If you plan to be out and active in rain for any length of time, breathable rain gear works best.
- Wearing a visored hat under a raincoat helps keep the hood of the raincoat out of a child's eyes.
- Wind protection is especially important when hiking or snowshoeing in the mountains or in exposed areas, paddling on the ocean or open water, bicycling, or cross-country skiing.

Dressing Babies for the Outdoors

- In hot weather, try thin, cotton one-pieces without feet to keep babies from overheating.
- In cooler weather, babies may need a hat or mittens before you do because they're not moving their bodies.
- In winter, babies stay warmer in snowsacks, rather than snowsuits with legs. If you ski or snowshoe with a child in a back carrier or open sled, remember that the child is not exercising and warming up as you are. Dress a baby in warm layers, minimize exposed skin, and check often to be sure the baby's nose, face, neck, and limbs are warm.
- Choose brimmed hats with a strap under the chin so they stay on.
- Pack twice as many diapers, covers, and clothing changes as you think you'll need. Bring several sturdy plastic bags to carry out soiled diapers and clothing.

PACKING

No single packing list can cover every activity in this book. The basic list below should work well for most day hikes. We've also provided specific tips for children's packs and for carriers, trailers, and sleds.

Basic Pack

You'll want to have the following items in your bag or backpack on outings in every season.

- ❏ Cell phone: Be sure to have emergency phone numbers on hand, though service is unreliable in rural and remote areas.
- ❏ Water: Bring enough for yourself, plus more to share. Two quarts per person is usually adequate, depending on the weather and the length of the trip.
- ❏ Food: Crankiness is increased by hunger. Pack high-energy snacks such as nuts, dried fruit, or granola bars. Pack a lunch for longer trips. Include children in this task as much as possible.
- ❏ Outerwear: wind protection, rain protection, warm jackets. Pack for the range of weather you're likely to encounter.
- ❏ Extra clothing: Extra socks, mittens, hats, and sunglasses come in handy and don't take up much room. Bringing extra warm clothes in all but the hottest weather is a good idea. If your activity takes you to a lake, river, stream, or ocean, a change of clothing may be required for everyone.
- ❏ Wet wipes
- ❏ Plastic bags
- ❏ Sunscreen
- ❏ First-aid kit: adhesive bandages, athletic or hospital tape, gauze, blister protection, small scissors, children's antihistamines, nonprescription painkillers, and tweezers for removing splinters
- ❏ Toilet paper or a pack of tissues
- ❏ Map and compass
- ❏ Whistle
- ❏ Flashlight or headlamp
- ❏ Insect repellent
- ❏ Extra clothes to leave in the car for the trip home

Optional Items

- ❏ Binoculars
- ❏ Camera
- ❏ Books: guidebooks, nature guides, picture books for young children
- ❏ Journal or loose paper, plus pens, pencils, or crayons
- ❏ Bandannas

❑ Fishing poles

❑ Trekking poles

Carriers, Trailers, and Pulks

At very young ages, for trips that don't involve a stroller, children are usually carried in a front pack or backpack, in a bike trailer, or on a sled behind skis. As children get older, bike seats and bike extensions may help you enjoy the outdoors together.

- Front packs are a good idea for babies up to about 6 months of age. They get the benefit of your body warmth, and you have a close-up view of them.
- You can move older babies to a child backpack when they're able to hold up their heads unaided.
- Children can ride in bike trailers as soon as they're able to hold their heads up independently. Be careful on bumpy terrain, however, and remember bike helmets, as with any cycling activity.
- Attached bike seats are appropriate when children can hold their heads upright while wearing a helmet and can comfortably sit upright on their own.
- For a period of a few years in between riding in a bicycle trailer and riding longer distances on a separate bicycle, your child may enjoy riding on a one-wheel child bike extension, complete with pedals, that attaches to the back of your bicycle. This may extend the distance you are able to enjoy riding together, but requires training and good communication.
- When cross-country skiing, it's easier and safer to use a sled built specifically for pulling children, called a pulk, than it is to ski with a baby in a backpack or front child carrier. You may start using a pulk with a child between 6 and 12 months old. The sled has two poles that are secured to the adult with a padded waist belt. Many cross-country ski areas have pulks available for rent.

Paddling Gear

- When paddling, store gear in specialized dry bags or in double-bagged, heavy-duty plastic bags.
- If you do a lot of paddling, you may want to invest in sized-down paddles so children can participate.
- Children should always wear personal flotation devices (PFDs). Parents should set an example by wearing PFDs as well.

Children's Packs

For many reasons—including safety, increasing skills and responsibility, and engaging them in the outdoors experience—children should carry some of their gear as early as possible.

- Food: Carrying their own snacks or lunches lets children replenish their energy on the go and also minimizes arguments among siblings over who has more of a favored food.
- Water: Carrying their own water encourages children to drink on the trail. You may want to try personal hydration systems for them.
- Clothing: When kids have their own jackets, rain gear, or wind protection, they're more likely to put them on and take them off when needed.
- Whistle: Teach children how to use a whistle for safety.
- Map and compass: Older children can help with route-finding (and learn a valuable skill while they're at it).
- Address and phone number: Put this important information in a water-proof bag and in a place (such as a pack or pocket) where your child knows to find it.
- Fun stuff: sketch pad, magnifying glass, binoculars, camera, Frisbee, ball, glow sticks, coloring books, harmonica. Young children may want to bring a favorite toy or stuffed animal.

SAFETY

Being prepared and taking a few precautions can reduce problems on your outings.

Sun and Heat

Children's sweat glands don't fully develop until adolescence, so they have a harder time managing extreme heat than adults.
- Apply sunscreen thoroughly before setting out for activities.
- During very hot weather, seek out shade or water to play in.
- Make sure children drink plenty of liquid to prevent heat exhaustion or heatstroke. Be alert for symptoms, including nausea, headache, dizziness, pale skin, and shallow breathing.
- If a child becomes overheated, move to a cool, shady spot. Apply wet cloths, loosen clothing, and have the child sip water.

Hypothermia

Hypothermia is a life-threatening condition that occurs when the body's core temperature drops. Hypothermia can happen in any season, even summer. Wet, windy conditions can be as dangerous as severe cold.
- The best treatment for hypothermia is prevention. Cool to cold temperatures combined with moisture and wind cause hypothermia, so stay dry and choose clothing that keeps you warm even when wet, such as wool and fleece. Remember your raincoats. Keep well hydrated and nourished.

- Know the signs: loss of judgment, shivering, stumbling, trouble speaking, and difficulty with motor skills such as unzipping a coat.
- A child who has become chilled should immediately be removed from the windy and cold conditions and changed into dry, warm clothes. Give the child warm, sweet liquids to drink and food with protein and sugar, if possible.
- To check a baby, feel the neck, torso, and limbs. If limbs feel cool to touch, a baby may be at risk for hypothermia.

Dehydration
- Make sure children drink plenty of water when active outdoors.
- Bring your own water. Never drink untreated water from outdoor sources.

Insects
- Mosquitoes can be a minor or significant nuisance, depending on seasonal and daily conditions. In the Northeast, some mosquitoes are infected with the eastern equine encephalitis virus, a rare but potentially fatal disease that can be transmitted to humans. The threat is generally greatest in the evening hours, when mosquitoes are most active.
- Ticks carry Lyme disease. Have children wear long sleeves, and long pants tucked into socks. After every outdoor adventure, don't forget to check for ticks (visit cdc.gov/ticks for tips).
- If any child on your trip is allergic to bee or wasp stings, he or she (or a designated adult) should carry an Epi kit.
- Insect repellent containing DEET is not recommended for children. Teach older children to wash their hands after applying repellent, if possible, and to avoid getting it in their eyes or mouths.

Plants and Animals
- Poison ivy is ubiquitous in the Northeast. Teach children to identify its clusters of three leaves that shine in the sun but are dull in the shade. If a child comes into contact with poison ivy, wash the affected area with soap as soon as possible.
- Train young children not to eat berries or plants.
- Teach children to observe, but not feed, wild animals. Explain that they shouldn't get between a mother and her young, such as a mother bear and cubs or a moose cow and calves.

Lightning
- If you're caught in a lightning storm, seek shelter, preferably in a building or car. If neither is nearby, seek shelter among trees that are of equal height. Avoid peaks, towers, and single trees in open areas. Remove packs or any-

thing containing metal. Squat down, if possible on a foam pad, with your heels touching, knees apart, and hands off the ground.

- If you're on water and see a storm approaching, immediately head for shore.
- Count the number of seconds between lightning and thunder to estimate how far you are from the storm. Estimate one mile for every five seconds. If the number of seconds is decreasing, the storm is headed your way.

Water Safety

Children should always be supervised while around water. Remember these swimming safety tips, adapted from the American Red Cross:

- Never leave a young child unattended near water and do not trust a child's life to another child; teach children to always ask permission to go near water.
- Have young children and inexperienced swimmers wear U.S. Coast Guard–approved life jackets around water and in boats, but do not rely on life jackets alone. Be sure a jacket fits the user. Check buckles and straps.
- The Coast Guard does not recommend taking infants on board recreational boats and cautions that Infant Type II personal flotation devices up to 18 pounds may not always perform as expected.
- Establish rules for your family and enforce them without fail. For example, no swimming unless you can touch bottom.
- Know how to safely operate the type of watercraft you will use. Plan what you will do if a boat capsizes. Enroll in a boating safety class.

If you are going to a New York City park with a pool and you think you might swim, it's important to plan accordingly:

- Pools are open from 11 A.M. to 3 P.M., and again from 4 to 7 P.M.
- You must wear a bathing suit to go onto the pool deck, even if you are not planning to swim.
- Bags are not permitted on the pool deck, and you cannot bring cameras, handheld devices, cell phones, e-book readers, or other electronic devices.
- Free day-use lockers are available, but you must bring your own padlock.
- Swimming aids, water toys, and flotation devices are prohibited.
- Books and bound periodicals are permitted on the pool deck, but newspapers are not.

Full regulations can be found at nycgovparks.org/sub_things_to_do/facilities/af_pool_rules.html or by calling 311.

Getting Lost

- When hiking, sign in and out at trail registers to leave a record in case of emergency.

- Adults in the group should be able to use a map and guidebook. Keep the group together, with everyone within eye sight. Try a game, such as everyone counting off, to keep track.
- Teach children to stay together, keep to the trail, and wait at trail junctions if the group gets spread out. Point out landmarks as you go along to help build images of the trail in children's minds.
- Teach children to stay in one place, preferably in the open, if they get lost and to blow their whistles (three short blasts). The best thing adults can do in this situation is to stay calm and to keep the rest of the group together.
- Consider enrolling in a program like AMC's Lost and Alone workshops, which teach children how to stay with a group in the outdoors and also what to do if they become separated from the group.

Manhattan

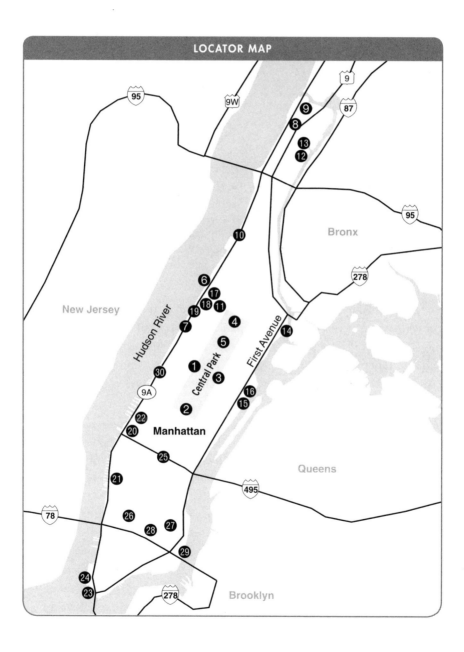

LOCATOR MAP

Trip 1

All Ages

Central Park (West)

The western section of New York's famous Central Park offers differing terrain for walks or bicycle rides, plus plenty of room for picnicking in beautiful landscapes.

Address: West 96th Street at Eighth Avenue (Central Park West), Manhattan, NY
Hours: 6 A.M. to 1 A.M. daily
Fee: Free
Contact: centralparknyc.org; 212-310-6600 or call 311
Bathrooms: Tennis courts (see Trip 5); Delacorte Theatre (see Trip 5)
Water/Snacks: Vendors throughout park; several restaurants and grocery stores one block west of Central Park West on Columbus Avenue
Maps: USGS Central Park; centralparknyc.org/maps
Directions by Car: Public parking is very limited; driving is discouraged. *GPS coordinates:* 40° 47.496′ N, 73° 57.884′ W.
Directions by Subway: Take the B or C train to West 81st Street/American Museum of Natural History, to West 96th Street, or to West 72nd Street.

The first public park built in America, Central Park receives about 35 million guests per year. At 843 acres—or 6 percent of Manhattan's total acreage—it offers room for everyone, and a great variety of outdoor activities. Bike routes wind throughout the park, and on weekends, the roads and parkways located inside park walls are closed to motor traffic so visitors can freely skate, bicycle, and ride scooters.

Starting at the West 96th Street entrance and heading south, you will soon encounter the Seneca Village Site, which was home to the first predominantly African American community in Manhattan. The village once stretched from West 89th and West 81st streets but was demolished in 1857 to make way for the park. A decade-long archeological dig that ended in June 2011 unearthed much evidence of the community's existence. Contact the Central Park Conservancy for free periodic tours of this area.

Continuing south, you will enter Naturalists' Walk, an outdoor classroom—complete with split-log benches—for teaching students about nature. A network of paths, which run from about West 81st to West 77th streets, takes you through a range of landscapes, from rocky outcroppings to a verdant valley.

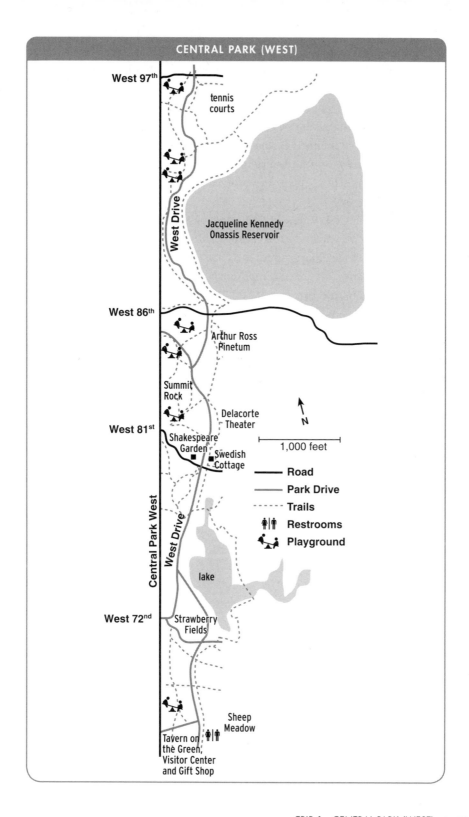

Near the park entrance at West 72nd Street is the legendary Strawberry Fields, a memorial to singer-songwriter John Lennon. It is located across from the Dakota Building where he resided.

Sheep Meadow, a 15-acre preserve that is open from May to mid-October, rounds out the walk through Central Park West. To give the park an English feel, sheep were maintained in this area for about seven decades, ending in 1934. The former sheepfold building became the renowned Tavern on the Green restaurant, which closed in 2010. The building is now an information center and gift shop.

Numerous themed playgrounds are throughout this area. From the north heading south, they include the Rudin Family Playground, the Wild West Playground, the Safari Playground, the Diana Ross Playground, the Abraham and Joseph Spector Playground, the Mariner's Playground, and the Tots and Adventure Playground. *Remember:* Strawberry Fields is a quiet zone, so postpone your visit if your children are rambunctious when you are in this area.

PLAN B: For an abundance of activities, diverse landscapes, and great walking trails, visit the south, north, and central areas of the park (see Trips 2, 4, and 5). The American Museum of Natural History at 79th Street and Central Park West is also a wonderful place to learn about outdoor, underwater, and space environments.

Trip 2

All Ages

Central Park (South)

The southern end of Central Park is home to the park's oldest and largest playground, as well as the Hallett Nature Sanctuary and the legendary Carousel.

Address: West 59th Street at Columbus Circle, Manhattan, NY
Hours: 6 A.M. to 1 A.M. daily
Fee: Free; some activities require fees (see below)
Contact: centralparknyc.org; Central Park Conservancy, 212-310-6600 or call 311; Wollman Ice Skating Rink, 212-439-6900; Victoria Gardens Amusement Park, 212-982-2229; guided tours of Hallett Nature Sanctuary, 212-360-1471; Central Park Zoo, 212-439-6500
Bathrooms: Heckscher Playground
Water/Snacks: Vendors inside park; Sheep Meadow Café; Ballfields Café and Merchant's Gate Plaza Café (just outside park)
Maps: USGS Central Park; centralparknyc.org/maps
Directions by Car: Public parking is very limited; driving is discouraged. *GPS coordinates:* 40° 46.094' N, 73° 58.890' W.
Directions by Subway: Take the A, B, C, D, 1, 2, or 3 train to 59th Street, Columbus Circle.

The southern region of Central Park extends roughly from 59th Street to the 65th Street Transverse Road, between Central Park West and Fifth Avenue. Enter on the western side at Columbus Circle and head east to the Heckscher Playground, which is both the oldest and largest in the park. In addition to playground equipment, it features an extensive jungle gym maze built into a large rock-climbing area. Beyond the maze, the rock-climbing area is so extensive that professionals and amateurs use it for training and practice.

Continuing east will bring you to the idyllic Pond, one of seven bodies of water incorporated into the park's design. To the north is the 4-acre Hallett Nature Sanctuary, which is open for guided tours only. The sanctuary contains several species of birds, along with raccoons, woodchucks, and rabbits.

The Central Park Zoo, which has an entrance fee, is farther along to the northeast. Animals that hail from an incredible diversity of climates call it home. You'll also find a petting zoo, a cafeteria, and restrooms. Leaving the zoo and heading southeast, you will arrive at the shady, bench-lined Wien

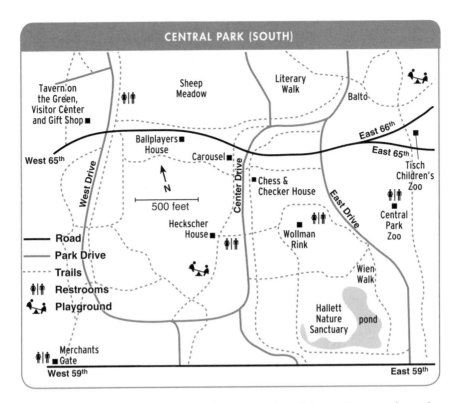

CENTRAL PARK (SOUTH)

Tavern on the Green, Visitor Center and Gift Shop ■

Sheep Meadow

Literary Walk

Balto

East 66th

Ballplayers ■ House

West 65th

Carousel ■

East 65th

Tisch Children's Zoo

West Drive

Center Drive

■ Chess & Checker House

East Drive

Central Park Zoo

N

500 feet

Heckscher House ■

Wollman Rink

Wien Walk

— Road
— Park Drive
--- Trails
Restrooms
Playground

Hallett Nature Sanctuary

pond

Merchants ■ Gate

West 59th

East 59th

Walk, which brings you to the southeastern edge of the park across from the Park Plaza hotel.

Heading back west from the zoo, you will encounter the Wollman Ice Skating Rink, which is open October through April (there are fees to enter and to rent skates). In summer the rink becomes Victoria Gardens Amusement Park, which also has a fee.

Continuing west you will reach the fabled Carousel, which has a small fee. Merry-go-rounds have been located at this site for well over 130 years. The present one was constructed in 1908 and brought in from Coney Island to replace another, which burned in 1950.

Adult bicycles are available to rent at Columbus Circle. Pedicabs and horse-drawn carriage rides also await passengers, for a fee, along 59th Street. *Remember:* Heckscher Playground is quite extensive, with a large variety of activities. It can be difficult for one adult to monitor children of different ages.

PLAN B: For more great places to explore, visit the west, east, and central areas of the park (see Trips 1, 3, and 5).

The natural world is often invoked to describe New York City: The grid of streets and buildings is called an urban or concrete jungle. Times Square has been described as a glittery canyon. The city itself has been called the Frontier City, calling to mind the wide-open spaces of the once-wild West.

In this vein, "urban hiking" has taken off as an outdoor activity. As part of the city's—and nation's—greater "green revolution," long stretches of streets in all five boroughs have been converted into "trails" for walking and biking. Urban hiking is more than just another metaphor, however. Adapting the outdoor mindset when walking on the accessible interior greenways is one way to reorient how you interpret space in the city and learn to appreciate your children's stamina for walking, biking, or riding a scooter great distances.

By design, many newly designated urban green zones connect to parks and waterfronts so pedestrians and cyclists can explore these traditional green spaces, which are growing in size and number throughout the Emerald Empire.

The 1.25-mile section of Broadway, from the Time Warner Center at 59th Street, Columbus Circle, to Macy's at 34th Street, Herald Square, is perhaps the most well-known urban hike in the city. Begin your walk at the southwest corner of Central Park, in the center of Columbus Circle, beneath the statue of Christopher Columbus. Proceed south on Broadway along the trail, which is designated by large green dots and huge pots of plants that double as traffic barriers in some areas. Within a few blocks, a great blue horizon opens above Times Square. This part of the trail features wide, tan-paved picnic spots with hundreds of chairs, as well as a few designated lanes where cars—an endangered species on this route—are allowed through heading east or west. In February 2010, Broadway, the city's great north–south thoroughfare, was permanently closed to traffic in this area. By 2014, the pavement in Times Square will be replaced by silver metallic tiles lined with sleek benches, and, if current plans continue, Midtown Manhattan should have become a pedestrian plaza by the time your kids are grown.

Continuing on the green-dotted path south, you'll find art installations set amid more densely packed café spaces. As the walkway opens out into Herald Square at West 35th Street, you will find, in the middle of the street, a wide-open "green space"—paint, covering the former roadway—which is a great spot to stop for a picnic or to sit and watch the world go by. It's worth hanging around Herald Square until the mechanical clock, cast in 1895 by renowned French sculptor Antonin Jean Carles, chimes on the hour.

Trip 3

Central Park (East)

Paved roads link together a chain of manicured lawns that roughly corresponds to Museum Mile along Fifth Avenue.

Address: East 66th Street at Fifth Avenue, Manhattan, NY
Hours: 6 A.M. to 1 A.M. daily
Fee: Free
Contact: centralparknyc.org; 212-310-6600 or call 311
Bathrooms: Bethesda Fountain; Metropolitan Museum of Art; near Conservatory Gardens
Water/Snacks: Drinking fountains throughout park during summer; vendors throughout park
Maps: USGS Central Park; centralparknyc.org/maps
Directions by Car: Public parking is very limited; driving is discouraged.
   GPS coordinates: 40° 46.119′ N, 73° 58.189′ W.
Directions by Subway: Take the 4 train to 68th Street/Hunter College and walk three blocks west.

Central Park's eastern portion runs along Fifth Avenue between East 66th and East 97th streets. The area has easy, rolling hills that are well shaded by mature trees.

Entering at East 66th Street and heading north, you will first encounter the East Green, one of eight designated quiet zones in Central Park. Loud music, talking, and running are prohibited in quiet zones. Stretching to East 72nd Street, the East Green is most fragrant and colorful in spring when magnolia and cherry trees bloom.

Crossing over East 72nd Street, you will head into an area that we call the "children's classics zone." First is the Conservatory Water, where, from April through October, children can rent remote-controlled mechanical boats to guide over the water. The setting is so idyllic that E.B. White used it as a backdrop in his 1945 classic, *Stuart Little*. The location also served as the set for the book's 1999 film version. In winter, the Conservatory Water is sometimes open for ice skating.

Continuing north, you will find an 11-foot-tall bronze statue of Alice and her famous entourage from Lewis Carroll's *Alice's Adventures in Wonderland*.

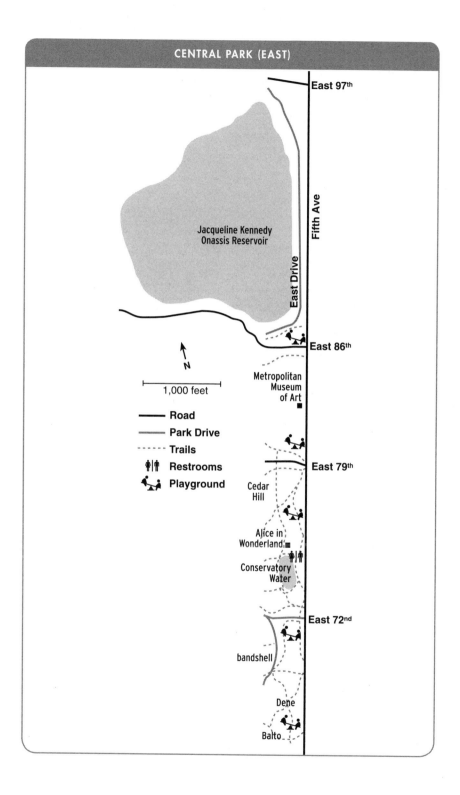

The Mad Hatter, the Cheshire Cat, the Dormouse, Dina the cat, and the White Rabbit are present and accounted for. Children are invited to climb and crawl all over Alice and her friends, unlike other statues in Central Park (and most everywhere else). Owing to more than a half century of such activity, the statues remain smooth and polished.

This area is also popular with bird-watchers catching views of red-tailed hawks that are wont to take flight from high atop buildings along Fifth Avenue.

Heading along East Drive or along the paved path that curves north, you will come upon the Metropolitan Museum of Art. This area has some terrific hills for sledding in winter. Destination playgrounds are on the north and south sides of the Met, in addition to playgrounds at East 76th Street and East 96th Street, the latter being one of the largest in the park. The Dene (which means "valley") is an area of the park with gentle hills and winding walkways perfect for strolling. It covers the area from East 66th Street to East 72nd Street. *Remember:* Tempting though it may be on a hot summer day, you cannot wade in the Conservatory Water. Don't forget to visit Balto, the statue of a dog that became a hero by helping to deliver life-saving medicine during an Alaskan blizzard in 1925. Children love to climb on the statue, and parents love to snap photos here. (See map on page 23.)

PLAN B: Central Park's west, south, and north sections (see Trips 1, 2, and 4) are all within an easy walk—and well worth the visit.

Trip 4

Central Park (North)

Paved roads and several ornamental bridges lead pedestrians and bicyclists over stunning natural and manicured hilltops and around two beautiful lakes.

Address: 110th Street (Central Park North) at Frawley Circle, Manhattan, NY
Hours: 6 A.M. to 1 A.M. daily
Fee: Free
Contact: centralparknyc.org; 212-310-6600 or call 311
Bathrooms: Charles A. Dana Discovery Center; near Conservatory Gardens; near Great Hill; North Meadow Recreation Center
Water/Snacks: Drinking fountains throughout park during summer; vendors throughout park
Maps: USGS Central Park; centralparknyc.org/maps
Directions by Car: Public parking is very limited; driving is discouraged. *GPS coordinates:* 40° 47.808′ N, 73° 56.981′ W.
Directions by Subway: Take the 4 train to 110th Street and walk three blocks west.

Central Park's northern reaches feature a great portion of rugged—but accessible—terrain. The area, which stretches between the park's east–west walls from 110th to 97th streets, is studded with rock outcroppings that can be traversed via a network of paved and dirt paths.

The Charles A. Dana Discovery Center, located in the northeast corner, offers free educational and family programs throughout the year. From April through October, poles and bait are provided for free catch-and-release fishing at the Harlem Meer. The tree-lined meer is also the perfect place to spot waterfowl and turtles. The hilltop remains of Fort Clinton, a fortification built during the War of 1812, are located on the meer's southern bank, providing panoramic views to the north.

The Lasker Rink and Pool, west of the meer, is a landmark destination in summer and winter. From July 1 through Labor Day, it is the only public swimming pool in Central Park, and admission is free. From October to March, it converts into an ice-skating rink (small admission fee; skates available to rent). Strollers are not permitted.

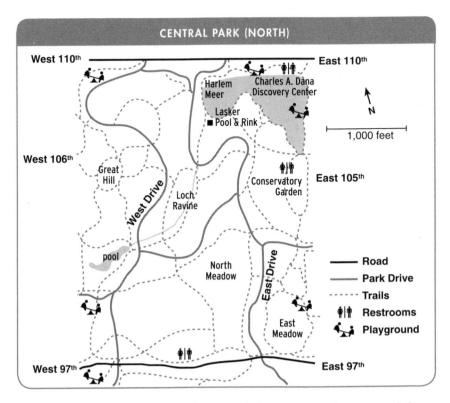

CENTRAL PARK (NORTH)

West 110th · East 110th
Harlem Meer · Charles A. Dana Discovery Center
Lasker Pool & Rink
N
1,000 feet
West 106th · Great Hill
West Drive
Loch Ravine
Conservatory Garden · East 105th
pool
North Meadow
East Drive
Road
Park Drive
Trails
Restrooms
Playground
East Meadow
West 97th · East 97th

To feel a world apart from the nation's largest city, take an easy hike or ride through the North Woods—also called Manhattan's Adirondack Mountains—which feature the picturesque Loch. Originally designed as a lake by the nineteenth-century landscape architects Frederick Law Olmsted and Calvert Vaux (see page xxiv), the Loch is now a stream with several waterfalls and pools. The shady, rocky banks make for cooler picnic spots on summer days.

The Conservatory Garden, along Fifth Avenue, is another destination that transports visitors in time and place. This well-manicured, 6-acre oasis features French, Italian, and English curatorial styles and a broad array of flowers and flowering trees and shrubs. It is a quiet zone with no bikes permitted and is open from 8 A.M. to dusk.

Destination playgrounds are inside park walls along Central Park's north, west, and east sections. *Remember:* If you plan to swim, come prepared per city pool regulations (see page 13).

PLAN B: For more wonderful walks, great playgrounds, and stunning landscapes, continue south to the west or east areas of the park (see Trips 1 and 3).

Trip 5

Central Park (Central)

The heart of Central Park features paved walkways and sidewalks, as well as a network of gravel bridle paths and several wooded areas with well-maintained nature trails.

Address: West 81st Street at Eighth Avenue (Central Park West) or East 79th Street at Fifth Avenue, Manhattan, NY
Hours: 6 A.M. to 1 A.M. daily
Fee: Free
Contact: centralparknyc.org; 212-310-6600 or call 311
Bathrooms: Delacorte Theater; Bethesda Arcade; Central Park Tennis Center
Water/Snacks: Vendors throughout park; Boathouse Restaurant at Loeb Central Park Boathouse on Lake
Maps: USGS Central Park; centralparknyc.org/maps
Directions by Car: Public parking is very limited; driving is discouraged. *GPS coordinates:* 40° 46.740′ N, 73° 58.123′ W.
Directions by Subway: From the West Side, take the B or C train to West 81st Street/American Museum of Natural History; from the East Side, take the 4, 5, or 6 train to East 86th Street and walk three blocks east to Fifth Avenue.

The heart of Central Park stretches from the Jacqueline Kennedy Onassis Reservoir through the Great Lawn and onto the Ramble and Lake. One day is not nearly enough time to see and do everything available here, especially once the wily charms of the Great Lawn pull you in.

The reservoir is a tremendously popular destination for walkers and joggers, including, at a time, Jackie O. It was built in the 1860s as a temporary water supply for the city—a purpose it couldn't possibly fill today—while the Croton water system underwent its two-week annual maintenance. Today the reservoir is surrounded by a 1.58-mile running track that offers fantastic views of the Manhattan skyline.

Heading south, you pass through the Arthur Ross Pinetum, an arboretum that has the largest collection of pine trees in Central Park. It also features sets of swings and many picnic tables.

The 55-acre Great Lawn, setting for many legendary concerts, is open mid-April through mid-November. It is a perfect place to picnic, fly kites, and play catch. Turtle Pond is on the lawn's southern edge and is, as the name suggests,

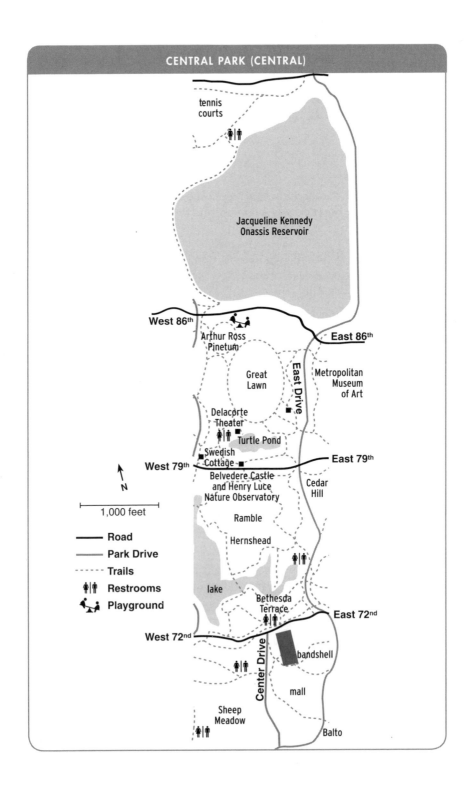

CENTRAL PARK (CENTRAL)

tennis courts

Jacqueline Kennedy Onassis Reservoir

West 86th

Arthur Ross Pinetum

East 86th

Great Lawn

East Drive

Metropolitan Museum of Art

Delacorte Theater

Turtle Pond

Swedish Cottage

West 79th

East 79th

Belvedere Castle and Henry Luce Nature Observatory

Cedar Hill

Ramble

Hernshead

lake

Bethesda Terrace

East 72nd

West 72nd

Center Drive

bandshell

mall

Sheep Meadow

Balto

N

1,000 feet

Road
Park Drive
Trails
Restrooms
Playground

home to many turtles. Overlooking the pond is the Belvedere Castle, which was built in 1865 as a stunning attraction without a specific purpose. Today it houses the Henry Luce Nature Observatory, which has natural history artifacts on display.

Farther south on West Drive or Central Park Driveway are the Shakespeare Garden and the Ramble—an extensive wild and wooded area with hiking trails that, in parts, overlook the Central Park Lake. Points of interest include the Azalea Pond and Bank Rock Bay. The Loeb Boathouse rents rowboats for a small fee.

Following Terrace Drive to Cherry Hill, you will come upon the Bethesda Fountain and Arcade. From there, you can follow the tree-lined Mall down to the sights in Central Park's south and east sections. (See page 24 for more information about Balto, the popular dog statue.) *Remember:* Strollers are not permitted on the reservoir or in the Ramble.

PLAN B: The west, south, east, and north areas of the park (see Trips 1, 2, 3, and 4) are all easily accessed from here, and feature numerous playgrounds.

Trip 6

Ages 5–8

Manhattan Waterfront Greenway (North)

The northern spur of the Manhattan Waterfront Greenway offers beautiful views of the Hudson River, the George Washington Bridge, and the landmark red lighthouse.

Address: West 130th Street and Marginal Street, Manhattan, NY
Hours: 6 A.M. to 1 A.M. daily
Fee: Free
Contact: nyc.gov/html/dcp/html/mwg/mwghome.shtml or call 311
Bathrooms: Fort Washington Park
Water/Snacks: None
Maps: USGS Central Park; nyc.gov/html/dcp/html/mwg/maps_2_1.shtml
Directions by Car: Public parking is very limited; driving is discouraged.
   GPS coordinates: 40° 49.137′ N, 73° 57.655′ W.
Directions by Subway: Take the 1 train to West 125th Street and walk three blocks west to the Hudson River. Enter the Greenway at West Harlem Piers Park at West 130th Street, which, due to the diagonal slant of West 125th Street, is the next street to the north (126th through 129th streets do not run in this area).

The Manhattan Waterfront Greenway, the longest section of the 32-mile Hudson River Valley Greenway, is the most heavily used bikeway in the United States. The section between West 125th and West 181st streets follows the Hudson River, providing idyllic views of the New Jersey shore on the opposite bank. The greenway is the product of recent efforts to transform the Manhattan coastline into a vibrant area for recreation and commuting.

Begin your walk or bike ride at West Harlem Piers Park. The route leading north initially involves following signs to navigate under an overpass, but soon resolves into a clear path leading north along the Hudson River to Fort Washington Park. The 183-acre park stretches between West 155th and West 179th streets and has athletic fields and courts, and a large playground. It also contains the famed Little Red Light House at West 178th Street, just below the awesome expanse of the George Washington Bridge.

West Harlem Piers Park features boardwalks along Manhattan Waterfront Greenway.

The lighthouse was the subject of a children's book by Hildegarde H. Swift, *The Little Red Light House and the Great Gray Bridge*, published in 1942. The 40-foot structure was built in 1880 on what was then an isolated rocky point on Manhattan's northern edge. After the George Washington Bridge was completed in 1931, the lights of the lighthouse were overwhelmed by the beams emanating from 600-foot towers above. Inspired by Swift's book, a nation-wide campaign prevented demolition of the lighthouse. Today the lighthouse, fronted by picnic tables, makes an ideal picnic spot.

To exit at West 181st Street, walk under the bridge and up a steep hill that curves through a tunnel and ultimately connects to a footbridge that spans the Henry Hudson Parkway. *Remember:* Winds off the Hudson River can make the greenway an unsuitable destination for small children during winter.

PLAN B: Fort Tryon Park (Trip 8) and Inwood Hill Park (Trip 9) are close to the northern terminus of this walk. Also consider walking or biking over the George Washington Bridge. The south side is open to pedestrians and bikers, and can be accessed by wending west on West 178th Street.

Manhattan Waterfront Greenway (South)

The Manhattan Waterfront Greenway is a thoroughfare, a promenade, and a spot for a long idyll watching boats and people—all at the same time.

Address: 89th Street and Riverside Drive, Manhattan, NY
Hours: 6 A.M. to 1 A.M. daily
Fee: Free
Contact: nyc.gov/html/dcp/html/mwg/mwghome.shtml or call 311
Bathrooms: 79th Street Boat Basin Café; on Greenway (77th Street)
Water/Snacks: Café at 70th street; shops and restaurants in neighborhood nearby
Map: USGS Central Park; nyc.gov/html/edc/pdf/greenway_mapside.pdf
Directions by Car: Public parking is very limited; driving is discouraged.
  GPS coordinates: 40° 47.504′ N, 74° 58.714′ W.
Directions by Subway: Take the 1 train to 86th Street and walk two blocks west toward the Hudson River.

The Manhattan Waterfront Greenway is by far the most extensive of many renovations within the larger Hudson River Valley Greenway Project. As the shores of Manhattan became less active as commercial and industrial hubs, these areas were neglected and went into steep decline. In 1993 the Department of City Planning (DCP) began designing the Greenway, and in 1997 the DCP and the New York City Department of Transportation produced the New York City Bicycle Master Plan, which incorporated the greenway into a 900-mile-long network of paths and bike lanes throughout New York City. Today, a large portion of this network is up and running—and biking—and the section of the greenway from 86th to 27th streets is among the most widely used areas of it.

You can reach the greenway by entering Riverside Park at 89th Street and Riverside Drive, where the ivory Soldiers and Sailors Monument, commemorating members of the Union army and navy who served during the Civil War, is perched majestically above the Hudson River. Follow the stairs around and behind the monument down into the park, heading south to arrive at the

Designated, paved bike lanes and pedestrian paths are separated by greenery along the southern section of the Manhattan Waterfront Greenway.

greenway above the 87th Street dog run. Parallel to 84th Street, the path will take you down to the shoreline of the Hudson. As you hike and bike along, you will enjoy scenic views of the Hudson and be entertained by numerous outdoor art installations, including a giant bottle with a fully furnished interior posed as though it simply washed up along the shore. At 59th Street you will arrive at Hudson River Park, a 550-acre park with many destination piers extending all the way down to Battery Park on the southern tip of Manhattan. *Remember:* In spring be sure to visit Cherry Walk, north between 100th and 125th streets.

PLAN B: Dip into Riverside Park South (Trip 19) for quieter walks, idyllic landscapes, and big playgrounds.

Trip 8

Fort Tryon Park

This all-seasons destination should not be missed during fall's foliage.

Address: Fort Washington Avenue and Cabrini Boulevard, Manhattan, NY
Hours: 6 A.M. to midnight daily
Fee: Free
Contact: nycgovparks.org/parks/forttryonpark or call 311;
   forttryonparktrust.org; 212-795-1388
Bathrooms: Anne Loftus Playground; The Cloisters museum; Fort Tryon Café
Water/Snacks: Water fountains at playground and throughout park; high-end
   restaurant New Leaf Restaurant and Bar on main walkway
Maps: USGS Central Park; nycgovparks.org/parks/M029/map/ft_tryon_map.pdf
Directions by Car: Public parking is very limited; driving is discouraged.
   GPS coordinates: 40° 51.563′ N, 73° 56.048′ W.
Directions by Subway: To get to the main entrance, take the A train to 190th
   Street. For a vigorous uphill hike, take the A train to Dyckman Street.

Fort Tryon Park is designed to be stunning year round, but our favorite season
to visit—autumn—owes its grandeur to the views of Palisades Interstate Park,
a dense forest preserve set along dramatic cliffs in New Jersey. When the trees
are dressed in yellow, orange, red, and fading green, it is a vista worth traveling for.

This is exactly what John D. Rockefeller Jr. wanted. Fort Tryon sits atop a
similar escarpment on the New York side of the Hudson River. Rockefeller donated Fort Tryon Park to New York City in 1935, and established the Palisades
in part to protect the views across the river. It can be said that Fort Tryon is a
descendant of Central Park, as it was designed by Frederick Law Olmsted Jr.,
son and namesake of Central Park's landscape architect. In 1983, it was designated an official city landmark.

At nearly 70 acres, Fort Tryon is renowned for its many distinct gardens
and lawns. These are most easily accessed via a network of paved and gravel
paths that begin at the main entrance at Fort Washington Avenue, one block
northwest of the 190th Street stop on the A train. This would be the best route
if you have a stroller or toddler.

Toddler-friendly paths wind through beautiful gardens at Fort Tryon Park.

You can also access the park by hiking up the trails, rough and steep in parts, from the entrance near the Dyckman Street stop on the A train. Exit the stop and walk two blocks south to Arden Street, and enter the park on your right. After a short distance, turn right and follow the path to an elevation of nearly 200 feet. The Cloisters, a branch of the Metropolitan Museum of Art that features medieval European art, commands this area. Follow the path to the western side, overlooking the Hudson, and absorb the view of the Palisades. *Remember:* Some of the gardens are designated quiet zones. If children need to burn off energy, playgrounds are near Dyckman Street and Fort Washington Avenue.

PLAN B: Leave Fort Tryon Park via the paths to the north to hike down to Inwood Hill Park (Trip 9).

Trip 9

Inwood Hill Park

This park is the only place in Manhattan where you can hike in old-growth forest and one of two places where you can observe a salt-marsh habitat.

Address: Payson Avenue and Dyckman Street, Manhattan, NY
Hours: Park: 6 A.M. to 1 A.M. daily; Nature Center: 10 A.M. to 4 P.M. Wednesday through Sunday
Fee: Free
Contact: nycgovparks.org/parks/inwoodhillpark or call 311; Nature Center, 212-304-2365
Bathrooms: Nature Center; tennis courts; Payson Playground
Water/Snacks: Water fountains throughout park; vendors often on the park's perimeter
Maps: USGS Central Park; USGS Yonkers; nycgovparks.org/parks/ inwoodhillpark/map
Directions by Car: Public parking is very limited; driving is discouraged. *GPS coordinates:* 40° 52.022′ N, 73° 55.71′ W.
Directions by Subway: Take the A train to 207th Street and turn west onto Seaman Avenue; walk north into the park. Or, take the 1 train to 215th Street and walk north to 218th Street; take a left on 218th Street and follow it to the end.

Largely nonlandscaped, Inwood Hill Park is home to the last natural forest and the only preserved salt marsh in Manhattan (see Trip 13). The rugged topography still bears the marks of the last ice age, which began 1.5 million years ago. The end of this era, roughly 10,000 years ago, left in its wake glacial potholes, caves, and deep rocky ridges that are still visible in the park—just as they are in the Adirondack Mountains and the Great Lakes region.

At nearly 200 acres, the park contains miles of trails and bike paths that take you from a busy city intersection into old-growth forest and onto the waterfront. The main pedestrian path, Bolton Road, is another vestige of an earlier era: It once led to the Bolton estate, one of several private summer homes that dotted the area in the nineteenth century. The entrance is on Payson Avenue near Dyckman Street (closer to the A train stop), and Bolton Road connects to a network of paved paths that was developed under the Works Progress Administration in the 1930s. To see both forest and river, head west

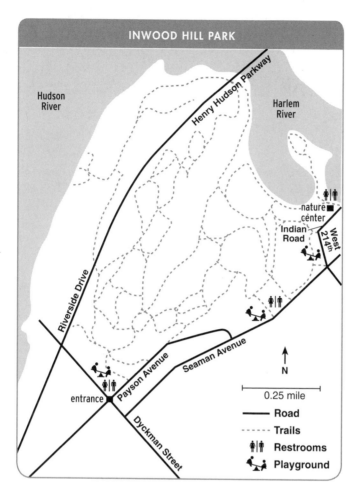

INWOOD HILL PARK

Hudson River

Harlem River

Henry Hudson Parkway

nature center

Indian Road

West 214th

Riverside Drive

Payson Avenue

Seaman Avenue

entrance

Dyckman Street

N

0.25 mile

—— Road

----- Trails

Restrooms

Playground

on the path (straight as you go in), and follow it as it curves to the right (north) to Spuyten Duyvel Creek. You can pass under the Henry Hudson Parkway bridge and continue on to the Hudson River. This path crosses back under the parkway near Dyckman Street.

Visit the Nature Center, near the salt marsh at 118th Street and Indian Road (closer to the 1 train stop), to learn more about the natural and human history of Inwood Hill Park. Playgrounds are at Payson Avenue and Dyckman Street, and at Seaman Avenue near 207th and 214th streets. *Remember:* Picnicking is discouraged in the forest areas but is encouraged on the manicured peninsula at the northern part of the park.

PLAN B: Fort Tryon Park (Trip 8) overlooks Inwood Hill Park and features a hardy walk up a wooded mountain.

Trip 10

Riverbank State Park

Riverbank State Park, among the newest and most popular of the New York State parks, features a variety of outdoor athletic activities and offers community gardening.

Address: 679 Riverside Drive, Manhattan, NY
Hours: 6:30 A.M. to 10 P.M. weekdays, 6:30 A.M. to 5 P.M. weekends
Fee: Free
Contact: nysparks.state.ny.us/parks/93/details.aspx; 212-694-3600
Bathrooms: Aquatics complex
Water/Snacks: Water fountains throughout park; the reasonably priced Tian Restaurant at the northern edge of park
Maps: USGS Central Park; nysparks.state.ny.us/parks/93/details.aspx
Directions by Car: Take the West Side Highway to 145th Street. A parking garage is underneath the park. *GPS coordinates:* 40° 49.628′ N, 73° 57.116′ W.
Directions by Subway: Take the 1 train to 137th Street and walk northwest toward the river.

Riverbank State Park is a quintessential "only in New York" destination. It is a 28-acre landmass built atop a sewage treatment facility on the Hudson River. Have space? Will use. Since opening in 1993, Riverbank—the only state park in Manhattan—has become one of the most popular parks in the state system.

Modeled after Japanese rooftop parks and gardens, Riverbank has several acres of "green roofs," or soil laid out in varying depths to support flora. It is the largest such roof in New York City. The treatment plant below it processes 125 million gallons of wastewater every day during dry weather, while emitting no odors. The park is part of a movement to renovate urban spaces to make them more sustainable, and to promote a healthy environment; it is the only park of its kind in the western hemisphere.

From a vantage roughly 70 feet above the Hudson River, Riverbank offers sweeping views of the New Jersey shoreline due east, and vistas of Manhattan's own shoreline to the south and north, up to the George Washington Bridge and beyond. To get the lay of the land, enter at either West 137th or West 145th Street and take the promenade along the perimeter of the park. Playgrounds and outdoor courts are near the southern entrance, and several major athletic

Visitors can enjoy views of the George Washington Bridge from Manhattan's only state park.

buildings are toward the north. Among the amenities (with small fees) are an Olympic-sized swimming pool, a fitness room, various ball courts, and a covered rink for roller-skating in warm weather and ice-skating during winter. Just south of the rink is a community gardening area.

As a special treat, visit the merry-go-round at the park's northeastern corner. Its design was inspired by children's artwork. *Remember:* Bicycles and pets are prohibited within the park.

PLAN B: Hike north on the Manhattan Waterfront Greenway (Trip 6) to see the George Washington Bridge up close, or south for a respite at the General Grant National Memorial (Trip 17).

Trip 11

Morningside Park

Morningside Park has excellent playgrounds, barbecue-equipped picnic spots, and a range of paved paths for easy strolling or more-vigorous uphill treks.

Address: West 110th Street and Manhattan Avenue, Manhattan, NY

Hours: 6 A.M. to 10 P.M. daily

Fee: Free

Contact: nycgovparks.org/parks/morningsidepark or call 311; morningsidepark. org; 212-937-3883

Bathrooms: At West 123rd Street and Morningside Avenue; at West 117th Street and Morningside Avenue; at athletic fields and lawns

Water/Snacks: Water fountains in playgrounds and at restrooms; vendors on park's perimeter

Maps: USGS Central Park; nycgovparks.org/parks/morningsidepark/map

Directions by Car: Public parking is very limited; driving is discouraged. *GPS coordinates:* 40° 48.075′ N, 73° 57.579′ W.

Directions by Subway: Take the A, B, C, or D train to 125th Street, or take the A, B, or C train to 110th Street or 116th Street.

Morningside Park is set along a dramatic cliff that sits between Harlem to the east and Morningside Heights to the west. Owing to this unusual topography, the park is named for the stunning sunrise views over Harlem that can be had from its elevated western edge.

Designed by landscape architect Frederick Law Olmsted and his senior partner, Calvert Vaux, the park's landscaping and ornamentation pick up seamlessly where nearby northern Central Park leaves off. The rugged cliff that drops down from Morningside Drive is thickly wooded, and cut through with paved paths and several sets of stone steps that make for a rigorous walk. Morningside Avenue, which forms the park's eastern edge, is, in contrast, a largely flat, easy stroll past well-manicured lawns and gardens. The park also provides easy paths for kids learning how to ride a bicycle.

Entering at West 110th Street and Morningside Avenue, you will first find an athletic field surrounded by a 470-yard fitness path that comprises a mile in 3.75 laps. The park's sidewalk perimeter, which has no through streets to interrupt the loop, forms another good walk of about 1.5 miles.

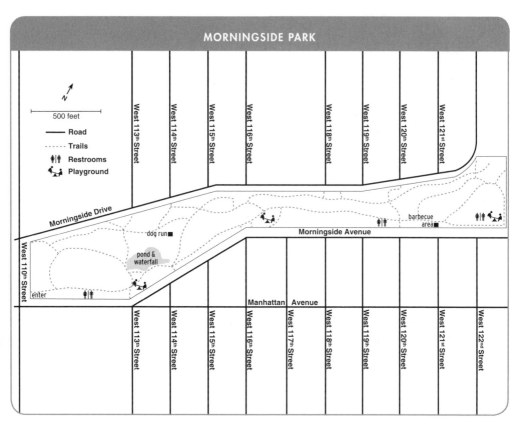

MORNINGSIDE PARK

500 feet

— Road
···· Trails
Restrooms
Playground

West 113th Street
West 114th Street
West 115th Street
West 116th Street
West 118th Street
West 119th Street
West 120th Street
West 121st Street

Morningside Drive

dog run■

pond & waterfall

barbecue area■

Morningside Avenue

West 110th Street

enter

Manhattan Avenue

West 113th Street
West 114th Street
West 115th Street
West 116th Street
West 117th Street
West 118th Street
West 119th Street
West 120th Street
West 121st Street
West 122nd Street

Just north of the athletic field are a pond and waterfall that appear to have been part of the original park design, but were actually added more than 100 years later. This site owes its beauty—and existence—to Columbia University student protesters who, in 1968, stopped the school from building a gymnasium over the park. The project had proceeded as far of the digging of a crater which, after demolition of the park was halted, was converted into the pond and waterfall.

Continuing north, at West 117th Street, is a large playground. Beyond this, many picnic tables and grassy fields continue north. A designated barbecue area is at West 121st Street and Morningside Avenue.

Another large playground with nearby basketball and handball courts is at West 123rd Street, which is the park's northern border. Smaller playgrounds are located at West 113th and West 110th streets. *Remember:* Barbecuing is allowed in designated areas only, and is not permitted under trees.

PLAN B: The northern section of Central Park (Trip 4) is just one block east from the southern end of the park. Riverside Park (Trip 18) is located four blocks west from the northern edge of the park.

In a modern twist on the treasure hunt, today's high-tech devices can help connect kids to nature.

Geocaching is an outdoor adventure that sends you in search of "caches" in parks and neighborhoods across the globe. This stash-and-seek game began on May 3, 2000, with a small black bucket hidden near Portland, Oregon. The U.S. government had, the day before, granted public access to previously restricted GPS (global positioning system) data. The coordinates for this bucket were posted online, and the hunt was on. (The terms "letterboxing" and "questing" are often used interchangeably with geocaching, but they are different. Letterboxing, for one, has a much longer history, dating back to the 1800s, and usually involves solving puzzles or elaborate clues. Participants use rubber stamps to record their discoveries.)

Caches can be found deep in the woods or in unusual spots throughout a city. Typically they hold small items or educational information about the area, and often a voluntary roster sheet to record who found the cache and when. Some ask participants to remove a cached item and add one of their own, and others contain only clues that guide seekers through a series of locations until the final cache is reached. No matter the type, the caches all help seekers hone GPS code-cracking skills and invite them to investigate an area.

To become one of the more than 5 million players worldwide, visit geocaching.com and sign up for a free membership that gives you access to over 1.5 million geocaches worldwide. In New York City, a bounty of caches are hidden in all five boroughs—some 25,000 in the summer of 2011, though stashes are continuously added and removed. From the "Hide and Seek a Cache" page on the website, type in a zip code and mile radius to find caches near you. Plug in the GPS coordinates, or send them to your device, and the search begins!

A final note: Geocaches are not supposed to be located in wilderness areas. Geocache hiders, and seekers, should respect the environment and follow Leave No Trace principles (see page xxvii).

Trip 12

Highbridge Park

Highbridge Park features the only mountain-biking trails in Manhattan.

Address: Dyckman Street and Nagle Avenue, Manhattan, NY; for the pool,
Amsterdam Avenue and West 173rd Street
Hours: Dawn to dusk daily
Fee: Free
Contact: nycgovparks.org/parks/highbridgepark or call 311; for the pool
call 212-927-2400
Bathrooms: None
Water/Snacks: Water fountains at playgrounds (between 190th and 188th streets;
at 157th Street)
Maps: USGS Central Park; nycgovparks.org/parks/highbridgepark/map
Directions by Car: Public parking is very limited; driving is discouraged.
GPS coordinates: 40° 51.692′ N, 73° 55.485′ W.
Directions by Subway: Take the 1 train to 157th Street to reach the southern part
of Highbridge, or get off at Dyckman Street to enter at the northern part.

The far reaches of Highbridge Park—so named after High Bridge, the city's
longest-standing span and bygone aqueduct—are as isolated and rustic as
anything you will find in New York City's parks. Many of the park's 119 acres
feature wooded escarpments crisscrossed by paved paths and trails that are
gaining fame as the only place to mountain bike in the city. From its upper
heights, the park offers spectacular views of the Harlem River. You can swim
at the Highbridge Recreation Center and Pool, a popular destination among
locals.

Enter the park near the intersection of 10th Avenue, Dyckman Street, and
the Harlem River Drive, and enjoy a rigorous walk up the paved path to your
left. The elevation reaches 150 feet. Turn around and return the way you came.
Rugged bike paths also run parallel to the paved route.

Six playgrounds are in the park, two along Amsterdam Avenue at 180th and
189th streets, two along Edgecombe Avenue at 164th and 167th streets, another
at the pool complex, and one at Fort George and Saint Nicholas avenues.

During a visit to Highbridge, you are likely to see volunteer groups clear-
ing underbrush and fixing paths—or field biologists from the City University

*Well-shaded paths along wooded escarpments at Highbridge Park
are ideal for robust hikes or bike rides.*

of New York who are there to study evolution. They view this park and others as living laboratories where they can research how urban geography impacts development and the selection of characteristics among our neighbors in the insect and animal worlds.

In its heyday, the park was as fashionable as Central and Prospect parks are today. The New York Restoration Project now describes it as "largely undiscovered" although efforts to revitalize it are changing that. Droves of visitors were once drawn to its boardwalk, a horse racetrack, and other outdoor sports venues. Urban planner Robert Moses (see page xxiv) turned parts of the racetrack into Harlem River Drive. He also developed the recreation center and pool. *Remember:* Many parts of Highbridge Park are too steep for strollers, and might be challenging for younger children on bicycles or scooters. Also, if you plan to swim, be aware of city park pool rules (see page 13).

PLAN B: Swindler Cove Park (Trip 13) is across Harlem River Drive, offering a respite among well-manicured gardens and lawns.

Trip 13

All Ages

Swindler Cove Park

A hidden gem in northeast Manhattan, Swindler Cove Park is free of bustle and is a great place to spend a few mellow hours with a picnic.

Address: 3703 Harlem River Drive, Manhattan, NY
Hours: 8 A.M. to 6 P.M. daily
Fee: Free
Contact: nyrp.org/Parks_and_Gardens/Parks/Swindler_Cove_Park/Park_
   Overview; 212-333-2552
Bathrooms: Riley-Levin Children's Garden
Water/Snacks: Water fountains at Riley-Levin Children's Garden
Map: USGS Central Park
Directions by Car: Public parking is very limited; driving is discouraged.
   GPS coordinates: 40° 51.472′ N, 73° 55.332′ W.
Directions by Subway: Take the 1 train to Dyckman Street. Turn right on
   Dyckman Street and walk one block to the Harlem River.

The New York Restoration Project calls Swindler Cove Park the "crown jewel" of its efforts, and it's right. What began as a project to clean an illegal dumping site has now become a 5-acre oasis along the Harlem River. The park is beautifully restored, tranquil, and meticulously landscaped. It features one of only two saltwater marshes in Manhattan. (Inwood Hill Park, Trip 9, has the other.)

The park runs along the Manhattan Waterfront Greenway—a cycling and walking route that nearly circumvents the island—and can be traversed along gravel footpaths. Boats, including the Circle Line tour, ply the Harlem River close by, and a lucky family may even spot a seal sunning itself on the dock of the Peter Jay Sharp Boathouse. The boathouse is the site of the annual Peter Jay Sharp Head of the Harlem Regatta. The regatta, held every September, attracts rowers from local colleges and high schools, and spectators from all over.

The Riley-Levin Children's Garden on the western edge of Swindler Cove Park has planting beds maintained by local school groups. The park also features picnic tables, restrooms, and a reflecting pool.

The Sherman Creek Nature Trail is a delightful path small children will love. No vigorous hikes are to be found here, but the trail leads to five outdoor animal "estates" designed to attract a range of birds and other wildlife. It is also

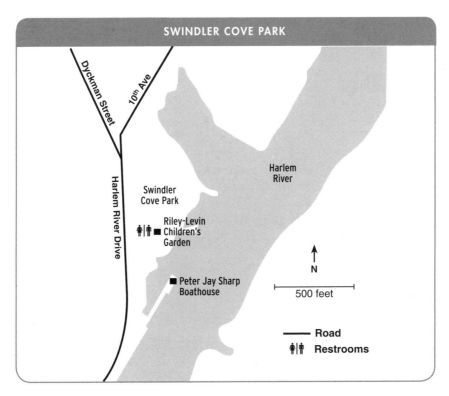

SWINDLER COVE PARK

Dyckman Street

10th Ave

Harlem River Drive

Swindler
Cove Park

Harlem
River

Riley-Levin
Children's
Garden

Peter Jay Sharp
Boathouse

N

500 feet

Road

Restrooms

part of the restoration project along the natural shoreline, and will ultimately connect Swindler Cove to an on-site nature center. *Remember:* The park does not have a playground, so pack a sketch pad and crayons and have your kids draw what they see on this nature walk through a diversity of landscapes.

PLAN B: For a serious uphill hike on a paved path, cross the Hudson River Parkway to visit Highbridge Park (Trip 12).

WHERE TO EAT NEARBY: Follow Dyckman Street to find shops and restaurants.

Trip 14

Ages 9–12

East River Esplanade (67th to 125th)

A hike along the East River Esplanade is a must-do to fully appreciate the Manhattan Waterfront Greenway project.

Address: East 120th Street and Paladino Avenue, Manhattan, NY
Hours: Dawn to dusk daily
Fee: Free
Contact: nyharborparks.org/visit/eari; 212-619-5000
Bathrooms: Jefferson Park (114th Street); Carl Schurz Park (90th Street)
Water/Snacks: Water fountains and vendors in parks
Maps: USGS Brooklyn; USGS Central Park
Directions by Car: Public parking is very limited; driving is discouraged.
   GPS coordinates: 40° 47.822′ N, 73° 55.776′ W.
Directions by Subway: Take the 4, 5, or 6 train and walk three blocks east. A footbridge leads over Harlem River Drive at East 120th Street; five footbridges lead over FDR/East River Drive: at East 111th Street, at East 102nd Street, in Carl Schurz Park at East 87th Street, at East 81st Street, and at East 71st Street.

The development of Manhattan's 508-mile shoreline—known as the Manhattan Waterfront Greenway project—has been among the most important initiatives intended to transform the city into an environment that not only invites, but encourages, outdoor activities. The project has taken place concurrent with the renovation and reinvention of other sites around New York—such as empty lots turned into outdoor art museums (Trip 42) and abandoned docks turned into parks exposing the visitor to forgotten history (Trip 43).

A journey along the East River Esplanade provides one of numerous answers to the oft-asked question, What is there to do outdoors in the city? Entering the paved Esplanade at 120th Street, head south along the East River. Directly ahead, you will see the endpoint of your walk 53 blocks south (approximately 3 miles) at Carl Schurz Park (Trip 16), where Manhattan juts out farther east. In the center of the river you will also see Mill Rock, an uninhabited 3.9-acre island that, along with neighboring Flood Rock, once made the area a notoriously treacherous passage for vessels heading northeast out of New York Harbor. In 1885 the U.S. Army Corps of Engineers destroyed Flood

Cast a line for flounder, bluefish, and striped bass along the East River Esplanade.

Rock with 500,000 pounds of explosives. The concussion from the blast was felt as far away as Princeton, New Jersey.

Today this area of the East River presents a placid vista and a lovely panorama of the Queens–Brooklyn skyline. You can walk or bike along the esplanade, or come prepared to join the many anglers fishing for flounder, bluefish, and striped bass. *Remember:* At 114th Street you will pass Thomas Jefferson Park, yet another triumphant example of a city park recently rescued from decline. It features a popular recreation center and pool.

PLAN B: Carl Schurz Park (Trip 16), at the end of this hike, is a great spot to picnic, play Frisbee, visit a large playground, and watch the boats go by.

Trip 15

John Jay Park and Pool

John Jay Park features a large public swimming pool and playgrounds.

Address: East 77th Street at Cherokee Place, Manhattan, NY
Hours: Pool: 11 A.M. to 3 P.M. and 4 to 7 P.M. daily
Fee: Free
Contact: nycgovparks.org/parks/johnjaypark; 212-794-6566 or call 311
Bathrooms: East side of park in bathhouse
Water/Snacks: Water fountains in park; vendors at park entrance
Maps: USGS Central Park; nycgovparks.org/parks/johnjaypark/map
Directions by Car: Public parking is very limited; driving is discouraged.
  GPS coordinates: 40° 46.170' N, 73° 56.996' W.
Directions by Subway: Take the 6 train to 77th Street and walk five blocks east.

At a mere 3 acres, John Jay Park and Pool may be small, but it makes up for that with its assets and intriguing details. The 145-foot, Works Progress Administration–era swimming pool is a neighborhood hot spot—or cool spot—in summer, as are the sprinklers in the playground. A second, smaller pool is more appropriate for teaching kids how to swim.

The playground itself has lots of different equipment, including rock-climbing structures suitable for young children. It is fenced off from the rest of the park, which makes for easier child minding. The wide, paved expanses outside the playground are good for teaching younger children how to ride a bike or scooter. The park is also well shaded in summer.

A visit to John Jay Park and Pool is also a good way for the intrepid urban explorer to enjoy strolling the long east–west blocks of the Upper East Side, while viewing intriguing architectural relics. Among these are the Cherokee Apartments, which reveal how New Yorkers have worked to incorporate the benefits of sun and fresh air into urban design. Consider getting there to be part of the destination.

After exiting the subway at 77th Street, walk east five blocks to Cherokee Place. Turn north and look west to observe the stunning array of green-iron balconies perched against the yellow-brick walls of the Cherokee Apartments. These beaux arts buildings date to the early 1900s, when Mrs. W.K. Vanderbilt provided $1 million to construct housing to help halt the spread of tuberculo-

Sprinklers and a pool make John Jay Park a great destination in summer.

sis in New York City. The buildings were laid out to provide maximum sunlight and airflow, and every apartment has a balcony.

Don't miss the Douglas Abdell sculptures lining the west side of the park, and be sure to watch the boats go by along the East River. *Remember:* If you plan to swim, be aware of city park pool rules (see page 13).

PLAN B: If you fancy sitting on the lawn, Carl Schurz Park (Trip 16) is located six blocks north, along the East River.

Trip 16

All Ages

Carl Schurz Park and Gracie Mansion

The massive and well-manicured front lawn and gardens of Gracie Mansion are a stunning place to walk, stroll, and picnic while taking in beautiful views of the East River.

Address: 90th Street and East End Avenue, Manhattan, NY
Hours: Park, all hours daily; mansion, call ahead
Fee: Free
Contact: carlschurzparknyc.org; 212-459-4455
Bathrooms: Catbird Playground
Water/Snacks: None
Maps: USGS Central Park; nycgovparks.org/parks/carlschurz/map
Directions by Car: Public parking is very limited; driving is discouraged.
   GPS coordinates: 40° 46.641′ N, 73° 56.573′ W.
Directions by Subway: Take the 4, 5, or 6 train to 86th Street.

Delightfully incongruous among the soaring steel and brick buildings of Manhattan, Gracie Mansion is a two-story, yellow-clapboard, Federal-style house that dates to 1799. It has served as the official residence of New York City's mayor since 1942, and today its lawns and gardens form Carl Schurz Park.

The 14.9-acre park is named for Carl Schurz, a general in the Union army during the Civil War who was the first German-born American elected to the U.S. Senate. His wife, Margarethe Schurz, was instrumental in founding the kindergarten system in the United States.

A waterfront promenade borders the east side of the park, which connects to the Manhattan Waterfront Greenway. Visitors can hike along the paths of the park, enjoying waterfront views and cool breezes off the river. The bench-lined, tree-shaded paved paths are perfect for strollers and young walkers, as are the stairways leading down to a small garden area, in the center of which is a statue of Peter Pan. The statue was created by renowned sculptor Charles Andrew Hafner (1889–1960). The statue briefly went missing in 1999, but was later recovered by the New York City Police Department at the bottom of the

A statue of Peter Pan is among the delightful features at this riverfront park.

East River. This mysterious act of vandalism caused the parks commissioner to comment: "We thought his only enemy was Captain Hook."

Also be sure not to miss Catbird Playground, situated at the north end of the park, which is named for the beautiful animal-themed artwork it contains. *Remember:* Gracie Mansion holds several public tours on most Wednesdays (small fee, but free for students). Call 311 or email gracietours@cityhall.nyc.gov for more information.

PLAN B: If you're in the mood for a long waterfront promenade, the East River Esplanade (Trip 14) runs north and south of Carl Schurz Park.

Trip 17

General Grant National Memorial

Grant's Tomb is a must-see stopover—or an off-the-beaten-path destination for a picnic—on a longer hike in Riverside Park.

Address: Riverside Drive at West 122nd Street, Manhattan, NY
Hours: Memorial and museum: 9 A.M. to 5 P.M. daily; park: sunrise to sunset daily
Fee: Free
Contact: nps.gov/gegr; 212-666-1640
Bathrooms: Overlook Pavilion across Riverside Drive to west; Claremont Dolphin Playground, just north of monument at West 124th Street
Water/Snacks: None
Map: USGS Central Park
Directions by Car: Public parking is very limited; driving is discouraged. *GPS coordinates:* 40° 48.755' N, 73° 57.778' W.
Directions by Subway: Take the 1 train to 116th Street/Columbia University, walk north to West 122nd Street, and turn left.

Perched at one of the highest points in Manhattan, the General Grant National Memorial—better known as Grant's Tomb—is a longtime tourist destination whose popularity has risen, declined, and risen again, along with that of the surrounding neighborhood. Established with great fanfare in 1897, the site was modeled on the original "mausoleum"—the tomb of Mausolus, a satrap, or governor, in the Persian Empire between 353 and 350 BC. It had fallen into serious decline by the 1970s, but its restoration and revival gained momentum in the 1990s.

Owing to its open, flat, paved surfaces, Grant's Tomb is popular with skateboarders, and the New York Unicycle Club holds its meetings there on the first Sunday and third Saturday of each month, from 1 P.M. to about 5 P.M. It is also an ideal place for young children to gain expertise on a scooter, tricycle, or toddler bike.

Grant's Tomb sits on an island that is surrounded by Riverside Drive. A bird sanctuary is due west in Riverside Park, and many massive mature trees surround the monument itself. Combined, these elements turn the airspace over Grant's Tomb into a flyway for migrating birds. The area just north of the

The lawns of Sakura Park near General Grant National Memorial provide plenty of space for games.

memorial has grassy hills and picnic tables, as well as sweeping views of the Hudson River to the George Washington Bridge. Beyond that, on the park's northern edge, is the Claremont Dolphin Playground. Sakura Park is due east.

The park can be reached from Riverside Park (Trip 18) to the west, or from West 122nd Street to the east. The National Park Service recently restored the Overlook Pavilion, across from the memorial in Riverside Park, providing space for a visitor center, a small museum, and a bookstore. *Remember:* Riverside Drive surrounds the park on all sides, and in the absence of nearby pedestrian crosswalks, you must watch traffic to cross into the park.

PLAN B: The Manhattan Waterfront Greenway North (Trip 6) and Riverside Park North (Trip 18) are just west of the memorial park, offering additional playground options and long stretches for hikes and bike rides.

WHERE TO EAT NEARBY: Grant's Tomb is an excellent, off-the-beaten-path picnic spot. Provisions can be purchased in grocery stores and restaurants along Broadway, from West 116th Street heading south. Convenience stores on Broadway between West 121st and 122nd streets are also an option.

Trip 18

Ages 0–4

Riverside Park (North)

The shady upper promenade features a series of small playgrounds and is great for toddlers.

Address: Riverside Drive at 116th Street, Manhattan, NY
Hours: Dawn to 1 A.M. daily
Fee: Free
Contact: nycgovparks.org/sub_your_park/vt_riverside_park/vt_riverside_park. html or call 311; riversideparkfund.org; 212-870-3070
Bathrooms: Across from General Grant National Memorial (Riverside Drive and 124th Street); Riverside Park Café (near Henry Hudson Parkway at 105th Street)
Water/Snacks: Water fountains every few blocks along top level starting at 120th Street and less frequently along middle level; vendors throughout park; seasonal outdoor café at 105th Street
Maps: USGS Central Park; riversideparkfund.org/visit/Park-Map/?c=Park-Map
Directions by Car: Public parking is very limited; driving is discouraged. *GPS coordinates:* 40° 48.532′ N, 73° 57.957′ W.
Directions by Subway: Take the 1 train to 116th, 110th, or 103rd Street. Exit to the left (west) side, and walk two blocks to Riverside Park.

Riverside Park North is home to one of the greatest sledding hills in Manhattan. To get there, enter the park at 116th Street and follow the sound of shrieks and cheers to the ornamental fountain erected by the Woman's Health Protective Association in 1910. Descend the sweeping staircase on either side of the fountain, get on your sled or snowboard, and look out below!

Some 4 miles long and with three distinct levels, including the Manhattan Waterfront Greenway along the shore, Riverside Park is an exuberance of landscapes, activities, views, and destination playgrounds. The original park, developed between 1872 and 1910 by Frederick Law Olmsted and Calvert Vaux, stretched from 125th to 72nd streets, and we divide this at 100th Street (see Trip 19 for the southern section). The northern- and southernmost parts of the park, from 125th to 158th streets and from 72nd to 59th streets, are covered under the Manhattan Waterfront Greenway (Trips 6 and 7).

At street level along Riverside Drive, Riverside Park North is a wide, shady promenade that features small but thoughtfully designed "tot lots" every few

Riverside Park North and its many hills create a sledding mecca in winter.

blocks between 119th and 105th streets. (The ones at 116th and 105th streets have equipment for older children.) A great stone wall lines the promenade to the west, and behind that is a hillside of mature trees, verdant undergrowth, and a maintained dirt path that takes you deep within.

Entrances with paved paths leading to the middle level are at 120th, 116th, 115th, and 103rd streets. Between 112th and 101st streets, the mid-level promenade overlooks basketball courts, a skate park, baseball diamonds, and soccer fields. Beyond that lies the Hudson River. You can cross the Henry Hudson Parkway to reach the Greenway at 125th and 100th streets. *Remember:* During spring and fall, the ground surrounding the walking paths can remain wet for days following rain.

PLAN B: Head to Riverside Park South (Trip 19) for bigger destination playgrounds, or to the General Grant National Memorial (Trip 17) to enjoy an uncrowded plaza and another great playground.

Trip 19

Riverside Park (South)

With big playgrounds, monuments, and gardens, this area of Riverside Park has something for everyone.

Address: Riverside Drive at 100th Street, Manhattan, NY
Hours: Dawn to 1 A.M. daily
Fee: Free
Contact: nycgovparks.org/sub_your_park/vt_riverside_park/vt_riverside_park.html or call 311; riversideparkfund.org; 212-870-3070
Bathrooms: All destination playgrounds (see below); tennis courts (Riverside Drive and 96th Street)
Water/Snacks: Water fountains at playgrounds and throughout park; Boat Basin Café at 79th Street; vendors throughout park
Maps: USGS Central Park; riversideparkfund.org/visit/Park-Map/?c=Park-Map
Directions by Car: Public parking is very limited; driving is discouraged.
GPS coordinates: 40° 47.914′ N, 73° 58.391′ W.
Directions by Subway: Take the 1 train to 96th, 86th, 79th, or 72nd Street. Exit to the left (west) side, and walk two blocks to Riverside Park.

Where Riverside Park North has playgrounds dotting its street level, Riverside Park South has monuments, starting with the 1913 Firemen's Memorial at 100th Street and ending with the Eleanor Roosevelt Monument at 72nd Street. The high dome of the 1902 Soldiers and Sailors Monument, at 89th Street, is a skyline landmark when you're topside in the Hudson. Other monuments are dedicated to Joan of Arc (93rd Street) and Robert Ray Hamilton (76th Street).

In the middle level, Riverside Park South is a series of gardens and lawns with paved paths that connect to big destination playgrounds. These are the Dinosaur (98th Street), the Hippo (91st Street), River Run (82nd Street), and the Elephant (86th Street). You can descend from street level to the middle level every few blocks, and you can cross the Henry Hudson Parkway to reach the Manhattan Waterfront Greenway at 100th, 92nd, 83rd, 79th, and 72nd streets.

And all throughout, beautifully landscaped paths take you wherever you want to go. As you explore this part of the park, it's almost impossible to imagine the ashes from which it rose—but do try. In his masterpiece, *The Power Broker: Robert Moses and the Fall of New York*, Robert A. Caro describes a

Hudson River breezes make kite flying easy at Riverside Park.

1913-era Riverside Park thus: "...the 'park' was nothing but a vast low-lying mass of dirt and mud. Running through its length was the four-track bed of the NY Central.... At seventy-ninth and ninety-sixth streets, untreated garbage mounded toward the sky; the Sanitation Department used those areas as dumping grounds from which the garbage was transferred to scrows which towed it out to the open sea, but somehow the rate of transfer was never fast enough to clear the refuse away entirely."

Eventually, city parks commissioner Robert Moses (see page xxiv) would change all that, and today, Riverside Park serves as inspiration for the many parkland redevelopment efforts described in this book (see page ix for our "10 Best" list of industrial lands reclaimed for parks). *Remember:* Dramatic escarpments are near the River Run Playground, and though you may see people sunning themselves up there, children shouldn't climb the rocks. Broken glass is often in the crevices.

PLAN B: Head to the northern section of Riverside Park (Trip 18) for playgrounds of a more manageable size—especially for young children—or to the Manhattan Waterfront Greenway (Trips 6 and 7) for a wonderful promenade.

Trip 20

Ages 5–8

Pier 84

Pier 84, the largest public pier in Hudson River Park, offers free catch-and-release fishing and interactive water play for children.

Address: West 44th Street and the Hudson River, Manhattan, NY
Hours: 6 A.M. to 1 A.M. daily
Fee: Free
Contact: hudsonriverpark.org/explore/pier84.html or call 212-627-2020
Bathrooms: Pier 84 concessions area
Water/Snacks: Food vendors in Hudson River Park; concessions near entrance to Pier 84
Maps: USGS Central Park; USGS Weehawken; hudsonriverpark.org/explore.html
Directions by Car: Public parking is very limited; driving is discouraged. *GPS coordinates:* 40° 45.796′ N, 74° 0.005′ W.
Directions by Subway: Take the A, C, or E train to 42nd Street; walk west on West 44th Street to the Hudson River.

Pier 84 is a slice of the outdoors situated between two of the river's most popular tourist destinations: the Circle Line Sightseeing Cruises to the south and the venerable Intrepid Sea, Air and Space Museum to the north. The pier extends 1,000 feet into the water and provides a mix of a park environment and waterfront activities.

Big City Fishing offers free catch-and-release fishing along the north side of the pier. Striped bass, American eel, bluefish, and flounder are among the variety of sea animals caught and turned back to their habitat. Poles are lined up along the rail, and trained volunteers are on hand to bait hooks and help you cast a line. The recommended age is 5 years and older. The program runs weekends from spring through fall, from 10:30 A.M. to 5 P.M., weather permitting, with a half-hour limit if others are waiting.

Toward the end of the pier, Floating the Apple offers classes for rowing and boat building, and, if volunteer staff is available, a free insider's look at the art and craft of building 25-foot-long wooden rowboats and sailboats.

Children can also explore a cluster of interactive, science-themed water-play equipment located at the pier's entrance. A variety of pumps, some of

Kids can cool off, splash around, and explore the physics of water at this science-themed pier.

which require a little teamwork, send water down chutes, through water-wheels, and into pools and rivers. An irresistible circular fountain features dozens of geysers that send choreographed streams of water high into the air. The spigots are set below the surface so children can run through without tripping. *Remember:* This is one of the few destinations in this book that is best experienced on a hot summer day.

PLAN B: To get a fuller appreciation for the Hudson River Park redevelopment effort, head north to Pier 96 (Trip 22) for seasonal community kayaking, or hike south along the Manhattan Waterfront Greenway (Trip 7) to visit other refurbished piers. It is also easy to spend a day at the Intrepid Sea, Air and Space Museum.

Trip 21

High Line

The High Line is an example of the successful conversion of urban space into a bucolic recreational environment, and a great place to teach children about the area's natural flora.

Address: Gansevoort Street and Washington Street, Manhattan, NY
Hours: 7 A.M. to 11 P.M. daily
Fee: Free
Contact: thehighline.org; 212-500-6035
Bathrooms: North side of 16th Street on High Line, just opposite Northern Spur Horticultural Reserve
Water/Snacks: Vendors at Chelsea Market
Maps: USGS Jersey City; thehighline.org/about/maps
Directions by Car: Public parking is very limited; driving is discouraged. *GPS coordinates:* 40° 44.362′ N, 74° 0.482′ W.
Directions by Subway: Take the L train to Eighth Avenue; the A, C, or E train to 14th Street; the C or E train to 23rd Street; the 1, 2, or 3 train to 14th Street; or the 1 train to 18th Street or 23rd Street.

Rising 30 feet above the ground, the High Line was built in the 1930s as an elevated line for freight trains. Trains stopped running there in 1980, and by the late 1990s the structure was scheduled for demolition.

In 1999, a community-based nonprofit, Friends of the High Line, organized to save the structure and turn it into an elevated urban park and walkway. The park's forebear is the Promenade Plantée in Paris. Since opening in 2009, the High Line has gained national attention as an example of how urban spaces can be renovated to create public recreational landscapes.

It offers not only dramatic views of Lower Manhattan, but also art exhibitions and so-called self-seeded landscapes, which are cultivated swaths of the flora that grew in the rail tracks in the years after the trains had stopped running. Children will enjoy seeing their surroundings from a higher vantage.

The best way to experience the High Line is to take the stairs at the West 30th Street entrance and walk south. Toward the southern end you will find 10th Avenue Square, an elevated amphitheater that allows a bird's-eye view of the city blocks below and is very popular with photographers and local artists.

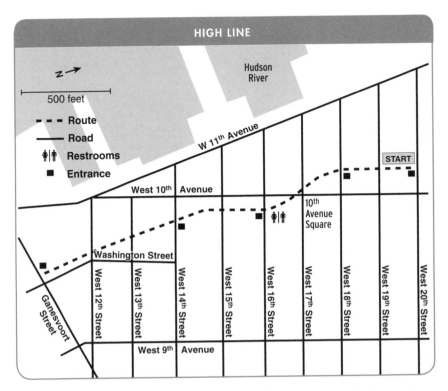

At the end you will descend into the Meat Packing District, a lively neighborhood with numerous restaurants.

Thanks to the recent opening of the upper half of the High Line, nine access points now exist: just north of Gansevoort street on Washington Street, as well as entrances along 10th Avenue at 14th, 16th, 18th, 20th, 23rd, 26th, 28th, and 30th streets. The 14th, 15th, and 30th street entrances include elevators; the others require walking up stairs. *Remember:* Dogs, bicycles, and scooters are not permitted on the High Line.

PLAN B: Because Manhattan is so narrow this far south, many alternate destinations are nearby, including Pier 96 (Trip 22), Battery Park (Trip 23), and Battery Park City Esplanade (Trip 24).

Trip 22

Pier 96: Downtown Boathouse

Experienced and first-time kayakers will agree: There is no better place to enjoy a cool river breeze than on the Hudson itself.

Address: West 55th Street and the Hudson River, Manhattan, NY
Hours: 5 P.M. to 7 P.M. weekdays, 9 A.M. to 6 P.M. weekends; open May through October, weather permitting.
Fee: Free
Contact: downtownboathouse.org/Pier96.html
Bathrooms: Portable toilet just north of pier
Water/Snacks: Food vendors along Manhattan Waterfront Greenway
Maps: USGS Central Park; hudsonriverpark.org/explore.html
Directions by Car: Public parking is very limited; driving is discouraged.
  GPS coordinates: 40° 46.209′ N, 73° 59.706′ W.
Directions by Subway: Take the B, D, or E train to Seventh Avenue or the C or E train to West 50th Street. Alternatively, you can take the 1, A, C, or E train to Columbus Circle (West 59th Street).

The shoreline has changed dramatically since the Lenni Lenapes, the American Indians who once populated much of the New York and New Jersey area, plied the waterway we now call the Hudson River. But settling into a kayak to bob and paddle around brings some perspective on how things were four centuries ago.

In 1995, the volunteer-run Downtown Boathouse effectively opened the river to individual use. That year, 100 people did what had become unthinkable to the modern mind: They stepped into a tiny craft to maneuver on the mighty Hudson—albeit, a designated nook of it—as cruise ships, large yachts, and ocean-bound barges chugged by mid-river. Since then, it is estimated that Downtown Boathouse has enabled several hundred thousand launches. Free walk-up boating is now available at Pier 96; at Pier 40, near West and West Houston streets; and at West 72nd Street. The 72nd Street location is open seasonally on weekends and holidays from 10 A.M. to 5 P.M.

Downtown Boathouse uses sit-atop kayaks for one or two people. Younger children can nestle in an adult's lap on a one-person kayak, but it is recommended that older children sit in the front of a two-person vessel. There is

Kayakers can launch at Pier 96 to paddle near cruise ships and ocean-bound barges on the Hudson River.

no age minimum or limit, but it is advisable that participants know how to swim. All participants must wear life preservers (available to borrow at the dock). Trained volunteers are on hand to give dockside paddling lessons, to help adults slide from a sitting position on the dock into the boat, and to help children in afterward. Boating is limited to 20 minutes when other visitors are waiting.

Clinton Cove Park, at the entrance to Pier 96, is a nice place to dry off on a bench or on the lawn afterward. *Remember:* You will get wet, so dress appropriately or bring a change of clothes.

PLAN B: To run and splash around in water, visit Pier 84 (Trip 20), and to see more of the Hudson's shoreline, hike or bike along the Manhattan Waterfront Greenway (Trip 7).

Trip 23

Battery Park

Located at the southern tip of Manhattan, Battery Park is steeped in more than 200 years of history and still teems with activity today.

Address: State Street and Battery Place (near the Staten Island Ferry Terminal), Manhattan, NY
Hours: 6 A.M. to 1 A.M. daily
Fee: Free
Contact: nycgovparks.org/parks/batterypark; thebattery.org; 212-417-2000
Bathrooms: At Battery Place and State Street
Water/Snacks: Vendors throughout park
Map: USGS Jersey City; thebattery.org/battery/battery_map.pdf
Directions by Car: Public parking is very limited; driving is discouraged. *GPS coordinates:* 40° 42.272′ N, 73° 0.851′ W.
Directions by Subway: Take the 4 or 5 train to Bowling Green, the R or W trains to Whitehall Street, or the 1 train to South Ferry.

Battery Park is the oldest public space in New York City, and one of the most historically significant locations in the United States. It was the birthplace of Manhattan more than 400 years ago. Today, the 20-plus-acre park offers plenty of space for walking and a playground at State and South streets. Concerts take place here throughout summer, and the park is studded with monuments that commemorate the area's and nation's history. Many are located within the 4-acre Battery Bosque Garden, a beautifully landscaped area that features woodland perennials, cultivated native plants, and a preservation of 140 London plane trees that, legend has it, owe their existence to Michael Rapuano, an Italian landscape architect who loved the species and designed it into various parks in New York City in the 1930s.

A network of stroller-friendly, paved and gravel paths all eventually lead to Castle Clinton National Monument at the northwest edge of the park. Originally built as a fortress during the War of 1812, the castle served as an assembly hall and open-air theatre before becoming an entry point for immigrants from 1855 to 1890. In 1896, the castle was reborn as the New York Aquarium, one of the nation's first public aquariums. It remained that way until 1941 when Robert Moses, who was then parks commissioner, closed the Battery and began

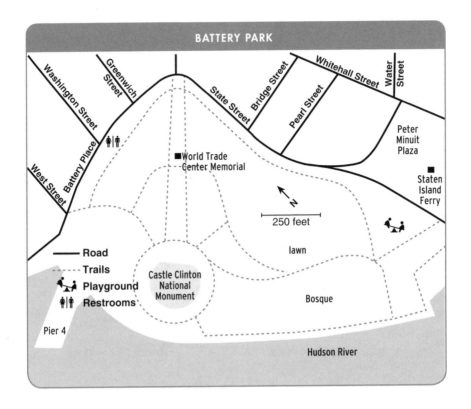

BATTERY PARK

Washington Street

Greenwich Street

State Street

Bridge Street

Whitehall Street

Water Street

Pearl Street

West Street

Battery Place

Peter Minuit Plaza

■ World Trade Center Memorial

■ Staten Island Ferry

N

|———| 250 feet

Road

Trails

Playground

Restrooms

lawn

Castle Clinton National Monument

Bosque

Pier 4

Hudson River

demolishing the fortress. Congress stopped the demolition, and the remains were taken over and developed by the National Park Service.

The shoreline around the castle has likewise evolved greatly, as landfill projects throughout the eighteenth and nineteenth centuries pushed it farther into New York Harbor. Today this extended coast serves as the launch point for ferries to Ellis Island, Liberty Island, and Governors Island, and for the free commuter ferry to Staten Island. It is also part of the Greenway bike path that nearly circumvents Manhattan. *Remember:* Battery Park is very popular and can get crowded with local and out-of-town visitors. It may be necessary to walk, rather than ride, bicycles through some areas.

PLAN B: Battery Park Esplanade (Trip 24) is a great place to walk and visit destination playgrounds along the Hudson River. Liberty Island (Trip 70), Governors Island (Trip 72), and Ellis Island (Trip 71) all provide opportunities for recreation and teaching your kids about the history of New York City and the United States.

Trip 24

All Ages

Battery Park City Esplanade

This pristine, 1.2-mile park runs the length of Battery Park City along the Hudson River. A paved bikeway runs along the water's edge, and boardwalk areas offer pedestrians brief detours from the main path.

Address: Battery Place and West Street (just west of Battery Park), Manhattan, NY

Hours: 6 A.M. to 1 A.M. daily

Fee: Free

Contact: bpcparks.org/bpcp/parks/parks.php; 212-267-9700

Bathrooms: At Battery Place and State Street; Robert F. Wagner Park; Winter Garden; The Solaire

Water/Snacks: Vendors throughout the park

Maps: USGS Jersey City; bpcparks.org/bpcp/map/picts/bpcpc_map_2010.pdf

Directions by Car: Public parking is very limited; driving is discouraged. *GPS coordinates:* 40° 42.278' N, 74° 1.001' W.

Directions by Subway: Take the 4 or 5 train to Bowling Green, the R or W train to Whitehall Street, or the 1 train to South Ferry.

Battery Park Esplanade is a 1.2-mile necklace of greenery that links a number of smaller parks, coves, harbors, and playgrounds along the edge of the Hudson River. It offers panoramic views of New Jersey's shoreline, which composes the river's western bank.

At the Esplanade's southern entrance is Robert F. Wagner Jr. Park, a blend of lawns and themed gardens. Visitors will first encounter the Hot Garden, which features flowers that bloom in yellows to reds. A little north is the Cool Garden, where blossoms are white, blue, and pink.

Continuing north along the esplanade, the South Cove has a boardwalk that leads pedestrians to a perch high atop a winding staircase. Farther along, West Thames Park includes community gardens and a destination playground. The restoration and reopening of this park in July 2010 was viewed as a local triumph following the damage the neighborhood sustained during the 9/11 attacks on the nearby World Trade Center buildings.

You will then pass through Rector Park; Monsignor John J. Kowsky Plaza, which has a small tot-lot playground; the Esplanade Plaza; and then the North Cove, which is a bustling marina area that will fascinate children who are in-

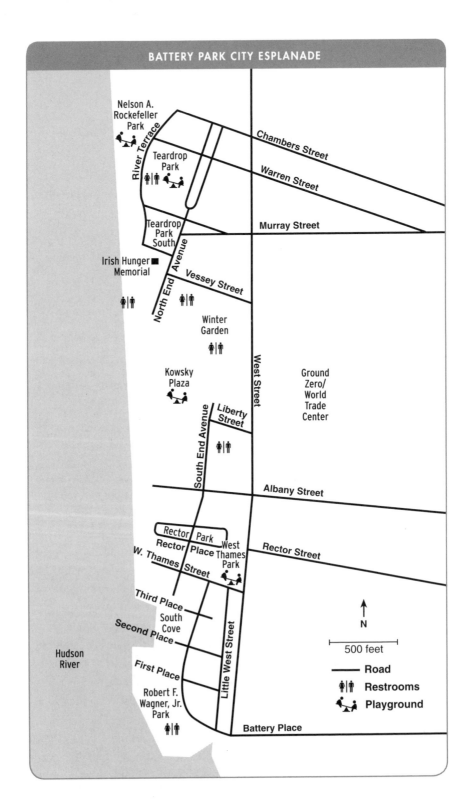

Nelson A.
Rockefeller
Park

River Terrace

Chambers Street

Warren Street

Teardrop
Park

Murray Street

Teardrop
Park
South

North End Avenue

Vessey Street

Irish Hunger ■
Memorial

Winter
Garden

West Street

Kowsky
Plaza

Ground
Zero/
World
Trade
Center

South End Avenue

Liberty
Street

Albany Street

Rector Park

Rector Place West

Rector Street

West
Thames
Park

W. Thames Street

Third Place

Little West Street

South
Cove

Second Place

Hudson
River

First Place

N

500 feet

━━━ Road

👫 Restrooms

👨‍👧 Playground

Robert F.
Wagner, Jr.
Park

Battery Place

terested in harbor activities. After the World Financial Center Plaza is the Irish Hunger Memorial, a miniature rural Irish landscape with remnants of a stone house and barren potato fields.

Nearing the north end of the esplanade is 2-acre Teardrop Park, which has both quiet lawns and a robust playground. Nelson A. Rockefeller Park, at the esplanade's northern tip, also contains a destination playground with a series of trampolines and a small merry-go-round that children can power by pedaling. *Remember:* The esplanade is less crowded and better for biking than Battery Park (Trip 23).

PLAN B: To add some history to your outdoor adventure, consider Battery Park (Trip 23), Liberty Island (Trip 70), Governors Island (Trip 72), and Ellis Island (Trip 71).

We believe that rain doesn't need to "go away," but rather people need to go outside despite the wet weather. Since most people don't, however, rainy days are a rare chance to have the city virtually to yourselves. On a hot day you can go out without a coat and get wet on purpose. Otherwise, a good raincoat is essential. You and the kids should be in boots, or sandals if it's warm. Head inside if there's lightning or severe weather, or if anyone starts to shiver.

Here are some ideas for rainy-day fun:

Rainy Day Art

Two toddler favorites—chunky colored chalk and bathtub crayons—take on new dimensions in the rain, even for older children. Let kids channel their inner artist by creating watercolors with chalk on the sidewalks, or indulge in body art with the crayons.

Playgrounds

Playgrounds—even tot lots—are likewise transformed in a soaking rain. Ordinarily sticky slides become quick water rides, and the sandbox is a landscape-in-waiting for lakes and estuaries.

Puddle Jumping

When puddles reach a respectable width, see who can jump over them—and for how long, as puddles inexorably grow. Then, hold a contest to see who can make the biggest splash by jumping in the middle or by kicking waves out of the center. How long does it take for the puddle to fill back up, or can you keep it from filling back up at all?

Nature in the Rain

Once energy is expelled, help kids note the natural environment. Are flowers open or closed? Are pigeons in their usual perches? And where have all the butterflies gone? Use a waterproof camera to take pictures and compare them with the same places on a sunny day, after a dry spell, or during another season.

Trip 25

All Ages

Bryant Park

A legendary social spot among the area's office workers, Bryant Park also holds many charms for children.

Address: 42nd Street and Fifth Avenue, Manhattan, NY
Hours: 7 A.M. to 7 P.M., 10 P.M., or midnight, depending on the month and day
Fee: Free (in winter, ice skate rentals are $13)
Contact: bryantpark.org/about-us/contact.html; 212-768-4242
Bathrooms: Near subway stop at 42nd Street; between Fifth and Sixth avenues
Water/Snacks: Upscale dining at Bryant Park Grill; casual dining at Bryant Park
    Café; four kiosks serving sandwiches, soups, salads, coffee, and ice cream
Maps: USGS Central Park; bryantpark.org/plan-your-visit/map.html
Directions by Car: Public parking is very limited; driving is discouraged.
    GPS coordinates: 40° 45.210′ N, 73° 58.853′ W.
Directions by Subway: Take the B, D, F, or M train to 42nd Street/Bryant Park,
    or take the 7 train to Fifth Avenue.

Within a relatively small space—only 9 acres—Bryant Park manages to pack in two seasonal favorites: the summer film festival and outdoor ice skating in winter. Both are free and wildly popular. Year round, on any day with reasonable weather, the impeccably clean park is a mecca for Midtown Manhattan office workers who flock there to enjoy lunch on the lawn, on a bench, or at one of the quaint picnic tables.

The land here was designated a public space very early in the city's history—in 1686—and so it has remained. Prior to that, it was wilderness.

To get a full sense of Bryant Park's charm and loveliness, first walk the perimeter on the sidewalks. Start at the corner of 42nd Street and Fifth Avenue, and walk south down Fifth to 40th Street. This will take you past the front of the behemoth-size central branch of the New York Public Library. Continue down 40th Street, turn right onto Sixth Avenue, and pass the grand entrance at Fountain Terrace. Turn right onto 42nd Street, and a little more than halfway up, enter the park. From here, wander the tree-lined gravel walkways around the lawn, or cross it at the center to take a spin on Le Carrousel, a recently installed treat for adults and children alike. *Remember:* During winter, lockers at the skating rink are free, but bring a lock or buy one there. Skate rentals are

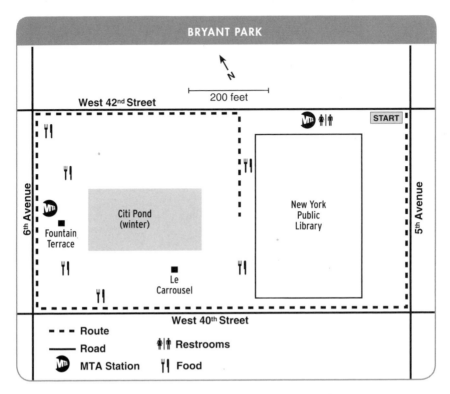

$13, or you can bring your own. You can check larger bags and have your own skates sharpened (each for a fee). A ride on Le Carrousel is $2 per person.

PLAN B: Head down Fifth Avenue to Washington Square Park (Trip 26)—especially in summer when the fountain is flowing.

Trip 26

All Ages

Washington Square Park

Washington Square Park is home to a legendary fountain in which children can play.

Address: Waverly Place and MacDougal Street, Manhattan, NY
Hours: All hours daily
Fee: Free
Contact: nycgovparks.org/parks/washingtonsquarepark
Bathrooms: Southwest of fountain
Water/Snacks: Water fountains in playground; vendors in and around park
Map: USGS Brooklyn
Directions by Car: Public parking is very limited; driving is discouraged.
    GPS coordinates: 40° 43.886′ N, 73° 59.817′ W.
Directions by Subway: Take the A, B, C, or D train to West Fourth Street; walk
    two blocks north and two blocks east.

Washington Square Park has two architectural landmarks: a great arch and an enormous fountain. While the former is the park's most prominent feature and can be seen from blocks away, it is the latter that draws children from all over the city during summer. Unlike most decorative fountains the world over, this one actually permits waders and bathers to climb in.

Located on the park's northern edge, the Washington Square Arch was designed by Stanford White, the legendary nineteenth-century American Renaissance architect. The arch was supposed to be temporary, made of plaster and wood and erected in 1889 over nearby Fifth Avenue in celebration of the centennial of George Washington's inauguration. The arch proved so popular that White was commissioned to design a permanent version for the park—which was already home to the fountain, created in 1872.

After arriving on the corner of MacDougal Street and Waverly Place, enter the park by heading south under the arch. Proceed past the fountain, then follow the path at the park's southern edge (along West Fourth Street) counterclockwise. The path will lead you back up to the northern edge of the park, where a popular playground is located. Continue your counterclockwise spin, now heading west across the top of the park. You will eventually turn south, and in this area you will find bathrooms and a dog run.

*Kids and adults alike enjoy wading and playing
in the Washington Square Park fountain.*

Park goers typically include a wide range of musicians, chess players, and street performers, as well as groups of students from nearby New York University who use the park as a place to study and socialize outdoors. The park is particularly good for parents with strollers, as all the paths are well paved. *Remember:* Biking is not allowed inside the park.

PLAN B: Tompkins Square Park (Trip 27), which has several good playgrounds, is located nearby. Walk eight blocks east on West Fourth Street, then three blocks north on Avenue E.

Trip 27

All Ages

Tompkins Square Park

Tompkins Square Park has a rich history, is conveniently located near other sites of interest in Lower Manhattan, and provides playgrounds suitable for different ages.

Address: 500 East Ninth Street, Manhattan, NY
Hours: 6 A.M. to 2 A.M. daily
Fee: Free
Contact: nycgovparks.org/parks/tompkinssquarepark; 212-360-8283
Bathrooms: Park Office building, toward northern edge of park
Water/Snacks: Vendors throughout park
Maps: USGS Brooklyn; itsmypark.org/brochures/tompkins_square.html
Directions by Car: Public parking is very limited; driving is discouraged.
   GPS coordinates: 40° 43.636′ N, 73° 58.962′ W.
Directions by Subway: Take the L train to First Avenue or the F train to Second
   Avenue.

Tompkins Square Park offers families with children of different ages numerous recreational activities within 10.5 acres. A 20-by-40-foot swimming pool (3 feet deep), fitness equipment, and several playgrounds will appeal to toddlers and older children. This park also boasts an expansive dog run and picnic tables, as well as basketball and handball courts.

Beautifully landscaped and, for the most part, well shaded, the park is located on what was originally marshland and open tidal meadows. Tompkins Square opened as a public space in 1834 and has undergone numerous renovations since then, but it is still home to three Sycamore trees from the original park: two on Tenth Street, and another at Avenue A and Ninth Street.

Begin your walk at the park entrance at Eighth Street and Avenue A. Follow the paths counterclockwise heading east and you will get a sense of the park's peculiar geography. Due possibly to its central location, particularly before the city fully expanded to the north, Tompkins Square Park served as the site for public demonstrations. Owing to its longtime reputation as a site for civil unrest, the park was redesigned by Robert Moses in 1936 to make it more conducive to crowd management. Visitors today will notice the attractive—yet, at a time, purposeful—wrought-iron fencing separating various areas of the park.

Shady, stroller-friendly paths, extensive playgrounds, and a dog run make Tompkins Square Park a hit with kids and animal lovers.

Tompkins Square Park was closed and renovated in the early 1990s, and has since reemerged as a wonderful destination for strolling and recreation. *Remember:* Do not climb or sit on the fences. Open-access areas have gates for entrance.

PLAN B: East River Park (Trip 29), three blocks due east, offers longer hikes along the East River, concessions, and more playgrounds to choose from.

Trip 28

Sara D. Roosevelt Park

Canal Street offers a bustling urban walk through Chinatown, making the beautiful gardens and well-themed playgrounds of Sara D. Roosevelt Park all the more delightful.

Address: Canal Street and Chrystie Street, Manhattan, NY
Hours: Dawn to 1 A.M. daily
Fee: Free
Contact: nycgovparks.org/parks/saradroosevelt or call 311
Bathrooms: South end of Hester Street Playground; north end of Lion's Playground
Water/Snacks: Water fountains throughout park and at playgrounds; vendors on surrounding streets
Maps: USGS Brooklyn; nycgovparks.org/parks/saradroosevelt/map
Directions by Car: Public parking is very limited; driving is discouraged.
    GPS coordinates: 40° 42.949′ N, 73° 59.692′ W.
Directions by Subway: Take the 1 train to Canal Street and walk six blocks east.

Some destinations pull you back in time, others bring you to a different landscape; visiting Chinatown is like experiencing another country. With borders currently defined as Grand, Allen, Worth, and Lafayette streets (north, east, south, and west, respectively), Manhattan's Chinatown is home to one of the highest concentrations of Chinese people in the western hemisphere. We refer to the borders as "current" because Chinatown shows no signs of stopping its expansion.

Canal Street is the spine of Chinatown. Though a walk down Canal may at times feel like wading against a powerful current, no matter which direction you're heading, it is the only way to truly experience the neighborhood's vibrancy. As you leave the subway station heading east, you will pass an eclectic array of shops selling everything from used cell phone rechargers to incense, pickled eel, diamond rings, golden Buddhas, herbal remedies, and more. The clog of automobile traffic in the streets will make you feel grateful you are using your two feet.

Sara D. Roosevelt Park (named for President Franklin D. Roosevelt's mother) starts at the intersection of Canal and Chrystie streets. This 7.8-acre

The courts at Sara D. Roosevelt Park offer a nice expanse for young bicycle riders or groups of children looking to enjoy a game of soccer.

park is made up of land acquired by the city in 1929 to widen Chrystie and Forsythe streets and build low-cost housing. In New Deal spirit, the plan was revamped to provide an inner-city idyll for parents and kids. The park is laid out around two playgrounds—Hester Street and Lion's. Before visiting the playgrounds, walk four blocks north to the intersection with Delancey Street to view the Hua Mei Bird Garden. In this space, local bird owners gather to display their fine feathered friends, a practice that is common in China. *Remember:* Don't miss the foot-activated xylophone at the Hester Street Playground.

PLAN B: Tompkins Square Park (Trip 27), which also has great playgrounds, is located two blocks east and five blocks north of the northern end of the park.

Trip 29

East River Park

Offering fresh river breezes and panoramic views of Brooklyn, East River Park is an excellent destination for hiking, walking, playgrounds, and fishing.

Address: FDR Drive between East Twelfth Street and Montgomery Street, Manhattan, NY
Hours: Park: 7 A.M. to 9 P.M. daily; running tracks: 8 A.M. to 9 P.M. daily
Fee: Free
Contact: nycgovparks.org/parks/eastriverpark; 212-529-7185 or call 311
Bathrooms: East Tenth Street; Broome Street (near tennis courts); East Sixth Street
Water/Snacks: Water fountains and vendors throughout park
Map: USGS Brooklyn
Directions by Car: Public parking is very limited; driving is discouraged. *GPS coordinates:* 40° 43.130′ N, 73° 58.479′ W.
Directions by Subway: Take the L train to First Avenue or the F train to East Broadway and walk three and a half blocks east toward the East River.

At nearly 57 acres, East River Park is a recreational mecca. Since opening in 1939, it has been immensely popular as a place for neighborhood residents to gather, particularly during summer, when fresh breezes blowing off the East River provide a much-needed respite from urban living.

Today the park provides many opportunities for easy and expansive walks, strolls, and bike rides along the East River, as well as for soccer, basketball, baseball, tennis, and football. It also features a recently renovated amphitheater and a great waterpark that has a wading pool and a collection of bronze seal statues that spray water on passersby. This destination, located near the fire house across from Grand Street, is also a huge hit with children.

As you go into the park, head directly east to the river. Depending on where you enter the park (several ways exist from north to south), you should follow the path either north or south. Going north will take you to the East River Greenway. Heading south, you will eventually pick up the southern spur of the East River Greenway. *Remember:* Crossing pedestrian bridges over highways can intimidate some children. It is helpful to tell them in advance what the plans are, and assure them that they will be safe and with you at all times. The

Anglers, pedestrians, and boat watchers enjoy East River Park.

bridges are well guarded from the highway below with high walls, rails, and/
or fences.

PLAN B: Tompkins Square Park (Trip 28) and the Imagination Playground at
South Street Seaport are close by. The former is one of New York's oldest and
most popular parks. The latter is a new park with a novel approach to children's recreation.

Trip 30

Ages 9–12

Hudson River Sloop *Clearwater*

This terrific family adventure blends history and environmental awareness aboard a stunning replica of an eighteenth-century sloop.

Address: West 79th Street Boat Basin, Manhattan, NY
Hours: Three-hour afternoon and evening sails; open seasonally, dates and times vary
Fee: Adults, $50; Clearwater members, $35; children ages 12 and under, $15
Contact: clearwater.org/about; 845-265-8080
Bathrooms: On board
Water/Snacks: Food and beverages allowed on board, but not available for purchase
Maps: USGS Central Park; clearwater.org/come-sailing/dock-directions
Directions by Car: Public parking is very limited; driving is discouraged. *GPS coordinates:* 40° 47.170′ N, 73° 59.116′ W.
Directions by Subway: Take the 1, 2, or 3 train to 79th Street and walk four blocks west to the Hudson River.

To step aboard the Hudson River sloop *Clearwater* is to step into the eighteenth century, when hundreds of similar vessels carried anglers, passengers, and cargo up and down the Hudson. Harking back to that era—a time when rivers were revered—the singer-songwriter Pete Seeger and other Hudson Valley residents built *Clearwater* with the purpose of raising awareness about the nation's threatened waterways. Launched in 1969, the sloop has been sailing to towns and cities along the Hudson, New York Harbor, and Long Island Sound ever since.

A three-hour cruise begins with a lesson on safety: the importance of keeping the boat's weight balanced, where to stand—and not stand—when the boom is in motion, and reacting quickly to the captain's calls.

Once offshore, the crew invites children amidships to learn boat architecture and terminology, the history of such vessels, and the need to protect the Hudson and all waterways. To that end, environmentalists once made a historic sail of *Clearwater* to Washington, D.C., to advocate for the passage of the Clean Water Act of 1972.

When it's time to raise the sail, everyone is invited to take a place along the thick rope to pull hand over hand, chanting "heave-ho," to make the heavy

Kids learn sea chanteys and the art of sailing aboard the sloop Clearwater.

cloth climb the mast. Children are also brought to the tiller to help crew members steer the boat, and are taught how to throw a vintage-style fishing net overboard. This comes with an important discussion on the restoration and preservation of fish populations.

Once the hard work is done, crew members settle down with the children to sing age-old sea chanteys and modern ballads. It is also a *Clearwater* tradition to observe a moment of silence to hear the sounds of the water as Henry Hudson himself may have heard them, except, perhaps, for the chop of a helicopter. *Remember: Clearwater* is propelled by the wind and tides. As such, it is best to prepare children for the possibility that the boat may not reach the George Washington Bridge, the southern tip of Manhattan, or any other destination they may hope to go to.

PLAN B: To walk off your sea legs, take a stroll through nearby Riverside Park (Trip 19) or along the Manhattan Waterfront Greenway (Trip 7).

Section 2

Brooklyn

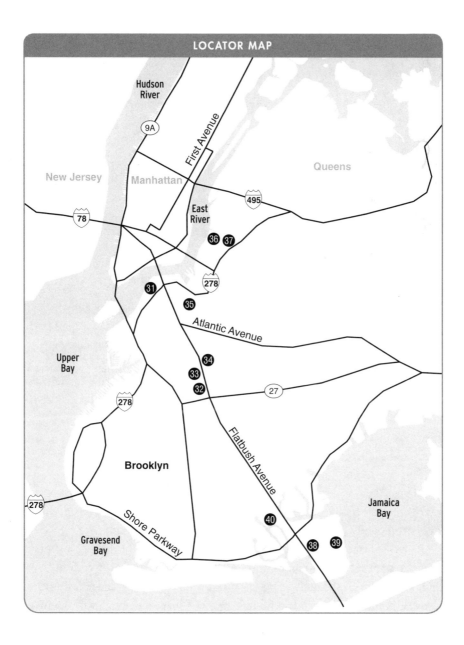

LOCATOR MAP

Trip 31

All
Ages

Brooklyn Bridge Park

Paved and gravel paths along the coast offer spectacular views of southern Manhattan and the landmark islands of New York Harbor.

Address: Plymouth Street and Washington Street, Brooklyn, NY
Hours: 6 A.M. to 1 A.M. daily
Fee: Free
Contact: nycgovparks.org/parks/brooklynbridgepark; brooklynbridgepark.org
   or call 311
Bathrooms: Near Fulton Ferry Landing
Water/Snacks: Concession buildings near Fulton Ferry Landing and Pier 6
Maps: USGS Brooklyn; brooklynbridgepark.org/go/the-park/the-park-plan
Directions by Car: Public parking is very limited; driving is discouraged.
   GPS coordinates: 40° 42.234′ N, 73° 59.373′ W.
Directions by Subway: To get to Pier 1, take the A or C train to High Street,
   the 2 or 3 train to Clark Street, or the F train to York Street.

Pier 1, the first section of this stunning waterfront rehabilitation project, opened in 2010. It brought to the area 6 acres of beautifully landscaped park, whose still-young trees and shrubs hold great promise of creating shady groves and paths in the years to come.

From the pier's 2.5-acre lawn and 1,300-foot promenade along the East River, families can enjoy breathtaking views of southern Manhattan, the islands of New York Harbor, and the awesome expanse of the Brooklyn Bridge. Free seasonal community boating and kayaking is offered at the boathouse at Pier 1 and Main Street.

The landscaped Interim Greenway Path stretches from Pier 1 at the northern tip to Pier 6 at the southern end, passing Piers 2 through 5, which are not yet open to the public. Walkers and riders get a good sense of the formerly active harbor, and of what will someday be an 85-acre waterfront park.

Pier 6 at Atlantic Avenue features a 1.6-acre cluster of destination playgrounds with different themes and equipment for children of various ages. Slide Mountain, as the name suggests, has several large chute slides in addition to two climbing nets for older children. Swing Village had a range of swings— from buckets to saucers—for children ages 2 through 12, and Sandbox Village

Brooklyn Bridge Park offers stunning views, great playgrounds, and plenty of space for picnicking.

has sand pits, wooden houses, and a stationary train for children to climb on. The Water Lab offers children ages 5 through 12 the chance to explore the physics of water through pumps, chutes, and water wheels. A tot-lot playground is at Pier 1.

For some sea-faring fun, hop the ferry to or from Manhattan's South Street Seaport. Service is available seasonally on Saturdays and Sundays; visit nyharborway.com for more information. Plans are also in place to add a water taxi dock at Pier 6 that would bring visitors to Governors Island (Trip 72). This is a park worth visiting frequently to watch it develop. *Remember:* Many areas of the park are designated as dog free. An enclosed dog run is at Pier 6. Also, the gravel paths are a challenge for some strollers and for children on scooters.

PLAN B: Prospect Park (Trip 32) offers a comparison with a very mature park, and the Prospect Park Audubon Center at the Boathouse and the Children's Corner (Trip 33) has many activities for children. You could also walk over the Brooklyn Bridge. Entrance to the elevated pedestrian boardwalk is at Tillary Street and Boreum Place.

Trip 32

All Ages

Prospect Park

Prospect Park is a mecca for day-hikers, bicyclists, picnickers, and lovers of geologic and human history.

Address: Eastern Parkway and Flatbush Avenue, Brooklyn, NY
Hours: 6 A.M. to 1 A.M. daily
Fee: Free
Contact: prospectpark.org; 718-965-8951; nycgovparks.org/parks/prospectpark or call 311
Bathrooms: Picnic House; bandshell; Harmony Playground; Lincoln Road Playground; Audubon Center at Boathouse; Prospect Park Zoo; Parade Ground; Parade Ground; playground; Litchfield Villa
Water/Snacks: Concessions at Audubon Center Boathouse, Prospect Park Zoo, Parade Grounds, and Picnic House
Maps: USGS Brooklyn; prospectpark.org/visit/interactive_map
Directions by Car: Public parking is very limited; driving is discouraged. *GPS coordinates:* 40° 40.369′ N, 73° 58.151′ W.
Directions by Subway: Take the F or G train to Seventh Avenue, Fifteenth Street/Prospect Park, or Fort Hamilton Parkway; the 2 or 3 train to Grand Army Plaza; the Q train to Parkside Avenue or Prospect Park; or the S or B train to Prospect Park.

At nearly 600 acres, most of them lush and accessible, Prospect Park is a destination you can visit many times, and still have much more to see. Frederick Law Olmsted and Calvert Vaux, the legendary nineteenth-century landscape architects (see page xxiv), developed Prospect Park in the mid-nineteenth century, coinciding with Brooklyn's rapid growth. It features their signature archways, forest walks, grassy meadows, and waterfalls.

Entering the park at Grand Army Plaza, Long Meadow, 1 mile in length, is a short walk south on East or West drive. Pedestrians can share the drives with bicyclists and skaters, or take to the network of well-groomed paths that circle and wind through the meadow. Lower Pool and Upper Pool, a pair of lakes that are popular birding sites, are at the western edge of the meadow. Just to the east is the more rugged Ravine, Brooklyn's only forest, which is heavily shaded by a wide variety of trees. The Ravine also has a network of streams and waterfalls.

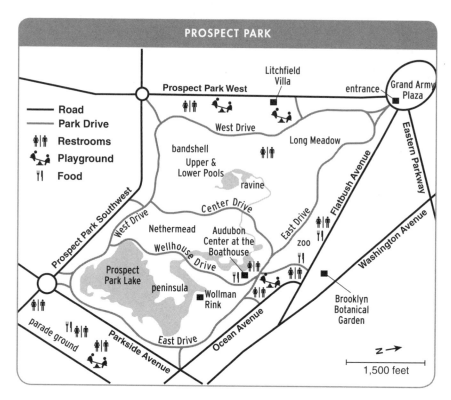

PROSPECT PARK

- — Road
- — Park Drive
- 🚹🚺 Restrooms
- 🛝 Playground
- 🍴 Food

Litchfield Villa

Prospect Park West

entrance

Grand Army Plaza

West Drive

Long Meadow

bandshell

Upper & Lower Pools

ravine

Center Drive

West Drive

Nethermead

Audubon Center at the Boathouse

East Drive

zoo

Wellhouse Drive

Prospect Park Southwest

Prospect Park Lake

peninsula

Wollman Rink

Flatbush Avenue

Eastern Parkway

Washington Avenue

Brooklyn Botanical Garden

parade ground

Parkside Avenue

East Drive

Ocean Avenue

N →

1,500 feet

Continuing south, cross over Center Drive, the Nethermead meadow, and Wellhouse Drive to reach the 60-acre lake, where all streams, pools, and waterfalls in the park eventually meet. This confluence is by no chance of nature; the park's water system was entirely human-made. The peninsula, which stretches into the lake, offers a view of waterfowl and provides more-secluded picnic spots. The lake is surrounded by both paved roads and footpaths.

From most spots along Prospect Park's perimeters, a playground is within easy walking distance. The park features a ring of seven playgrounds, most suitable for children of varied ages. The park is also a welcome stop while traversing the Brooklyn–Queens Greenway, a 40-mile bicycling and pedestrian path that connects those two boroughs. *Remember:* In winter, great sledding can be had near Picnic House, in the center of Long Meadow, and in the Nethermead.

PLAN B: Big and beautiful, Brooklyn Botanic Garden (Trip 34) is on the same tract of land as Prospect Park, though not accessible from within the park. To take in beautiful waterfront vistas, visit Brooklyn Bridge Park (Trip 31).

Trip 33

All Ages

Prospect Park Audubon Center and the Children's Corner

The Children's Corner in Prospect Park is a destination unto itself. On weekends, the Audubon Center at the Boathouse runs free drop-in educational programs geared toward nature.

Address: Lincoln Road and Ocean Avenue, Brooklyn, NY
Hours: Prospect Park: 6 A.M. to 1 A.M. daily; boathouse hours vary throughout the year
Fee: Free
Contact: prospectpark.org/visit/places/audubon; 718-287-3400
Bathrooms: Lincoln Road Playground; Audubon Center at Boathouse; Prospect Park Zoo
Water/Snacks: Concessions at Boathouse and at Prospect Park Zoo
Maps: USGS Brooklyn; prospectpark.org/visit/interactive_map
Directions by Car: Public parking is very limited; driving is discouraged.
  GPS coordinates: 40° 39.630′ N, 73° 57.774′ W.
Directions by Subway: Take the Q, S, or B train to Prospect Park. Exit at Lincoln Road and follow Lincoln Road to the park entrance on Ocean Avenue.

A good swath of eastern Prospect Park is devoted to children. From the Willink Entrance on Flatbush Avenue, follow the pedestrian path east, over East Drive, to the Audubon Center at the Boathouse—the National Audubon Society's first urban location. It is a great first stop to learn about nature, ecology, and preservation before heading off on the nearby trails to see nature in situ. The Boathouse also has trail maps, and all trails are well marked throughout the area.

Waterfall and Midwood trails both begin and end at the Audubon Center, taking day-hikers on an easy excursion along paved paths. Waterfall Trail is a 45-minute walk that showcases streams and, as the name suggests, waterfalls within the park's network of artificially designed waterways. Midwood Trail, which takes about a half hour, circles and winds through the oldest indigenous forest in Brooklyn.

Several easy hikes offer stunning views of the nation's first urban-area Audubon Center.

Half-hour boat tours of Lullwater Lake (which fronts the Boathouse) are available for a fee. An easy path around the lake's perimeter features viewing platforms and bridges that enable walkers to adjust the length of their trip.

Heading back over East Drive is the Children's Corner, home to the Lefferts Historic House, which dates to the eighteenth century, when the area was farmland. The grounds have replica gardening tools and sturdy wooden stilts that children and adults can use to experience how people more than 200 years ago worked the land when it was particularly waterlogged. On the right side of the house is an American Indian wigwam that children can enter to get an idea of how the area's original residents lived.

The Prospect Park Zoo, which has an entrance fee, is also located in the Children's Corner, as is a stunning antique carousel that was relocated from Coney Island in 1952. *Remember:* If you are interested in guided tours and nature programs, contact the Audubon Center at the Boathouse in advance to hear about the options.

PLAN B: Prospect Park at large (Trip 32) and Brooklyn Botanic Garden (Trip 34), both located on the same great tract of land, are within walking distance of the Children's Corner.

Trip 34

Brooklyn Botanic Garden

The Brooklyn Botanic Garden is a treat for the eyes, nose, and ears; in designated areas, it offers explorations of touch as well.

Address: 1000 Washington Avenue, Brooklyn, NY
Hours: Hours vary widely during the year depending on the day and season; closed most Mondays
Fee: Adults and children ages 12 and older, $10; students, $5; children under age 12, free
Contact: bbg.org; 718-623-7260
Bathrooms: Steinhardt Conservatory; southeastern edge of garden
Water/Snacks: Beverage vending machines; Terrace Café at southeastern edge of the garden open Tuesday through Sunday
Maps: USGS Brooklyn; bbg.org/discover/gardens
Directions by Car: Public parking is very limited; driving is discouraged.
  GPS coordinates: 40° 40.063′ N, 73° 57.710′ W.
Directions by Subway: Take the B or Q train to Prospect Park, or the 2 or 3 train to Eastern Parkway.

The Brooklyn Botanic Garden comprises 52 acres of sensory stimulation. As you enter along Eastern Parkway you will see a cycle of flowers that keep the Osborne Garden vibrant and fragrant from spring through summer. Visit in fall and winter for guided tours that explore the reasons why and how the plants and flowers react to the changing seasons.

The so-called whispering benches are set in a semicircle around a fountain and provide a trick for the ears: If you sit at one end of a limestone bench, your child, sitting at the other end, can hear you speak in a mere whisper. This is a good activity to do when entering the park, to underscore the need to use "inside voices" in a botanical garden even though you're outside.

Coming out of the Osborne Garden, to the left is The Overlook, which provides a stunning panorama of the Cranford Rose Garden and Cherry Esplanade before it. April is *Hanami* ("cherry blossom season"), which celebrates traditional and contemporary Japanese culture. Contact the garden's visitor services department or check the website for more information about the weekend-long Sakura Matsuri festival.

Children can explore nature at the Brooklyn Botanic Garden.

Take the path heading east off the Rose Arc, at the end of Cherry Esplanade, to visit the Steinhardt Conservatory, which features a series of pavilions housing plant that thrive in various climates. They include the Tropical Pavilion, Desert Pavilion, Temperance Pavilion, Bonsai Museum, and Aquatic House and Orchid Collection. Guides and labels describe a great variety of plants from around the world.

Exit the conservatory area and head left to find the Children's Garden, which has been in operation since 1914. Today it focuses on environmental stewardship and sustainable horticulture for all visitors, and for a fee, children ages 2 through 17 can participate in a gardening and harvesting program.

At the nearby Discovery Garden, children can, with supervision, explore their sense of touch. The garden features plants from a range of climates and habitats, as well as a nature center equipped with gardening tools so children can really get into the earth beneath them. Year-round drop-in workshops are included with the garden entrance fee. *Remember:* Plants cannot be touched outside the Children's Garden and Discovery Garden.

PLAN B: Prospect Park (Trip 32), where children can use outside voices in most areas, is around the corner, and Brooklyn Bridge Park (Trip 31) offers incredible views of one of New York's famous bridges.

Trip 35

Fort Greene Park

Fort Greene Park offers great hikes, a Revolutionary War–themed playground, scenic views, and an information center packed with local history.

Address: Dekalb Avenue and Washington Park, Brooklyn, NY
Hours: Dawn to 1 A.M. daily
Fee: Free
Contact: fortgreenepark.org; nycgovparks.org/parks/FortGreenePark or call 311
Bathrooms: Northwest Playground
Water/Snacks: Water fountains throughout park
Maps: USGS Brooklyn; nycgovparks.org/parks/FortGreenePark/map
Directions by Car: Public parking is very limited; driving is discouraged.
    GPS coordinates: 40° 41.393′ N, 73° 58.616′ W.
Directions by Subway: Take the 2 or 3 train to Nevins Street. After exiting the
    subway, head one block toward the Brooklyn Bridge to DeKalb Avenue. Turn
    right and walk six blocks to the main entrance to the park.

For a relatively small space (30.2 acres), Fort Greene Park packs in a lot. The winding paths provide a vigorous walk up and down a hilly landscape, and the monuments and displays inside the Information Center offer lessons in natural history, military history, landscape design, and the enormous strides the city has made in the past few decades in converting neglected space into inviting destinations. Phew! All of that just a few blocks from the Brooklyn Bridge.

A few things you should know before acquainting yourself with the wonders of Fort Greene: There never was a fort named Greene on this site (it was named Putnam), and when the park opened in 1847 it was named Washington. Fort Greene Park acquired its current moniker 49 years later in honor of General Nathanael Greene, who had supervised construction of the original fort. As for the lessons on landscape and natural history, the park is centered on the Prison Ship Martyrs Monument (a tower as magnificent as the story behind it is grim), and on the tree map inside the Information Center, with corresponding markers set beneath the trees around the park. As you walk through the park, the markers will enable you to identify the various types of trees.

At the entrance to the park off Willoughby Avenue is a map showing you the distance of various paths you can follow through the park. To orient your-

Visitors to Fort Greene Park enjoy relaxing on the park's shaded grass.

self, go directly to the Information Center by heading up the path to the right, then take the first left continuing uphill. You will notice that the same features that made the site important militarily (steep hills rising above the surrounding landscape) now make a good place for a vigorous urban hike. *Remember:* Don't miss the pillars in the Northwest Playground displaying the official animal and tree of each of the twelve colonies that fought in the American Revolution.

PLAN B: The Brooklyn Bridge is located a short walk away. A round-trip journey on the bridge over the East River provides not only views of Manhattan, but also an approximately 2.5-mile walk.

Trip 36

East River State Park

This park offers plenty of green space where kids can fly kites, run around, watch a concert, or enjoy a picnic.

Address: Kent Avenue at North Eighth Street, Brooklyn, NY
Hours: 9 A.M. to dusk daily
Fee: Free
Contact: nysparks.state.ny.us/parks/155/details.aspx; 718-782-2731
Bathrooms: In trailer near North Tenth Street
Water/Snacks: None
Map: USGS Brooklyn
Directions by Car: Public parking is very limited; driving is discouraged.
   GPS coordinates: 40° 43.293′ N, 73° 57.724′ W.
Directions by Subway: Take the L train to Bedford Avenue and walk four blocks
   northwest to Kent Avenue.

Located on the edge of Williamsburg, Brooklyn, East River State Park offers spacious views of the Williamsburg Bridge and Midtown Manhattan. The seven-acre park was opened in 2007 on the former site of the Brooklyn Eastern District Terminal, a railroad terminal that closed for good in 1983. New York State purchased the site in 2001.

The park is still a work in progress, though the results so far are promising. Enter the park at North Eighth Street and follow the gravel pathway down to the river. Walk north and south along the East River, then follow the pathway back to Kent Avenue. Picnic tables are available, as well as open areas where you can play catch or fly kites. In summer, East River State Park hosts open-air music concerts.

Keep an eye out for remnants of the park's past as a shipping dock, including cobblestone streets and railroad tracks embedded in the concrete. Though biking is not allowed in the park, the surrounding neighborhood is paved with bike lanes that are popular with cyclists, as are those surrounding nearby McCarren Park (Trip 37) in Greenpoint.

Near the Eighth Street entrance you will also spot the Chimney Swift tower. The tower is designed to help preserve chimney swifts, a migratory bird whose

Visitors can enjoy concerts or even make their own music on a Pop-Up Piano, part of the city's largest public art project.

population is in decline due to the loss of their habitat. Chimney swifts originally built their nests in large, hollow trees, but they get their name from the fact that brick chimneys also served as favored nest-building sites. Unfortunately, new steel chimneys are not suitable for this purpose, but the wooden tower serves as an ideal alternative for the swifts to roost and build their nests. *Remember:* Dogs and bicycling are not allowed.

PLAN B: Head to McCarren Park (Trip 37), just a few blocks to the east, for excellent biking.

Trip 37

All Ages

McCarren Park

McCarren Park offers wonderful opportunities for walking in what is fast becoming one of New York City's hippest neighborhoods.

Address: Bedford Avenue and North Twelfth Street, Brooklyn, NY
Hours: 6 A.M. to 1 A.M. daily
Fee: Free
Contact: nycgovparks.org/parks/mccarrenpark or call 311
Bathrooms: Toward northwestern section of park
Water/Snacks: None
Map: nycgovparks.org/parks/mccarrenpark/map
Directions by Car: Public parking is very limited; driving is discouraged.
   GPS coordinates: 40° 43.238′ N, 73° 57.281′ W.
Directions by Subway: Take the L train to Bedford Avenue and walk five blocks
   northeast.

McCarren Park, a 38-acre green space in Brooklyn's Greenpoint neighborhood, is rimmed by culturally diverse neighborhoods and is home to a gigantic pool that most recently was a wildly popular concert venue.

Enter the park at the corner of Twelfth Street and Bedford Avenue. Curve left (northeast) along the paved path circling the outer perimeter of the park. In the center of the park are numerous ball fields, with groups of picnickers and people-watchers of every demographic description.

As you reach the top of the park, you are closer to the traditionally Polish neighborhood of Greenpoint. These streets contain an abundance of Polish restaurants and specialty shops, which could provide excellent ingredients for a picnic. Circling back down toward where the park begins, walkers arrive at the part of Greenpoint populated by the new generation drawn by the neighborhood's creative energy and comparatively low rents. You are apt to spot more bicyclists than in any other New York City neighborhood, thanks to recently installed bike lines—including on some routes in the park—and to local enthusiasm for not owning cars.

The landmark pool, a onetime gem of the Depression-era Works Progress Administration program, is located in the western section of McCarren Park. As of this writing, the pool is still being restored to its original purpose. The

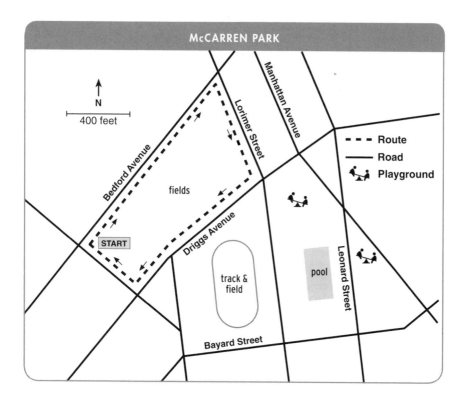

McCARREN PARK

N
|——————|
400 feet

Manhattan Avenue

Lorimer Street

Bedford Avenue

Route
Road
Playground

fields

Driggs Avenue

START

track & field

pool

Leonard Street

Bayard Street

pool's completion, scheduled for spring 2012, will represent the rebirth of an outdoor recreation space—a model of New Deal generosity—capable of accommodating 6,800 swimmers. *Remember:* Planned park renovations also include a skate park and an ice rink.

PLAN B: For cool river breezes, head five blocks east to East River State Park (Trip 36).

Trip 38

Ages
9–12

Floyd Bennett Field (North)

Part of the Gateway National Recreation Area, Floyd Bennett Field was New York City's first municipal airport; now it is home to the first and only public campground in the city.

Address: 3159 Flatbush Ave., Brooklyn, NY
Hours: Visitor center: 9 A.M. to 5 P.M. daily
Fee: Free
Contact: nyharborparks.org/visit/flbe.html; 718-338-3799
Bathrooms: Visitor Contact Station; Visitor Contact Station parking lot; near Park Nursery (adjacent to Archery Range)
Water/Snacks: Concessions in Visitor Contact Station and Aviator Sports and Events Center
Map: USGS Brooklyn
Directions by Car: Take the Belt Parkway to Exit 11S, then Flatbush Avenue south. Take the first left inside the park, and park in the lot of the Visitor Contact Station. *GPS coordinates:* 40° 35.356′ N, 73° 53.979′ W.
Directions by Subway: Take the 2 train to Flatbush Avenue, then take the Q35 bus to the stop across from the Aviator Sports and Events Center.

Floyd Bennett Field is named for a Brooklyn-born aviator whose dubious claims to fame include faking what would have been the first flight to the North Pole, and failing to win the Orteig Prize for the first successful nonstop flight from France to the United States (the honor went to Charles Lindbergh). Despite this ignominy, a Floyd Bennett Memorial Airport is near his birthplace in Queensbury, New York, and a Navy destroyer, the USS Bennett, was named in his honor. Go figure. Or, as the sign says when you exit Brooklyn: "fuhggedaboudit."

In any case, the site is rich with aviation history and offers interesting trails. The best way to experience this is by exploring the north section to discover abandoned airplane hangars and vacant runways that stretch into the horizon. Many of the buildings are considered among the finest examples of aviation architecture from the early days of commercial air travel, and they now constitute a district listed on the National Register of Historic Places.

After entering the park, turn right and walk along Hangar Row Historic District, a stretch of abandoned airplane hangars that will make you long for

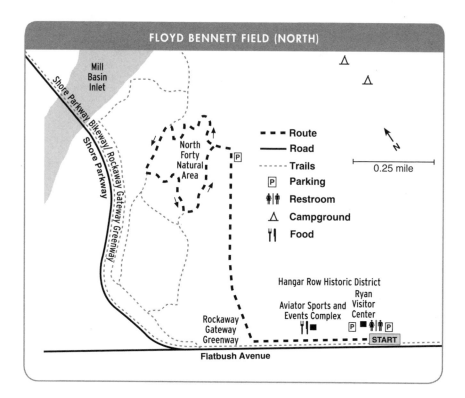

FLOYD BENNETT FIELD (NORTH)

Mill Basin Inlet

Shore Parkway Bikeway/Rockaway Gateway Greenway

Shore Parkway

Rockaway Gateway Greenway

North Forty Natural Area

- - - Route
——— Road
- - - - Trails
P Parking
🚹🚺 Restroom
△ Campground
🍴 Food

0.25 mile

N

Hangar Row Historic District

Ryan Visitor Center

Aviator Sports and Events Complex

Rockaway Gateway Greenway

START

Flatbush Avenue

the golden age of flight. When you reach the end, turn around and retrace your steps northwest along the paved road approximately 0.4 mile to the bottom of the abandoned runway. Turn right, walking northeast up the runway for about another 0.4 mile, to reach the entrance to a network of hiking trails that lead into the North Forty Natural Area, which is designated by a sign. In 1986, this area was developed with shrubs and a man-made pond to attract robins, northern cardinals, mockingbirds, and more. If everyone's feeling up for it, walk the loop trail (less than 1 mile; see map). *Remember:* To turn your day trip into an overnight, consider camping here. See page 102 for further information.

PLAN B: Try the south side of Floyd Bennett Field (Trip 39) for a hike with views of Jamaica Bay and Manhattan. If you are driving, nearby Marine Park (Trip 40) offers the opportunity to experience a rare and fragile ecosystem that is in the process of being restored.

WHERE TO EAT NEARBY: No restaurants or shops are within walking distance. Concessions are available at the Aviator Sports and Events Center and the Visitor Contact Station, but it's best to bring your own food and beverages.

Trip 39

Ages 9-12

Floyd Bennett Field (South)

This former airfield has now been turned back over to nature. Visitors can walk or bike along interesting trails, or camp at the public campground.

Address: 50 Aviator Road, Brooklyn, NY
Hours: Visitor center: 9 A.M. to 5 P.M. daily
Fee: Free
Contact: nyharborparks.org/visit/flbe.html; 718-338-3799
Bathrooms: Visitor Contact Station; Visitor Contact Station parking lot; near Park Nursery (adjacent to Archery Range)
Water/Snacks: Concessions in Visitor Contact Station and Aviator Sports and Events Complex
Map: USGS Brooklyn
Directions by Car: Take the Belt Parkway to Exit 11S, then Flatbush Avenue south to the main entrance. The parking lot is just after the Visitor Contact Station. *GPS coordinates:* 40° 35.033′ N, 73° 53.606′ W.
Directions by Subway: Take the 2 train to Flatbush Avenue, then take the Q35 bus to the main entrance of the park.

Dredged up from the shallow depths of Rockaway Inlet to create New York City's first municipal airport (launching pad of Amelia Earhart's ill-fated final flight), Floyd Bennett Field will strike you as a space suspended in time. The surrounding waters have clearly begun to retake what was once theirs. Weeds thrive happily in the cracks of former runways, and the low-slung forest—thick, humid—thrives incognizant of the abandoned buildings.

For this hike, begin at the Visitor Contact Station at the main entrance near Flatbush Avenue. Walk northeast on Floyd Bennett Boulevard 0.5 mile toward Jamaica Bay. Pass Ranger Road and Enterprise Road, then turn left past the Park Nursery on your right. Take the first right and continue the 0.5-mile loop. From there, take the disintegrating paved path clockwise past the Gateway Environmental Study Center.

The park is hardly crowded, but along the way you will pass people enjoying diverse activities. On one visit, adult hobbyists were racing remote-controlled cars around a miniature Daytona; golfers were hitting shots across empty baseball fields; adventurous mountain bikers were exploring crumbling parking lots; and archers were lined up aiming at a row of targets. All this ac-

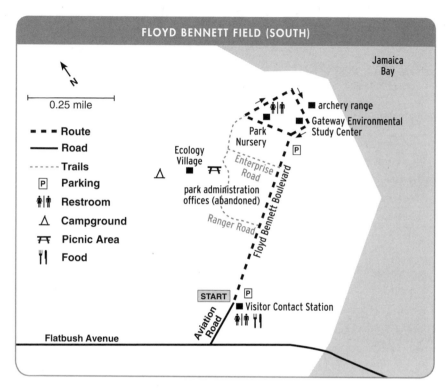

FLOYD BENNETT FIELD (SOUTH)

Jamaica Bay

0.25 mile

- **- - - Route**
- **——— Road**
- **----- Trails**
- **P Parking**
- **Restroom**
- **△ Campground**
- **Picnic Area**
- **Food**

N

Ecology Village

Park Nursery

archery range

Gateway Environmental Study Center

Enterprise Road

park administration offices (abandoned)

Ranger Road

Floyd Bennett Boulevard

START

Visitor Contact Station

Aviation Road

Flatbush Avenue

---

tivity went on a few hundred feet away from vacant structures that are packed with mazes of rusty pipes and surrounded by determined plant life.

Looking east across Jamaica Bay you will see the Jamaica Bay Wildlife Refuge (Trip 51 and Trip 52), and looking north you will spot skyscrapers looming over Manhattan. Following Floyd Bennett Boulevard back the way you came, you can take a second look at the abandoned park administration offices, slowly being reclaimed by the salt marsh they were built upon. A short hiking trail is north beyond Ecology Village Campgrounds, a pine grove area that is the only public campground in the five boroughs. Owing to its remote location, Floyd Bennett Field is an ideal location for stargazing. The Amateur Astronomers Association of New York meets there one night a month from May to December. *Remember:* A great way to reach this destination is by biking along the Shore Parkway Bikeway/Rockaway Gateway Greenway.

PLAN B: Walk across to the north side of Floyd Bennett Field (Trip 38) for the historical Hangar District and a short hike. If you are driving, try nearby Marine Park (Trip 40), which is a great spot for hiking and bird-watching.

WHERE TO EAT NEARBY: You may encounter a vending truck catering to archers near the Archery Range.

Camping conjures images of the simple life: walking along streams in thick forests, pitching a tent, cooking outdoors, waking up to the sound of birds, and generally leaving the modern world behind. But if you've never camped, getting started can seem overwhelmingly complicated. What should you pack? How do you set up a tent? How do you start a fire?

For urbanites who are daunted by questions such as these, two free family camping programs can provide the answers. Urban Park Rangers, part of the city Department of Parks and Recreation, hosts free camping excursions Friday and Saturday nights from May through August, starting between 5 and 7 p.m. About 30 participants are selected by lottery, and the recommended age is 4 and older.

Tents and food are provided but campers must bring their own sleeping bags and flashlights or headlamps (the event features a night hike). Campgrounds are located near restrooms, such as at the Great Hill in Central Park, near Picnic House in Prospect Park, on Orchard Beach in Pelham Bay Park, and at the nature centers at Alley Pond Park, Marine Park, Pelham Bay Park, Fort Greene Park, Inwood Hill Park, Cunningham Park, and Wolfe's Pond Park.

A team of rangers rotates sleeping throughout the night so someone is always available for questions or an escort. For more information, visit nycgovparks.org or call 311.

A team of National Park rangers also runs a family camping program at Floyd Bennett Field, part of the Gateway National Recreation Area, one weekend per month from June through September. The recommended age is 6 and older. Campers bring their own food but all other equipment, including cooking utensils, is provided. Sleeping bags are available to rent for $8, or you can bring your own. Restrooms and drinking water are across from the campsite.

The program starts at 2 p.m. on Saturday. Sunday morning's begins at 8 a.m. with a birding and nature hike. After breakfast, rangers drive everyone to nearby Jacob Riis Park to lead them in several hours of kayaking and seining (catch-and-release fishing using large nets). For more information, visit nps.gov/gate or call 718-338-4306.

Floyd Bennett is also the only place in the five boroughs with a public campground, Ecology Village Campground, with about 40 tentsites and six RV sites and plans for more. Reservations and permits are required in advance. Visit nps.gov/gate or call 718-338-3799.

Trip 40

Ages 9–12

Marine Park and the Salt Marsh Nature Center

Marine Park, a bird-watcher's paradise, offers visitors the opportunity to see a rare and fragile ecosystem preserved right in New York City.

Address: Avenue U and East 33rd Street, Brooklyn, NY
Hours: Nature Center: 11 A.M. to 5 P.M. daily; grounds and nature trail: dawn to dusk daily
Fee: Free
Contact: saltmarshalliance.org; 718-421-2021
Bathrooms: Salt Marsh Nature Center
Water/Snacks: Water fountain in Nature Center
Map: USGS Coney Island
Directions by Car: Take the Belt Parkway to the Kings Plaza exit (11N). Go north on Flatbush Avenue. Turn left onto Avenue U and continue west for ten blocks past East 33rd Street. Free parking is available in the lot next to the Nature Center. *GPS coordinates: 40° 36.306′ N, 73° 55.793′ W.*
Directions by Subway: Take the 2 train to Flatbush Avenue/Brooklyn College, then take the B41 bus to Kings Plaza or the B44 to Avenue U. Transfer to the B3 to East 33rd Street and Avenue U; or take the Q or B train (the B train does not run on weekends) to Kings Highway and take the westbound B3 bus to Burnett Street and Avenue U.

The Salt Marsh is located in Marine Park, which, at 798 acres of marsh and grassland, is the largest park in Brooklyn. Here you can hike through a rare and fragile ecosystem that was only recently reclaimed after decades of environmental degradation.

Fed by Gerritsen Creek, which runs into Jamaica Bay, the marsh served as Lenape fishing grounds for centuries before being occupied by Dutch settlers in the seventeenth century. In the center of the marsh lie the remains of a tidewater gristmill, which was the first tide-powered mill built in North America. The mill operated for close to 100 years, supplying flour to the neighboring towns of Flatbush, Flatlands, and Gravesend. It also supplied flour for George Washington's troops during the American Revolution. In 1935, the mill burned to the ground, and following that, the area became an illegal dumping ground for decades.

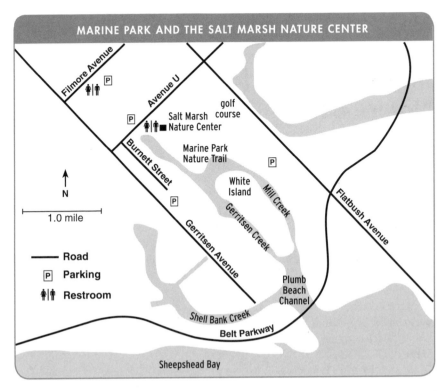

MARINE PARK AND THE SALT MARSH NATURE CENTER

Filmore Avenue

Avenue U

golf course

Salt Marsh Nature Center

Marine Park Nature Trail

N

1.0 mile

Burnett Street

White Island

Mill Creek

Gerritsen Creek

Flatbush Avenue

Gerritsen Avenue

Plumb Beach Channel

—— Road

P Parking

Restroom

Shell Bank Creek

Belt Parkway

Sheepshead Bay

Today it is the definition of land rejuvenated. More than 350 species of birds—among them, loons and Canada geese in winter, and herons and egrets in summer—as well as 100 species of butterflies can be spotted in the area. The waters are also home to about 100 species of fish, in addition to crabs, eels, and turtles.

Visitors can begin their 1-mile tour of the Salt Marsh at the Nature Center, where displays describe the history of the preservation effort, and you can view dioramas and exhibits of the marsh's flora and fauna. Exit the center to the back and turn right. Walking along gravel paths and crossing the occasional bridge, you will pass the gristmill remains, which are partially submerged in Gerritsen Creek. At a T intersection, go right to stop at a viewing platform, and then continue following the path around to return to the intersection and then back to the Nature Center. Be sure to bring your binoculars. *Remember:* Though strollers are fine for the paved pathways running around the outer rim of the Salt Marsh, they cannot be used on the trail past the Nature Center.

PLAN B: If you are traveling by car, Floyd Bennett Field (Trips 38 and 39), part of the Gateway National Recreation Area, provides another window on nature's reclamation of former industrial sites.

Section 3

Queens

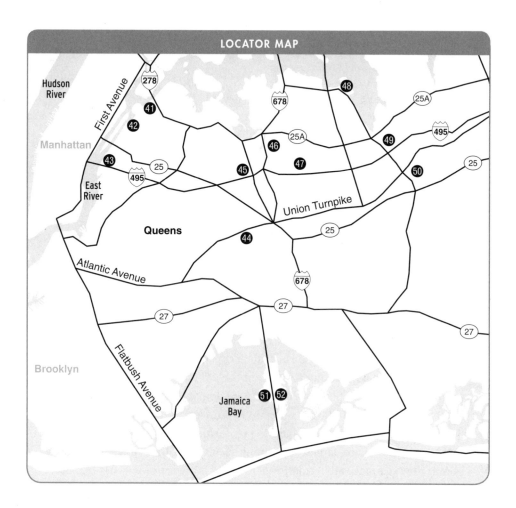

Trip 41

Astoria Park

Long considered to be a great neighborhood destination, Astoria Park's atmosphere and views are well worth traveling for.

Address: Astoria Park South and Shore Boulevard, Queens, NY
Hours: Park: 6 A.M. to 1 A.M. daily; pool: 11 A.M. to 3 P.M. and 4 to 7 P.M. daily in season
Fee: Free
Contact: nycgovparks.org/parks/AstoriaPark or call 311; pool, 718-626-8620
Bathrooms: Charybdis Playground; Shore Boulevard (opposite 23rd Road)
Water/Snacks: Snack bar at pool; vendors throughout park
Maps: USGS Central Park; nycgovparks.org/parks/AstoriaPark/map
Directions by Car: Public parking is very limited; driving is discouraged.
   GPS coordinates: 40° 46.606′ N, 73° 55.668′ W.
Directions by Subway: Take the N or Q train to Astoria Boulevard. Leave by the north exit and walk west nine short blocks on Hoyt Avenue to Astoria Park.

Astoria Park is a place of grand proportions. At nearly 60 acres and 1.5 miles around, it is one of the largest parks in Queens. Two massive bridges stretch over the park—the RFK to the south and Hell Gate to the north—and from its long eastern shoreline, Astoria Park offers expansive views of Manhattan. It is also home to the biggest outdoor swimming pool in the city, which is part of a stunning (if slightly time-worn) art deco complex. Its creator, former parks commissioner Robert Moses (see page xxiv), was a powerful swimmer and believed that everyone should have the opportunity to swim, and so he built for Astoria one of the largest swimming facilities in the United States. The pool is now the main attraction for park goers in the summer. At 3 feet deep, the pool is subdivided by ropes—a necessity for keeping track of children on crowded days.

A stroll along Shore Boulevard to take in the East River views is a must. To get a sense of the park's size, walk north (the river will be to your left) toward Ditmars Boulevard. As you do this, on your right will be the pool complex (site of the 1936 and 1964 U.S. Olympic trials), a shady grove, and a wide-open field. At the top of the field, curve right on the paved path and take the easternmost path, down nineteenth Street, south to the pool. Playgrounds, bocce

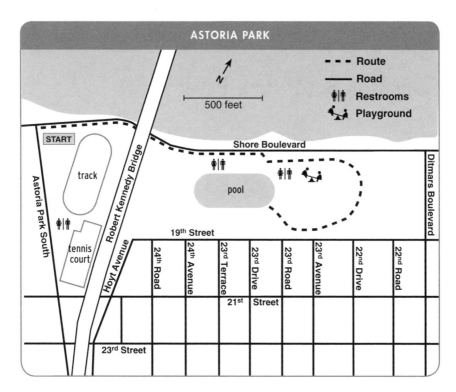

ball courts, tennis courts, and a running track offer lots of other activities too. *Remember:* If you are planning to swim, observe city pool rules (see page 13).

PLAN B: Flushing Meadows Corona Park (Trip 45) and Kissena Park (Trip 47) offer plenty of excellent walks and playgrounds, and the Queens Botanical Garden (Trip 46) provides some educational structure.

Trip 42

Socrates Sculpture Park

This park is among the most inspiring examples of how New Yorkers are reinventing defunct industrial spaces as areas for outdoor recreation and creativity.

Address: Broadway and Vernon Boulevard, Queens, NY
Hours: 10 A.M. to sunset daily
Fee: Free
Contact: socratessculpturepark.org; 718-956-1819
Bathrooms: Portable toilets just inside park's south entrance
Water/Snacks: None
Map: USGS Central Park
Directions by Car: Public parking is very limited; driving is discouraged.
  GPS coordinates: 40° 46.061′ N, 73° 56.170′ W.
Directions by Subway: Take the N or R train to Broadway, then walk eight
  blocks west toward the East River.

Socrates Sculpture Park is an eccentric gem developed from land that, by the mid-1980s, had become an abandoned riverside landfill.

After ascending from the Broadway stop of the N or R train, walk west on Broadway eight blocks (nearly 1 mile) toward the East River to the park entrance. Along the way you will see an extraordinary variety of shops and restaurants representing just a few of the racial and ethnic communities inhabiting Queens, New York's most diverse borough. No single group maintains a majority, and the ten most widely spoken languages include Greek, Tagalog, and Hindi.

At the park, a coalition of artists and community members transformed neglect and urban blight into an outdoor museum. It is the only location in the city dedicated exclusively to giving artists an outdoor space to exhibit their work. Socrates Sculpture Park sponsors many outdoor events, from film screenings to periodic kayak trips on the East River. The Community Works Initiative Program also holds workshops to teach basic landscaping and horticultural skills to neighborhood residents.

Follow the stone paved path to the river. Across the water you will see Roosevelt Island (Trip 73), identifiable from the backdrop of Manhattan by the diminutive lighthouse on its northern tip. Follow the path north and then re-

*Eclectic sculptures and horticultural workshops
help kids explore the outdoors at this park.*

turn the way you came to wander around the sculptures throughout the park. *Remember:* Most of the time, artworks are not cordoned off, but they shouldn't be touched unless a sign grants permission to do so.

PLAN B: Follow Vernon Boulevard approximately 2 miles south (head west at 48th Avenue) along the East River to Gantry Plaza State Park (Trip 43). This walk, past many power distribution centers, will give you an idea of the massive industrial undertaking required to electrify New York City.

Trip 43

All Ages

Gantry Plaza State Park

This park features abundant recreation opportunities, as well as gantries, a fascinating footnote in the history of technology.

Address: Center Boulevard at 49th Avenue, Queens, NY
Hours: 8 A.M. to 10 P.M. daily
Fee: Free
Contact: nysparks.com/parks/149/details.aspx; 718-786-6385
Bathrooms: Bathrooms under construction west of Fishing Pier
Water/Snacks: Vendors throughout park
Map: USGS Brooklyn
Directions by Car: Public parking is very limited; driving is discouraged.
    GPS coordinates: 40° 44.662′ N, 73° 57.510′ W.
Directions by Subway: Take the 7 train to Vernon Boulevard/Jackson Avenue
    (see below).

Gantry Plaza State Park was created from the ruins of a Long Island Railroad facility, used to transfer cargo from ships onto railcars for transport. The two large metal structures hovering above the park are gantries. During the heyday of railway shipping, these giant cranes raised and lowered transfer bridges so cargo cars could be rolled on and off barges.

The journey is part of this destination. Exit the subway at the Vernon Boulevard–49th Avenue exit. Walk west on 49th Avenue two blocks, passing the Andrews Grove Playground on your right. The playground is shady and has sprinklers, so it makes a good stopping point on your way to or from the park. When you arrive at Gantry (which also has a playground) walk or bike along the paved path, which quickly turns to gravel, south through a tiny forest of trees and benches until you reach the southernmost of four piers around which the park is designed. As you do so, you will observe railroad tracks that have been left behind, as well as the smaller of two gantries hovering above, evidence of the park's former life.

The first pier, Fishing Pier, is, as the name suggests, designated for fishing (bring your own pole). When you return to shore, continue heading north and head out onto each of the next three piers: Sunning Pier, Café Pier, and Overlook Pier. All four offer great views of several landmark New York City

Wave-style benches complement the sound of water below the pier at this fascinating East River park.

buildings across the river in Manhattan, including the Chrysler, the Empire State, and the United Nations. Next is a large grassy area intercut with paved stone pathways—Piers Park—which includes a large destination playground. *Remember:* For a good view of the famous Pepsi sign—a landmark on the Queens waterfront—walk to the southern end of Peninsula State Park and face southeast.

PLAN B: Socrates Sculpture Park (Trip 42) is a 45-minute walk due north on Vernon Boulevard.

No matter where you are—in a park or in a kayak—clue and search games are great ways to get kids to home in on the details of where they are.

SCAVENGER HUNTS: Whether a hunt is planned ahead or played ad hoc, kids enjoy cracking clues to discover the world around them. To plan a hunt, plot out a reasonable geographic zone—a small corner of the Naturalists' Walk in Central Park West (Trip 1) for younger children, or the whole of Gantry Plaza State Park (Trip 43) for older kids—and select a dozen or more things they can identify: varieties of trees, trees with no leaves, rocks of certain shapes, pebbles of a particular color, conical pine cones, acorns, berries, flowers of different colors—the possibilities are endless. Older kids can also be expected to read informational signs to uncover facts that are not readily apparent.

Once you've chosen the "answers," write your clues. For example, "In summer we all have leaves, you know, but I keep my leaves even when the weather turns to snow." (Answer: a pine tree.) Ad hoc hunts—spot an object, and design a leading question—are a good way to recharge and redirect kids when patience wanes. These also allow you to set kids in search of living creatures, which you can't count on being present during a planned hunt.

I SPY: This classic can be played anywhere. From a kayak, "I spy with my eye something that begins with L." First clue not enough? "Something that is shaped like a plate." Still need more? "Something that is also green." (Answer: a lily pad.)

SEEK AND FIND: This one we kind of made up. Within a set area, equip kids with a tape measure or long pieces of string and send them out in search of the widest tree trunk, the longest rock, the tallest flower, the shortest shrub. Taking great care, older kids can also count the number of leaves on a flower stem or on a young sapling tree. If you don't have a tape measure or string, invent measuring tools, such as sticks or rocks of the same size. For instance, a shrub might be "six rocks" tall. The measuring tool can then itself be measured at home to determine the real size of the natural object.

Trip 44

All Ages

Forest Park

This thickly forested park features a network of blazed hiking trails and instructions on how to follow them, making it a good "starter park" for more-serious hikes outside the city.

Address: Park Lane and Forest Park Drive, Queens, NY
Hours: Dawn to 9 P.M. daily
Fee: Free
Contact: nycgovparks.org/parks/forestpark; 718-846-2731 or call 311
Bathrooms: Near playground at park entrance; visitor center
Water/Snacks: Vendors on both sides of Woodhaven Boulevard
Map: USGS Jamaica
Directions by Car: Public parking is very limited; driving is discouraged.
   GPS coordinates: 40° 42.693′ N, 73° 50.145′ W.
Directions by Subway: Take the E or F train to Kew Gardens/Union Turnpike. As you exit the subway, follow Queens Boulevard south one block to 80th Road. Follow 80th Road three blocks to the entrance of Forest Park at Park Lane.

Forest Park is aptly named for its profound wilderness. It is one of only a few largely untouched and densely forested parks in the city, and it contains an enormous continuous oak forest (413 acres) that boasts some specimens more than 150 years old. Forest Park also features 4.75 miles of forested hiking trails, as well as trails for mountain biking and horseback riding. Forest Park Drive, which leads you through the park, is reminiscent of the drives circulating Central Park (see Trips 1–5), and provides easy access to the trails.

From the entrance of Forest Park at Park Lane and 80th Road, follow the paved path past ball courts and the William Sobelsohn Playground. You will arrive at Forest Park Drive, which soon intersects with Metropolitan Avenue. After crossing Metropolitan, Forest Park Drive becomes pedestrian-only. On your right will be the yellow-blazed trail leading through the Northern Forest. This trail takes you on a 1.5-mile hike, and begins with an explanation of how to read and understand trail blazes—a great help for first-time hikers. As you continue along Forest Park Drive you will next come to the longer, blue-blazed Gully Trail, which provides a 1.75-mile hike through thick forest. Both of these

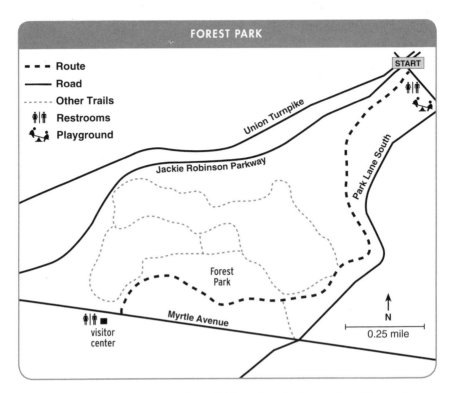

FOREST PARK

- - - Route
— Road
····· Other Trails
🚹🚺 Restrooms
🛝 Playground

Union Turnpike

START

Jackie Robinson Parkway

Park Lane South

Forest
Park

Myrtle Avenue

visitor
center

N

0.25 mile

trails also connect to a 0.5-mile, red-blazed trail. *Remember:* If you do not take either of the side trails, but instead stay on Forest Park Drive to Myrtle Avenue, you will have walked 1.5 miles, and you will arrive at the visitor center. Past the visitor center, you'll find an antique carousel, the Victory Field Sports Complex (opened in 1927 and dedicated to veterans of World War I), and an 18-hole golf course that dates to 1905.

PLAN B: Return to coastal Queens to visit Gantry Plaza State Park (Trip 43), where you can fish, explore the piers leading out into the East River, and visit a delightful playground.

Trip 45

Flushing Meadows Corona Park

Home of two World's Fairs and the U.S. Open Tennis Tournament, this park also has vast areas to explore on foot, on bike, or by boat.

Address: 47th Avenue and 111th Street, Queens, NY
Hours: Dawn to 9 P.M. daily
Fee: Free
Contact: nycgovparks.org or call 311
Bathrooms: Near Playground for All Children; near 111th Street
Water/Snacks: Vendors throughout park
Maps: USGS Jamaica; nycgovparks.org/sub_your_park/vt_flushing_meadows/vt_flushing_meadows_park.html
Directions by Car: Public parking is very limited; driving is discouraged.
GPS coordinates: 40° 44.855′ N, 73° 51.212′ W.
Directions by Subway: Take the 7 train to 111th Street. Walk four blocks southeast on 111th Street.

In *The Great Gatsby,* F. Scott Fitzgerald referred to the site of Flushing Meadows Corona Park as "the valley of the ashes," owing to its history as a former dumping ground. Flushing Meadows triumphed over this ignoble start, and was the site of the 1939 and 1964 World's Fairs. Many of the exhibits and institutions constructed for these fairs—the New York Hall of Science, the Rocket Thrower sculpture, and the massive Unisphere globe among them—thankfully remain as riveting attractions today. At 1,255 acres, the park is ideal for biking and urban hiking. It also contains Meadow Lake, which is very popular for boating.

Enter the park where 47th and 49th avenues intersect with 111th Street. As you head northeast along United Nations Avenue, you will pass Arthur Ashe Stadium and the U.S. Tennis Association Billie Jean King National Tennis Center on your left and the Unisphere, a gigantic, glistening metal globe, on your right. Walk around this topographically representative globe—several times. Can you spot the Rocky Mountains? Mount Everest? Returning to the route, you will pass several fields. When you reach the top of United Nations Avenue, you can either continue walking clockwise back toward the entrance of the park or follow paths northeast toward Industry Pond. If you follow the

World's Fair landmarks, such as the massive steel Unisphere globe,
are found throughout this extraordinary park.

bike path leading southeast through this area—and beneath a mind-boggling highway cloverleaf—you will eventually arrive at Meadow Lake. At 93 acres, the artificially constructed Meadow Lake is New York City's largest lake. The boathouse, where you can rent paddle boats, is located on the eastern shore.

At the southern edge of the park, near 111th Street, is the Playground for All Children. The playground was opened in 1997, and is one of only a handful in the United States that is designed for children with and without disabilities. *Remember:* You cannot launch private boats in Meadow Lake.

PLAN B: A carousel and the Queens Zoo, run by the Wildlife Conservation Society, are also located in the park, near the entrance at 47th and 49th streets. The New York Hall of Science is also located on 111th Street near that entrance. Gantry Plaza State Park (Trip 43) is easily accessible by subway, offering cool river breezes.

Trip 46

Queens Botanical Garden

There may not be any greenhouses with rare and exotic plants here, but green is very much the theme of this rejuvenated botanical garden.

Address: 43–50 Main Street, Queens, NY
Hours: 8 A.M. to 6 P.M. April to October, 8 A.M. to 4:30 P.M. November to March; closed Mondays
Fee: Adults, $4; students and children over age 3, $2; children under age 3, free
Contact: queensbotanical.org; 718-886-3800
Bathrooms: Visitor center
Water/Snacks: Water fountains and snacks at visitor center
Maps: USGS Jamaica; USGS Flushing
Directions by Car: From Manhattan, take I-495 east to Exit 23. Merge onto Horace Harding Expressway, then take a left onto Main Street. The lot (fee) is ahead on the left. *GPS coordinates:* 40° 45.093′ N, 73° 49.570′ W.
Directions by Subway: Take the 7 train to Main Street–Flushing and walk eight blocks south to the Main Street entrance.

Smaller and homier than its renowned counterparts—the New York Botanical Garden (Trip 62) and the Brooklyn Botanic Garden (Trip 34)—the Queens Botanical Garden offers nice walks among beautiful plants and green-oriented programming for home gardens and environmental conservation practices.

Serving as the nexus between Flushing Meadows Corona Park (Trip 45) and Kissena Park (Trip 47), the Queens Botanical Garden was developed as part of the Gardens in Parade exhibit for the 1939 World's Fair. Monuments to the fair's theme, "Building the World of Tomorrow," are still very much visible at Flushing Meadows, but until earlier this millennium, the Queens Botanical Garden looked more like a forgotten part of yesteryear than an emblem of the future—or even a well-maintained part of the present.

A major rejuvenation begun in 2004 brought renovations to many gardens and paths, the entrance fountain, and notably, the Visitor and Administrative Center. The new center harked back to the futuristic World's Fair theme by instituting green facilities and practices that were ahead of their time—at least as far as LEED (Leadership in Environmental and Engineering Design)

*Hands-on programming at this botanical garden
teaches children about plants and nature.*

construction goes. The building was the city's first to receive a platinum rating from the U.S. Green Building Council.

Entering the 40-acre garden at Main Street, the visitor center will be on your right, and immediately after is the Cleansing Biotope, where rainwater is recycled through a wetland environment and channeled to the entranceway fountain before ultimately returning to the visitor center. Farther along the main path is the composting area that presents alternatives to water-consuming front and back lawns, as well as easy at-home composting techniques. The path circles the Meadow, then comes back to an area of themed gardens across from the visitor center. Along these smaller paths, gardens have been landscaped along various themes, including roses, perennials, ornamental grasses, the backyard—and to attract very busy bees. *Remember:* The greenhouse is not open to the public.

PLAN B: For a fuller understanding of the 1939 World's Fair, visit Flushing Meadows Corona Park (Trip 45). Nearby Kissena Park (Trip 47) also offers idyllic walks in a former arboretum.

Trip 47

Kissena Park

The rich horticultural history of this lovely and spacious park is very much visible today.

Address: Rose Avenue and Kissena Boulevard, Queens, NY
Hours: 6 A.M. to 1 A.M. daily
Fee: Free
Contact: nycgovparks.org/parks/kissenapark
Bathrooms: Tennis courts (on Rose and Oak Avenues); the lake (on Oak Avenue and on 104th Street)
Water/Snacks: Water fountains at restrooms and at playgrounds at 164th Street and Lithonia Avenue, at Booth Memorial Avenue and 160th Street, and at Rose and Oak avenues
Maps: USGS Jamaica; USGS Flushing; partnershipsforparks.org/brochures/kissena.html
Directions by Car: Public parking is very limited; driving is discouraged.
  GPS coordinates: 40° 44.771' N, 73° 48.850' W.
Directions by Subway: Take the 7 train to Main Street. Use the left exit, and walk down Main Street toward the railway bridge. Make a left onto Kissena Boulevard just after the bridge and walk about 0.75 mile to the park entrance at Kissena and Rose avenues. Or take the Q17, Q25, or Q34 bus to the same entrance.

In full bloom or draped in snow, Kissena Park is a confection. The park's natural geography is that of a two-tiered cake, with an elevated centerpiece surrounded by thick woods on three sides. Graceful willows bow down to Kissena Lake below, and whether covered in leaves or snow, these mature trees give this park the air and feel of "a wilderness of sweets," to borrow from the poet John Milton.

This atmosphere no doubt stems from the park's history as an internationally acclaimed horticultural nursery in the nineteenth century. Many of the original trees were moved to Central and Prospect parks, but today more than 100 species grow in this 230-acre park, with community-led efforts expanding the diversity of bushes, flowers, and trees.

Entering at Rose and Kissena avenues, follow the marked bike path to the right, behind the baseball fields. Where this splits, stay to the left to connect

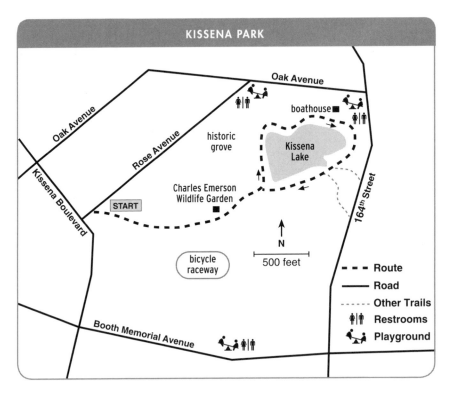

with the paved path that circles the lake. Walking clockwise, thick reeds and trees are between you and the lake, but these give way to scenic overlooks and a wider open stretch where people fish and watch the abundant marine life, including snapping turtles, ducks, herons, egrets, and gallinules.

After passing the boathouse, which is no longer in operation, you will come to the 14-acre historical tree grove on your left. In the 1870s, this plot was developed as a nursery of exotic trees and was one of the first to grow Japanese maples and cultivate rhododendron. It is well worth wandering around this area.

Continuing back around the lake, you will cross a bridge and return to the starting point. You can leave the way you came, or go up the stairs embedded in the thickly wooded hill to your left. The Charles Emerson Wildlife Garden is here, along with memorials to local veterans of the Korean War and World War I. *Remember:* Kissena Park is also home to the city's only bicycle raceway, which was built for the 1964 Olympic trials. Mountain bikes are not permitted, and minors cannot ride without signed parental permission.

PLAN B: The Queens Botanical Garden (Trip 46) and Flushing Meadows Corona Park (Trip 45) are all within a vast Y shape of parks in central Queens.

Trip 48

Fort Totten Park

Located on a high peninsula, the Fort Totten fortress was originally planned by Confederate General Robert E. Lee. Today the fort offers visitors an opportunity to walk through Civil War history.

Address: Weaver Road and Totten Avenue, Queens, NY
Hours: Park: 6 A.M. to 9 P.M. daily; battery hours vary (call 718-352-1769 for availability)
Fee: Free
Contact: nycgovparks.org/parks/forttotten; 718-352-4793
Bathrooms: At pool; next to visitor center
Water/Snacks: Water fountains at pool and at visitor center
Maps: USGS Flushing; nycgovparks.org/parks/forttotten/map
Directions by Car: Take Cross Island Parkway to Exit 33 toward I-295. Turn onto Bell Boulevard, then take a left onto Totten Avenue. Free public parking is available at the park entrance. *GPS coordinates: 40° 47.385′ N, 73° 46.921′ W.*
Directions by Subway: Take the 7 train to Flushing/Main Street, and then the Q13 or Q16 bus to Fort Totten Park.

A notable trope in the nomenclature of New York City parks is the word "fort." Fort Greene, Fort Tryon, Fort Totten—these names raise the question, Why are parks so often built where once there was a fort?

The geography makes sense: High points provide a panoramic view of a surrounding area, which is ideal for defense purposes, and such stunning vistas also work well if you're looking for dramatic scenery to picnic near. Forts also had to be isolated from population centers to best serve their purpose. This criterion is evident in all fort entries, with the notable exception of Fort Greene (Trip 35), where the city has grown up around it.

At Fort Totten, head first to the visitor center, which doubles as a museum of Civil War naval history. Exit the center downhill to your right to enter the fort remains. After passing through a tunnel that provides the perfect environment for teaching your children about echoes, you arrive at the lower interior section of the old fort. A period cannon resides here in a room overlooking Little Neck Bay.

This fortress basement belies the rolling lawns and wide river views at ground level.

Ascend the staircase, which will put you in mind of a medieval castle. On the top level, the roof is gone, providing a wide-open view of the bay, far different than the sight provided from windows below. From here, you can teach your kids about perspective.

While the fort was never used for its intended purpose—to defend New York Harbor—the peninsula was an outpost for a range of military activities for more than a century. A network of paved paths take you around the 60-acre park, passing many historical buildings such as the Commanding Officer's House and the castlelike Officers' Club, which now houses the Bayside Historical Society. The pool complex, which has a shallow wading pool and a larger pool with a diving area, is located near the middle of Shore Road, at the intersection with Story Avenue, overlooking Little Neck Bay. *Remember:* If you're planning to swim, be aware of city pool regulations (see page 13).

PLAN B: Return to Main Street in Flushing to visit Kissena Park (Trip 47) to walk within a historical arboretum, or Flushing Meadows Corona Park (Trip 45) to take in some outstanding World's Fair sites.

WHERE TO EAT NEARBY: Food and ice cream vendors may be in the parking lot. Otherwise, return to Main Street on the Q16 or Q13 for many restaurants and convenience stores.

Trip 49

Alley Pond Park and Environmental Center

Enormous Alley Pond Park offers hiking trails, playgrounds, an adventure course, and more. Start with an afternoon at the Environmental Center and its surrounding grounds to learn about the natural history of the area.

Address: 228-06 Northern Boulevard, Queens, NY

Hours: Environmental Center: 9 A.M. to 4:30 P.M. weekdays, weekend hours vary; trails: dawn to dusk daily

Fee: Free

Contact: alleypond.com; 718-229-4000

Bathrooms: Inside Environmental Center

Water/Snacks: Water fountain and beverage vending machine inside Environmental Center

Maps: USGS Flushing; USGS Sea Cliff; USGS Jamaica; USGS Lynbrook

Directions by Car: Take the Cross Island Parkway south to Exit 31E for NY 25A/ Northern Boulevard. The Environmental Center—and free public parking— is ahead on the right. *GPS coordinates: 40° 45.721′ N, 73° 45.216′ W.*

Subway: Take the 7 train to Main Street in Flushing, then the eastbound Q12 bus, which stops in front of the Environmental Center.

Alley Pond Park is enormous, with vast sections that are close to pure wilderness and others that are highly developed with outdoor activities and amenities: playgrounds, picnic and barbecue areas, ball fields and courts, and the largest high-ropes adventure course in the northeastern United States.

Set apart from all of this activity, the Alley Pond Environmental Center gives visitors the opportunity to see and learn how plants and animals interact, and how nature can reclaim the land after human development. During the highway construction booms of the 1950s, '60s, and '70s, this area and others of Alley Pond Park were used as dumps for construction debris.

The trails outside the center are easy to follow and well maintained, with boardwalks over creeks and wetlands. From the parking lot, go to the trailhead marker and turn left to enter the wooden Cattail Pond Trail. This quarter-mile loop circles Cattail Pond and features a detour to an observation deck on the Alley Creek. Continue the loop to pass through a meadow that attracts many

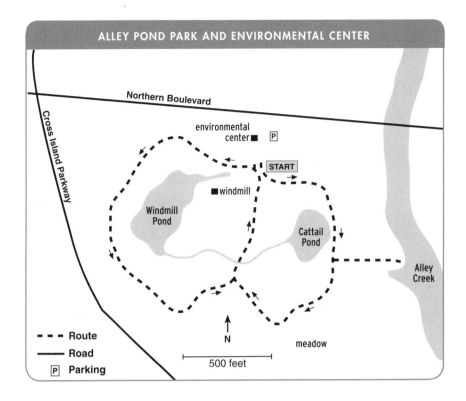

Northern Boulevard

Cross Island Parkway

environmental
center ■   P

START

■ windmill

Windmill
Pond

Cattail
Pond

Alley
Creek

- - - Route
——— Road
P Parking

N

meadow

500 feet

bird species, and return to where you started. From here, the slightly longer Windmill Trail will take you on a forested walk around Windmill Pond. The pond and the trail owe their name to the 1870s-era agricultural windmill that remains standing near the pond.

Environmental Center staff can help you spot and identify the animals that may be outdoors during a given season. Inside, the Animal Room is a big hit with children. This mini-zoo introduces them to local snakes, birds, lizards, rabbits, gophers, and more. *Remember:* The reeds and wetlands leading up to the Alley Creek viewing deck attract insects in summer. It is advisable to bring insect repellent.

PLAN B: If you are driving and fancy a swim or some Civil War history, visit Fort Totten Park (Trip 48). If you'd like to feed animals and stock up on fresh produce, visit Queens County Farm Museum (Trip 50).

WHERE TO EAT NEARBY: Shops and restaurants are along Northern Boulevard, and on Douglastown Parkway, which intersects Northern Boulevard heading east.

Trip 50

All Ages

Queens County Farm Museum

Young children love feeding the adorable animals, and in early fall, older children are thrilled to find their way through the maize maze.

Address: 73-50 Little Neck Parkway, Queens, NY
Hours: 10 A.M. to 5 P.M. daily; historical farmhouse tours available 11 A.M. to 4 P.M. weekends
Fee: Free (unless for a special event; call ahead)
Contact: queensfarm.org; 718-347-3276
Bathrooms: Near main entrance past historical farmhouse on right
Water/Snacks: Water fountain across from farmhouse; snacks and beverages in gift shop near main entrance; farm stand selling produce near main entrance
Maps: USGS Lynbrook; queensfarm.org/pdf/map.pdf
Directions by Car: Take the Grand Central Parkway to Exit 24 for Little Neck Parkway. Make a left onto the parkway and drive three blocks to the museum. The parking lot is closed unless a special event is under way. Street parking is free. *GPS coordinates:* 40° 44.876′ N, 73° 43.414′ W.
Directions by Subway: Take the E or F train to Kew Gardens/Union Turnpike Station, and then the eastbound Q46 bus to the Little Neck Parkway stop. Cross Union Turnpike and walk north on Little Neck Parkway three blocks.

When you think of getting outside in New York City, a working farm within city limits probably doesn't leap to mind as a possible destination. Even more impressive: The Queens County Farm Museum is believed to be the oldest continuously farmed site in the state, having started as a family farm in 1697.

Today it is an enjoyable all-seasons destination, though it is perhaps best to visit in early fall, when the amazing maize maze makes its annual comeback. To keep regular visitors guessing, each year the 3-acre maze is groomed to a different theme, such as a maple leaf or baseball. Prior to setting off, guides deliver a "stalk talk" that prepares you to look for clues and solve puzzles to find the way out. (Other exit strategies exist, however.) Apple and pumpkin picking are also seasonal favorites. The hayrides operate year round, weather permitting.

The farm is on a 47-acre plot of land that includes pear and apple orchards, a vineyard, an herb garden, and planting fields with more than 50 varieties of vegetables. Among the animal attractions are a cow pasture, a horse barn,

Children enjoy spotting farm animals along the paved path that begins at Queens County Farm Museum's entrance.

chicken and duck coops, and pens for alpacas, goats, sheep, and pigs. You can see—and feed—most of the animals along the paved path that starts at the entrance. Smaller gravel paths take you around and closer to the animal pens, as well as past the gardens, pastures, and orchards.

The butterfly garden is somewhat off the beaten path, located behind the gift shop. Perennials and thick bushes, specifically chosen to attract butterflies, line a small network of narrow gravel paths, forming a maze that younger children enjoy puzzling through. *Remember:* Colorful buckets of animal feed are available for a small fee at the gift shop.

PLAN B: If your children would like to hold animals, the petting zoo at next-door Green Meadows Farm is sometimes open to the public for a small fee. Call 718-470-0224 or go to visitgreenmeadowsfarm.com.

WHERE TO EAT NEARBY: Restaurants and shops are along Union Turnpike, three blocks south of Little Neck Parkway (turn right out of the parking lot).

Trip 51

Jamaica Bay Wildlife Refuge: West Pond Trail

The West Pond of the Jamaica Bay Wildlife Refuge juxtaposes an expanse of natural wilderness with views of the Manhattan skyline.

Address: 1 Cross Bay Boulevard, Queens, NY
Hours: 8:30 A.M. to 5 P.M. daily
Fee: Free
Contact: nps.gov/gate/planyourvisit/thingstodojamaciabay.htm; 718-338-3799; nyharborparks.org/visit/jaba.html; 718-318-4340
Bathrooms: Visitor center
Water/Snacks: Water fountains inside visitor center
Maps: USGS Far Rockaway; brooklynbirdclub.org/westpondmap.htm
Directions by Car: From Manhattan, take I-495 east to Exit 22A. Take I-678 south to Exit 1W. Take a slight right onto North Conduit Avenue, then take the ramp on the left on the Verrazano Bridge. Merge onto the Belt Parkway and take Exit 17S. Merge onto Cross Bay Boulevard and drive 3.4 miles. The parking lot is outside the visitor center. *GPS coordinates:* 40° 37.038′ N, 73° 49.426′ W.
Directions by Subway: Take the A train to Broad Channel. Exit the station to the right and walk along Noel Road through two lights to Cross Bay Boulevard. Cross over to the far side of Cross Bay Boulevard and turn right. The entrance to the visitor center is about a mile up the road on the left.

The Jamaica Bay Wildlife Refuge is a 9,155-acre tract within the Gateway National Recreation Area, a preserve of some 26,000 acres of waterways, wetlands, beaches, woodlands, and historical areas in New York and New Jersey.

The refuge is a natural wonder within the city that was never completely "paved over." The views of massive housing blocks and the Manhattan skyline hovering on the horizon will make you appreciate this all the more. The refuge is an important example of how natural wonders may be not only preserved in a city, but also made easily accessible by public transportation.

As you exit the back of the Visitor Contact Station, head west (clockwise) along the 1.5-mile path that circles the pond. The flat gravel trail that you will follow is renowned for bird-watching—swans, egrets, herons, osprey, and owls

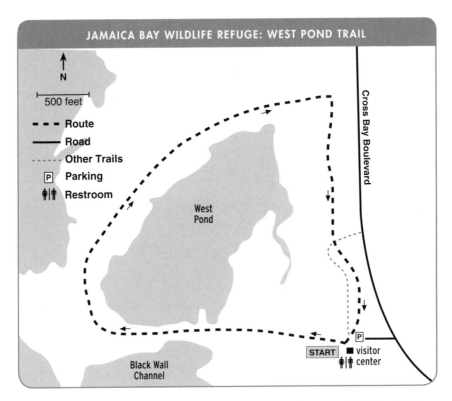

JAMAICA BAY WILDLIFE REFUGE: WEST POND TRAIL

N

500 feet

- - - Route
——— Road
········· Other Trails
P Parking
🚹🚺 Restroom

West Pond

Cross Bay Boulevard

START ■ visitor 🚹🚺 center

P

Black Wall Channel

among them—and it may make you feel you are closer to the Florida Keys than to Times Square. The trail is dotted with numerous bird houses and bat sanctuaries that have been built to attract local birds and bats whose domiciles elsewhere have been diminished by the encroachment of human civilization. Your stroll may be interrupted by the occasional gaggle of geese making their way across the path, and you may need to skirt dozens of nesting spots marked by flags and covered with steel cages to protect the terrapin eggs within. The full trail comprises a 1.5-mile loop. *Remember:* You need a free permit from the Visitor Contact Station to explore Jamaica Bay.

PLAN B: For more-rugged walks with children who are older, visit the East Pond (Trip 52). If you are traveling by car, you can also take in Floyd Bennett Field (Trips 38 and 39) or Marine Park (Trip 40).

WHERE TO EAT NEARBY: Some food establishments are along Cross Bay Boulevard.

The National Park Service (NPS) created its Junior Ranger program to encourage children to explore and learn about national parks—from art and history, to science and nature, to transportation and even dinosaurs. The hope is that children who do so will become invested in protecting and preserving those special places. Fifteen NPS sites offer Junior Ranger activities in New York alone, with many other sites across the country participating. Modeled on scout programs, the Junior Ranger program awards children badges, patches, and certificates for their involvement. For example, at Ellis Island (Trip 71), Junior Rangers are awarded a badge after completing a booklet of activities that guide children through the museum, to give a first-hand experience of what it was like for immigrants to arrive at the island.

At Floyd Bennett Field (Trips 38 and 39), Junior Rangers are asked to take notes on the variety of flying things—bats, airplanes, butterflies, and helicopters—they might see on the property, which was New York City's first municipal airport. The Junior Ranger booklet also covers semaphore and alpha codes, bird migration, and how to make a paper airplane. Other Junior Ranger activity books—such as the one designed for the Statue of Liberty (see Trip 70)—are not only site-specific, but also ask children to think more about the National Park Service and the history of the United States. For example, kids are told that the arrowhead is the symbol of the National Park Service, why copper turns green, and who gave the Statue of Liberty to the United States. Visit nps.gov/learn/juniorranger.cfm for more information.

Another city-based Junior Ranger program is run through the Urban Park Rangers, who offer a number of family programs throughout the year. On Friday and Saturday nights through July and August, families can camp for free in many of the parks covered in this book (see page 102). An internship program, called The Ranger Conservation Corps, is offered to high school students; through it, interns do restoration work in "Forever Wild" sites around the city one day a week after school. In the Junior Rangers Adventure Program, kids ages 8 through 11 learn outdoor skills like how to paddle a canoe or use a compass during day camp or overnight outings throughout the summer. For details and sign-up information, visit nycgovparks.org/rangers or call 311.

Trip 52

Jamaica Bay Wildlife Refuge: East Pond Trail

East Pond Trail of the Jamaica Bay Wildlife Refuge is a shorter, rougher, wilder alternative to neighboring West Pond Trail.

Address: 1 Cross Bay Boulevard, Queens, NY
Hours: 8:30 A.M. to 5 P.M. daily
Fee: Free
Contact: nps.gov/gate/planyourvisit/thingstodojamaciabay.htm; 718-338-3799; nyharborparks.org/visit/jaba.html; 718-318-4340
Bathrooms: Visitor center
Water/Snacks: Water fountains inside visitor center
Maps: USGS Far Rockaway; brooklynbirdclub.org/maps/eastpond.pdf
Directions by Car: From Manhattan, take I-495 east to Exit 22A. Take I-678 south to Exit 1W. Take a slight right onto North Conduit Avenue, then take the ramp on the left onto the Verrazano Bridge. Merge onto the Belt Parkway and take Exit 17S. Merge onto Cross Bay Boulevard and drive 3.4 miles. The parking lot is outside the visitor center. *GPS coordinates:* 40° 37.038' N, 73° 49.426' W.
Directions by Subway: Take the A train to Broad Channel. Exit the station to the right and walk along Noel Road through two lights to Cross Bay Boulevard. Cross over to the far side of Cross Bay Boulevard and turn right. The entrance to the visitor center is about a mile up the road on the left.

Jamaica Bay—stretching across Brooklyn and Queens—offers a wide variety of wild spaces on the outskirts of the great metropolis. The Jamaica Bay Wildlife Refuge is not only the largest open space in all of New York City, but as part of the Gateway National Recreation Area, it is also the only national park accessible by subway.

East Pond Trail is a terrific jaunt. Much shorter and less developed than neighboring West Pond Trail, East Pond Trail offers a rustic alternative suggesting what much of the salt marsh looked like before human encroachment.

Enter the trail off Cross Bay Boulevard. Follow it east for 0.2 mile and to the north, you will see Big John's Pond, a freshwater pond named after the bulldozer operator who dug it. It is home to some 300 species of birds that migrate

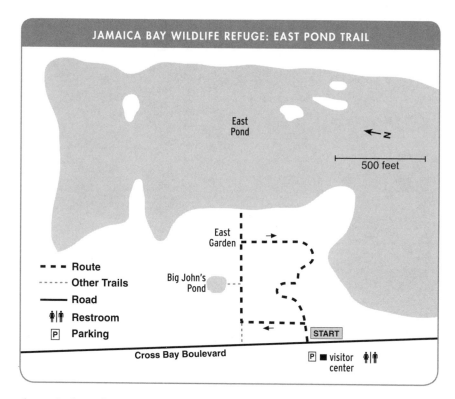

JAMAICA BAY WILDLIFE REFUGE: EAST POND TRAIL

East
Pond

← N

500 feet

East
Garden

Big John's
Pond

- - - Route
----- Other Trails
—— Road
♀|♂ Restroom
P Parking

START

Cross Bay Boulevard

P ■ visitor
center ♀|♂

through the refuge every year. Continue east another 0.2 mile and you will reach a junction; the trail on the right will be your return route. Walk straight ahead for views of the East Garden, then out onto the boardwalk for a view of East Pond. Afterward, turn back to follow the trail south then west, finishing the loop back where you began.

In June and September, the water level in East Pond is lowered to invite thousands of migrating birds. During these months visitors can also walk around the pond. Otherwise, call ahead to make sure the trail is open. *Remember:* You need a free permit from the Visitor Contact Station to explore Jamaica Bay. Note too that East Pond Trail is not suitable for strollers, and it is advisable to wear boots if you do the full loop when it's open.

PLAN B: For an easy and satisfying walk on maintained paths, visit the West Pond (Trip 51). If you are traveling by car, you can also take in Floyd Bennett Field (Trips 38 and 39) or Marine Park (Trip 40).

WHERE TO EAT NEARBY: Some food establishments are along Cross Bay Boulevard.

Section 4

Staten Island

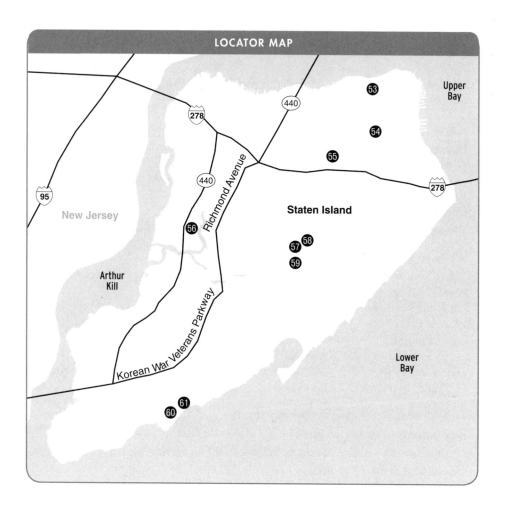

Trip 53

All Ages

Snug Harbor Cultural Center and Botanical Garden

It shouldn't be a secret: Children will love puzzling their way through the Secret Garden hedge maze.

Address: 1000 Richmond Terrace, Staten Island, NY
Hours: 8 A.M. to 4:30 P.M. Tuesday through Friday, 10 A.M. to 4:30 P.M. Saturday and Sunday, November to March; 8 A.M. to 6 P.M. Tuesday through Friday, 10 A.M. to 6 P.M. Saturday and Sunday, March to November
Fee: Free (General Grounds and Botanical Garden)
Contact: snug-harbor.org; 718-448-2500
Bathrooms: Buildings C, D, G and T along Shinbone Alley; gift shop and Chinese Garden entrance, in building Y on Cottage Row; other locations throughout the park
Water/Snacks: Water fountains in building C; café at the Children's Museum
Map: USGS Jersey City; snug-harbor.org/visit
Directions by Car: From NY 9A South, take I-278 West to Exit 14. Turn right onto Fingerboard Road, then left onto Bay Street in 2.4 miles. Continue onto Richmond Terrace and drive 1.7 miles to the entrance on the left.
GPS coordinates: 40° 38.676′ N, 74° 6.123′ W.
Directions by Bus: From the St. George Ferry Terminal, take the S40 bus at Gate D and disembark at Snug Harbor.

Tucked within this 83-acre park are diverse gardens—Tuscan, Chinese, and herb among them—an inspired hedge maze, the Staten Island Children's Museum, and much more. It's an eclectic lot and an intriguing place to roam around and make discoveries.

Most of the lawns and horticultural exhibits are on the western and southern edges of the park. From the entrance at Snug Harbor Road, walk southwest along Cottage Row. New York Harbor will be behind you. When you see the greenhouse, turn left onto Chapel Road and then make a quick right onto Gazebo Road. Take this path through the herb garden and into the tunnel of trees that have been cultivated to curve over a series of wire frames. Exit to the right, and you will be back on Cottage Row.

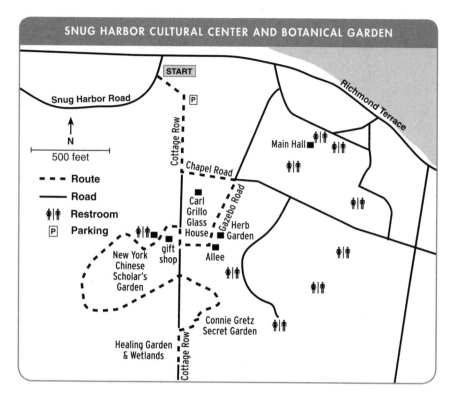

SNUG HARBOR CULTURAL CENTER AND BOTANICAL GARDEN

Continuing south along Cottage Row, you cannot miss the half-acre Secret Garden maze, marked by a 38-foot-tall, medieval-style castle that you can ascend to get a bird's-eye view of the park. A sure hit with kids, this charming horticultural feature is based on Frances Hodgson Burnett's 1911 novel, *The Secret Garden*. The shrubs are about 4 feet high, so adults can see over them and offer younger children a guiding hand—and voice—for getting through.

To the west of the Secret Garden is a series of switchback paths that take you down a hill and through wetlands, and to the east is a thoughtfully re-created Tuscan garden. The southern and eastern sections of Snug Harbor offer a grassy campus of Greek Revival and Beaux Arts buildings in various stages of redevelopment and use that earned Snug Harbor its place on the list of National Historic Landmarks. *Remember:* The Secret Garden has some thorny rosebushes near which children should be careful.

PLAN B: The Staten Island Children's Museum is located in Snug Harbor, behind Chapel Road.

WHERE TO EAT NEARBY: If you are driving, visit the shops along Richmond Terrace. A year-round farmers market is near the ferry terminal.

Trip 54

All Ages

Silver Lake

Silver Lake offers enormous oaks, walking and cycling paths, tennis courts, ball fields, and a golf course, as well as a dog run and sledding in winter.

Address: Victory Boulevard at Forest Avenue, Staten Island, NY
Hours: Dawn to dusk daily
Fee: Free
Contact: nycgovparks.org/parks/silverlakepark; call 311 or 718-447-5686
Bathrooms: Golf club at 915 Victory Boulevard
Water/Snacks: Water fountains at the playground, University Place, Revere Street, and throughout the park; café at the golf club
Map: USGS Jersey City and The Narrows
Directions by Car: From NY 9A South, take I-278 West to Exit 13 onto Narrows Road North. Bear right onto Clove Road, then take a right onto Victory Boulevard. The park is ahead on the left. Parking is available on the surrounding streets. *GPS coordinates*: 40° 37.614′ N, 74° 5.483′ W.
Directions by Bus: From the St. George Ferry Terminal, take the S46 bus at Ramp C, Bay 3, and disembark at Castleton Avenue and Havenwood Road.

About a third of 151-square-mile Staten Island is devoted to parks; in 1900, Silver Lake Park was the first among them. The park surrounds Silver Lake, a spring-fed reservoir that formed at the end of the last ice age (approximately 10,000 years ago) and served as a source for the ice industry in the nineteenth century. The oaks that line its banks are so thick that three children forming a circle around the trunk cannot reach one another's hands. You don't see many trees this big in the other boroughs.

Enter the park on Victory Boulevard near Forest Avenue, and follow the paved paths that slope toward the water. Turn right, and begin walking around the lake by crossing over the wooded northern rim. This connects to a paved path that follows Silver Lake Park Road. The reservoir along this side is encircled by a high chain-link fence, except for an opening where pedestrians and cyclists can traverse the reservoir on a high stone bridge. On the other side, you can explore more than 2 miles of trails that loop along the well-shaded bank.

One of Staten Island's two newest playgrounds, opened in summer 2011, is located at University Place and Revere Street. The facility joins tennis courts,

Miles of paths wend around this spring-fed reservoir.

ball fields, and an 18-hole golf course to make Silver Lake Park a destination for people of all interests. *Remember:* The seventh fairway of the Silver Lake Golf Club, adjacent to the park, is open in winter for sledding. The dog run is located along Victory Boulevard, across from the Parkview Apartments.

PLAN B: Clove Lakes Park (Trip 55) has paved paths marked by blazes that offer a good introduction to hiking and reading trail signs.

WHERE TO EAT NEARBY: A restaurant is at the golf club, and if you are driving, others dining options are along Victory Boulevard.

Trip 55

All Ages

Clove Lakes Park

A "Forever Wild" site nestled within the busy streets of Staten Island's south shore, this park features a paved, blazed trail along the lake, where you can rent paddle boats.

Address: 1150 Clove Road, Staten Island, NY
Hours: Dawn to dusk daily
Fee: Free
Contact: nycgovparks.org/parks/CloveLakesPark; call 311 or 718-390-8000
Bathrooms: Lake Club, near the park entrance
Water/Snacks: The Lake Club restaurant; food vendor near the playground and ball fields at the park entrance
Map: USGS Jersey City and The Narrows; nycgovparks.org/parks/ CloveLakesPark/map
Directions by Car: From NY 9A South, take I-278 West to Exit 13 onto Narrows Road North. Bear right onto Clove Road. The park is ahead on the left. Free parking is available at the lot for the Staten Island Zoo at the intersection of Clove Road and Martling Avenue. *GPS coordinates (park entrance):* 40° 37.094′ N, 74° 6.454′ W.
Directions by Bus: From the St. George Ferry Terminal, take the S61 at Ramp A, Bay 5, and disembark at Victory Boulevard and Clove Road.

Clove Lakes Park offers nearly 200 acres of green space as one of New York City's 51 "Forever Wild" sites. Deemed the most ecologically valuable lands, these parcels are protected by the state constitution from sale or development. Clove Lakes earned this designation thanks to its attractive outcroppings of serpentine rock (so named for its green color and snakeskin texture) and the presence of what is reputedly the oldest living thing on Staten Island—a 107-foot tulip tree more than 300 years old, located in the northwest section of the park.

From the corner of Martling Avenue and Clove Road, follow the paved paths lined with old-growth trees leading either northwest or southeast into the park. Easy-to-follow paved paths and a network of dirt trails take you around the park and up and down hills that encircle its signature lakes. The section of the park south of Martling Avenue features a bridge that traverses lovely artificial waterfalls.

Paved trails, studded with scenic overlooks, take you around the lovely lakes of this park.

To teach children how to read trail signs, follow the innermost blue-blazed trail that hugs the southern lake. Many entry and exit points to this paved and pleasantly hilly route are along the way.

From May to October, you can rent paddleboats at the Lake Club for $10 per hour. The outdoor World War II Veterans War Memorial Ice Skating Rink, on Victory Boulevard west of Clove Road, is open in winter. Call 718-720-1010 or 718-720-1014 for schedule and details. Admission is $8, and skate rentals are $5. *Remember:* You cannot ride bikes on the paths that circle the lakes. Cycling is restricted to Clove Road and Victory Boulevard.

PLAN B: The Staten Island Zoo at 614 Broadway is a fifteen-minute walk northwest of the park. It features an aquarium and habitats as diverse as a rain forest and a New England farm, complete with a petting zoo.

WHERE TO EAT NEARBY: A number of restaurants are outside the Staten Island Mall, at Richmond Avenue and Ring Road.

Trip 56

All Ages

Freshkills Park

Schmul Park, the first parcel to open under the massive Freshkills Park project, offers a state-of-the-art playground, ball fields, gardens, and grassy areas for picnicking.

Address: Wild Avenue, Pearson Street, and Melvin Avenue, Staten Island, NY
Hours: Dawn to dusk daily
Fee: Free
Contact: nyc.gov/parks/freshkillspark; freshkillspark.wordpress.com; 212-788-8277
Bathrooms: Schmul Park playground
Water/Snacks: None
Map: USGS Arthur Kill
Directions by Car: From NY 9A South, take I-278 West to Exit 7 onto Richmond Avenue. Drive 1.7 miles and turn right onto Travis Avenue. Parking is available on the streets surrounding Schmul Park. *GPS coordinates:* 40° 35.182' N, 74° 11.513' W.
Directions by Bus: From the St. George Ferry Terminal, take the S62 bus at Ramp A, Bay 3, and disembark at Victory Boulevard and Carteret Ferry.

Opened in 1947, Fresh Kills landfill eventually became the primary dump for New York City. In 2001, the landfill was closed and the work of turning it into Freshkills Park began. The 2,200-acre park project is one of the largest public works efforts in the United States and is scheduled to open in phases through 2036.

At the time of this writing, an overhauled Schmul Park, an 8-acre tract that traded a blacktop playground for thoroughly modern equipment, was on track to be the first area of Freshkills to open in spring 2012. This area will eventually serve as the pedestrian gateway to North Park, whose development was launched in 2011. The North Park design features miles of hiking and biking trails that have panoramic views of the William T. Davis Wildlife Refuge tidal flats. It is one of five major components of Freshkills Park. South Park will have trails and athletic fields, East Park will have woodland walks, and West Park will feature a World Trade Center memorial—the landfill was briefly reopened to process debris from the September 11, 2001, attacks. The Confluence will

Flying kites is just one of the many activities to enjoy at Freshkills, one of the city's largest parks.

form the center of Freshkills Park, offering kayaking, a visitor center, educational facilities, and restaurants.

Throughout the year, the Department of Parks and Recreation hosts free events so visitors can witness the birth of a park, join bird-watching tours, or hike, kayak, fly kites, and bike in the areas that are under development. It is an exceptional treat to be among the first Freshkills Park users to see, firsthand, the work it takes to convert a former industrial site into a stunning and multifaceted green space. *Remember:* Before heading to Freshkills, contact the park office for an update on the restoration. For a list of upcoming tours and events, visit nycgovparks.org/park-features/freshkills-park.

PLAN B: A hike up Moses Mountain (Trip 58) ends with 360-degree views.

WHERE TO EAT NEARBY: A number of restaurants are outside the Staten Island Mall, at Richmond Avenue and Ring Road.

Trip 57

Greenbelt Nature Center

The Greenbelt Nature Center trails are ideal for young children who are ready to try hopping across flat rocks or balancing on the occasional log crossing.

Address: 700 Rockland Avenue, Staten Island, NY
Hours: 10 A.M. to 5 P.M. Tuesday through Sunday, April to October
Fee: Free
Contact: sigreenbelt.org; 718-351-3450
Bathrooms: Nature center
Water/Snacks: Water fountain in nature center
Map: USGS Arthur Kill and The Narrows; sigreenbelt.org/Trails/trailmap.pdf
Directions by Car: From NY 9 South, take I-278 to Exit 11 onto Bradley Avenue. Take a right onto Brielle Avenue, then another right onto Rockland Avenue. The nature center and parking lot are ahead on the left. *GPS coordinates:* 40° 35.336′ N, 74° 8.399′ W.
Directions by Bus: From the St. George Ferry Terminal, take the S74/S84 bus from ramp B or the S61/S91 bus from ramp A and disembark across from the nature center.

Two bands of contiguous parks totaling 2,800 acres compose the Staten Island Greenbelt, with the nature center at its hub. This vast tract—the largest wooded area in New York City—offers 35 miles of hiking trails that range from easy to moderate.

Start at the nature center, which features displays on the ecosystem—wetland, forest, tree canopy—of the Greenbelt. The center also offers educational programs for toddlers, teens, adults, and seniors, and is a city composting demonstration site. The easy, mile-long Nature Center Trail begins to the left (east) of the modern and information-packed center. The trail is marked by a white N painted in a blue square on trees throughout. After you cross a wooden footbridge, a dirt path immediately takes you into a thick canopy of mature trees. Several hundred yards into the walk, you will see an E blaze (a blue E painted in a white square on a large tree) for a trail heading to the left. This is a short, beginner trail that is good for preschool children.

To complete Nature Center Trail, continue on the N path, which gets narrow at points, until you reach Blue Trail, which in this link doubles as the N. Turn right and follow it through a native fern garden and among towering

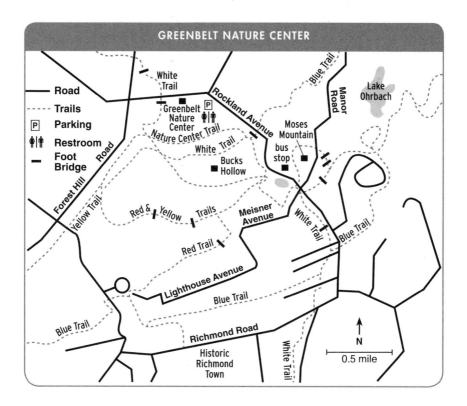

Road
Trails
P Parking
Restroom
Foot Bridge

White Trail
Rockland Avenue
Greenbelt Nature Center
Nature Center Trail
White Trail
Bucks Hollow
Moses Mountain
bus stop
Manor Road
Lake Ohrbach
Blue Trail

Forest Hill Road
Yellow Trail
Red & Yellow Trails
Red Trail
Meisner Avenue
White Trail
Blue Trail

Lighthouse Avenue
Blue Trail
Blue Trail

Richmond Road
Historic Richmond Town
White Trail
N
0.5 mile

birch and beech trees. In spring, numerous types of wildflowers and songbirds thrive here because of the ponds that lie off the trail. The trail ultimately forms a semicircle that leads back to the nature center.

Another option is Multipurpose Trail, a wide, crushed-gravel, pedestrian-friendly trail that is great for biking (the only Greenbelt trail on which biking is permitted). The trail is mostly flat and begins near the intersection of Rockland Avenue and Forest Hill Road, due west of the nature center entrance, and runs along Forest Hill Road to Richmond Avenue. Experienced hikers could also try the full 12.3-mile Blue Trail, which takes you up to Todt Hill (410 feet), the highest point of elevation on the eastern seaboard between Maine and Florida. *Remember:* A branch of Multipurpose Trail also runs east toward Historic Richmond Town (Trip 59).

PLAN B: From May through October, the Carousel for All Children, in nearby Willowbrook Park at Eton Place off Richmond Avenue, is a fun destination.

WHERE TO EAT NEARBY: If you are driving, visit the shops and restaurants along Victory Boulevard. A number of restaurants are outside the Staten Island Mall, at Richmond Avenue and Ring Road.

Trip 58

Greenbelt: Moses Mountain

An uphill but easy hike brings you to great views at the top of a mountain built of construction debris.

Address: 700 Rockland Avenue, Staten Island, NY
Hours: Dawn to dusk daily
Fee: Free
Contact: sigreenbelt.org; 718-351-3450
Bathrooms: Greenbelt Nature Center
Water/Snacks: Water fountain in the Greenbelt Nature Center
Map: USGS Arthur Kill and The Narrows; sigreenbelt.org/Trails/trailmap.pdf
Directions by Car: From NY 9 South, take I-278 to Exit 11 onto Bradley Avenue. Take a right onto Brielle Avenue, then another right onto Rockland Avenue. The nature center and parking lot are ahead on the left. *GPS coordinates:* 40° 35.336′ N, 74° 8.399′ W.
Directions by Bus: From the St. George Ferry Terminal, take the S74/S84 bus from ramp B or the S61/S91 bus from ramp A and disembark across from the nature center.

Though the name Robert Moses has come up frequently in this book (see page xxiv), there is probably no more appropriate monument to his impact—for better or worse—on New York City geography than Moses Mountain. The 260-foot-high mound, among the most popular hikes in the Greenbelt, is made of debris from the construction of the Staten Island Expressway (I-278). The trail map available at the nature center notes that the name was mockingly bestowed, presumably because Moses deserves no honor after having sacrificed many Staten Island neighborhoods for highway projects. This relatively easy, up-and-back hike can be done in 90 minutes.

Pick up Blue Trail behind the nature center and follow it east until a junction with Red Trail. Turn right (south) onto Red Trail and continue onto White Trail. White Trail will lead you to the top of Meisner Avenue. Walk northeast until you reach Yellow Trail at the corner of Meisner and Rockland avenues.

You will see a yellow stripe on the guard rail on the other side of Rockland Avenue, beyond a traffic light. Enter the dirt trail to the left of the guard rail, and in short order, the dense forest will make you forget you're in the city. Fol-

Thickly wooded Moses Mountain offers a popular hike to panoramic forest views.

low the periodic yellow blazes on trees and rocks to the top of the mountain. Early on, the trail is flat, heading basically due north with a few bends along the way. After about fifteen minutes, the trail turns to the right and begins a gentle ascent up the mound. From here, parts of the trail are rocky and tree-rooted but manageable for young children. At the summit you will be treated to breathtaking 360-degree views of Greenbelt's thick canopy of red maple, oak, and hickory trees. It is particularly beautiful in fall. *Remember:* The flat part of the trail can be swampy if the weather has been rainy.

PLAN B: Greenbelt Nature Center (Trip 57) is an easy alternative if it recently has rained and you fear that Moses Mountain might be too slippery. If you are driving, Historic Richmond Town (Trip 59) is a nearby alternative for outdoor adventures in a rolling parklike setting.

WHERE TO EAT NEARBY: If you are driving, visit the shops and restaurants along Victory Boulevard. A number of restaurants are outside the Staten Island Mall, at Richmond Avenue and Ring Road.

Trip 59

All Ages

Historic Richmond Town

This outdoor museum preserves 300 years of New York history while providing visitors with bucolic parkland to enjoy.

Address: 441 Clarke Avenue, Staten Island, NY
Hours: 1 to 5 P.M., Wednesday through Sunday
Fee: Free for grounds-only access
Contact: historicrichmondtown.org; 212-360-8201
Bathrooms: 3rd County Courthouse in front of the parking lot
Water/Snacks: Café at the corner of Richmond Road and Court Place
Map: USGS Arthur Kill; historicrichmondtown.org/village-map
Directions by Car: From NY 9 South, take I-278 to Exit 12 onto Slosson Avenue. Continue onto Todt Hill Road and drive for 2.0 miles. Take a slight right onto Richmond Road, then bear left onto Amboy Road. Turn right onto Clarke Avenue. The parking lot (free) is on the right. *GPS coordinates: 40° 34.205′ N, 74° 8.709′ W.*
Directions by Bus: From the St. George Ferry Terminal, take the S74 bus to Richmond Road and St. Patrick's Place.

Seventeenth-century Historic Richmond Town provides visitors with more than 100 acres of green space and quaint village streets that are much as they were more than three centuries ago. Children are amazed to learn that they are walking on the very paths and lawns that villagers traversed between the blacksmith, the grocery store, the rail station, and what is today the oldest school house in the United States.

Start at the visitor center in the 3rd County Courthouse facing the parking lot. Here you can purchase tickets ($8 for adults, $5 for children over 4, and free for those younger) to enter the various buildings where docents in period clothing make furniture or print posters and pamphlets using old-time tools. However, the destination is worth seeing from the outside alone.

Exit the visitor center onto Center Street (opposite the parking lot) and turn right to begin a pleasant 45-minute loop. This tree-lined road eventually meets St. Patrick's Place. Turn right, and on your right (across the street) will be the Stephens-Prier House, whose big and beautiful lawn speaks to the wealth of the onetime occupants. Take St. Patrick's Place to Richmond Road

A docent in period dress demonstrates a basket-weaving method.

and turn left. This takes you past a farm and a number of historical homes that doubled as workshops for various trades.

On your left you will come to Court Street (which stretches from the visitor center); take the path to your right and then make a quick left to find your way to Dunn's Mill and Mill Pond. This is one of 16 watersheds in the Staten Island bluebelt program aimed at controlling flooding by rehabilitating and protecting designated waterways. Landscaped with plants that are indigenous to Staten Island, Mill Pond is a magnet for birds and other wildlife.

Return the way you came, and take Court Street back to Center Street. Turn right, and a few hundred yards on your left will be one of two designated picnic areas set within a grove of trees. *Remember:* Low-cost programs for children (including a camp in summer and workshops in winter) are offered throughout the year.

PLAN B: A hike up Moses Mountain (Trip 58) would make a nice complement to this destination.

WHERE TO EAT NEARBY: A number of restaurants are outside the Staten Island Mall, at Richmond Avenue and Ring Road.

Trip 60

Ages 9–12

Mount Loretto Unique Area: Waterfront Walk

Mount Loretto is one of the first stops in New York State for northbound birds and butterflies in spring, and one of the last for those going south in winter.

Address: 6450 Hylan Boulevard, Staten Island, NY
Hours: Dawn to dusk daily
Fee: Free
Contact: dec.ny.gov/outdoor/8291.html; 718-482-7287
Bathrooms: Portable toilet at the entrance
Water/Snacks: None
Map: USGS Arthur Kill; dec.ny.gov/outdoor/8273.html
Directions by Car: From NY 9 South, take I-278 to Exit 5 and merge onto NY 440 South. Take Exit 3 and merge onto Veterans Road. Turn left onto Bloomingdale Road and drive for 1.8 miles, then turn left onto Amboy Road. Take the first right onto Sharrot Avenue, then turn right onto Hylan Boulevard. The parking lot will be ahead on your left. *GPS coordinates*: 40° 30.536′ N, 74° 13.294′ W.
Directions by Bus: From the St. George Ferry Terminal, take bus S78 and disembark at Mount Loretto.

A *New Yorker* article about harbor seals returning to New York inspired us to visit Mount Loretto, a nearly 200-acre park and nature preserve with grasslands, wetlands, and a mile of shoreline. We didn't encounter any seals, but we were impressed by the red-clay bluffs that are reputedly the only ones in the New York City area.

To enjoy the waterfront and the bluffs, walk, bike, or stroll south along the gravel path (Kenny Road to Beach Loop) that leads from the entrance gate to Raritan Bay on the horizon. At trail marker 8 on the left, a pond is obscured by shrubs. The grass here is a popular feeding spot for ducks. At any given moment, you may see more webbed feet than beaks, as the ducks dive into the muck to nibble for food.

When you reach the grassy stretch overlooking the shore, Sandy Hook, New Jersey, will be in the distance. The red-clay cliffs and beach will be beneath you, although you may not see much of the beach during high tide.

The grasslands at Mount Loretto Unique Area attract many colorful birds and butterflies.

Return to the gravel path and go left. You will pass a small shrine on your left. This is the only vestige of the property's former owner, the Archdiocese of New York, which held the title from 1890 to 1999. A fire in 2000 destroyed the building that had once served as orphanage dormitories and a hospital. The land is now under protection by the state's Department of Environmental Conservation, allowing trees and tall grasses to erase traces of the area's human history.

From the building site (marked by an informational sign), continue to the end of the path, then make the steep walk up to the Prince's Bay Lighthouse. Built in 1828, and modernized from wood to brownstone in 1864, the lighthouse is fenced off and no longer used, but the views from the surrounding grounds are spectacular. *Remember:* This route is the only one at Mount Loretto that permits bicycle riding. See map on page 151.

PLAN B: Within the park, the Grassland and Wetlands trails (Trip 61) are excellent nature hikes.

WHERE TO EAT NEARBY: Pack a picnic, or, if you are driving, visit the shops and restaurants along Hylan Boulevard.

Trip 61

Ages 5–8

Mount Loretto Unique Area: Grassland and Wetlands Loops

These two loops offer a variety of terrain, including a moderately steep hill. The view at the top is worth the climb.

Address: 6450 Hylan Boulevard, Staten Island, NY
Hours: Dawn to dusk daily
Fee: Free
Contact: dec.ny.gov/outdoor/8291.html; 718-482-7287
Bathrooms: Portable toilet at the entrance
Water/Snacks: None
Map: USGS Arthur Kill; dec.ny.gov/outdoor/8273.html
Directions by Car: From NY 9 South, take I-278 to Exit 5 and merge onto NY 440 South. Take Exit 3 and merge onto Veterans Road. Turn left onto Bloomingdale Road and drive for 1.8 miles, then turn left onto Amboy Road. Take the first right onto Sharrot Avenue, then turn right onto Hylan Boulevard. The parking lot will be ahead on your left. *GPS coordinates*: 40° 30.536′ N, 74° 13.294′ W.
Directions by Bus: From the St. George Ferry Terminal, take bus S78 and disembark at Mount Loretto.

Grasslands—a rare landscape in the New York City area—cover more than half of the Mount Loretto Unique Area. This environment is a wonderland for sparrows, bobolinks, swallows, and other grassland birds. This is also a prime habitat for wildflowers, which, in turn, attract numerous butterflies from spring through early fall.

Grassland Trail is on your right, about 30 yards south of the entrance gate. When you turn right onto this short dirt trail, you will be heading west. An expanse of grasslands will be to your left. After about a quarter-mile, the trail comes out onto a paved path; turn left and follow it south toward the shoreline.

From here you can follow the paved path to the main route along the shore (Trip 60), or return the way you came. The wetlands trailhead is directly across from the entrance to the grasslands trail. Wetlands Trail, which takes you east, has numbered markers that point to a freshwater pond; brackish water tidal wetlands; a larger freshwater pond that is home to frogs, turtles, salamanders,

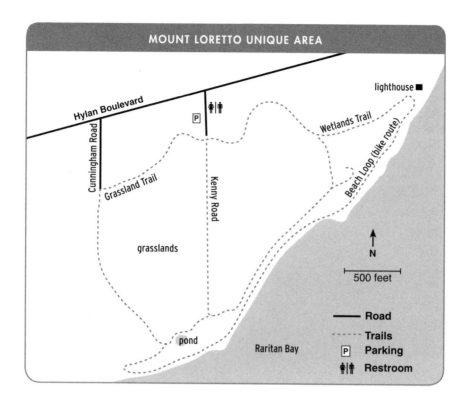

and insects called water striders (when you see them, you will understand how they earned this name!); a higher overview of the wetland system; and a tidal inlet. From this marker, retrace your steps to the freshwater pond, turn left and go uphill to a scenic view of the entire park. Descending along a dirt road, you will see Raritan Bay on your left.

Evidenced by the cracked shells on the ground throughout Mount Loretto, the wetlands are a good habitat for crabs and, by extension, the long-legged birds such as egrets and herons that like to feed on them. *Remember:* Bicycles are not permitted on the nature trails.

PLAN B: Kenny Road and Beach Loop (Trip 60) are easier for toddlers, young children, and strollers.

WHERE TO EAT NEARBY: Pack a picnic, or if you are driving, visit the shops and restaurants along Hylan Boulevard.

Section 5

Bronx

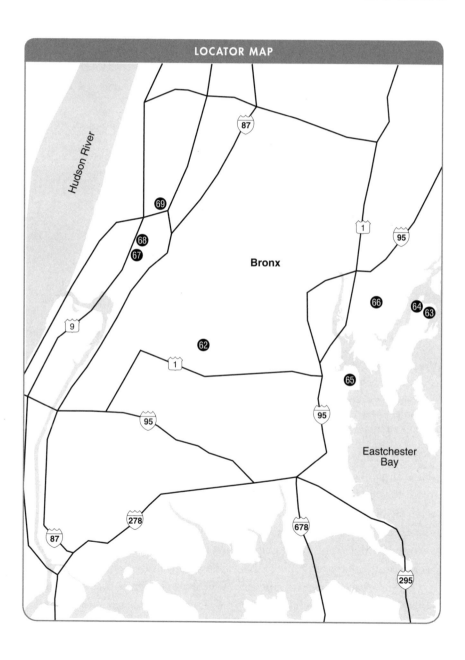

LOCATOR MAP

Hudson River

Bronx

Eastchester Bay

Trip 62

New York Botanical Garden

Explore a wilderness that has, in parts, remained largely untouched since before the arrival of the Dutch in about 1624.

Address: 2900 Southern Boulevard, Bronx, NY

Hours: 10 A.M. to 6 P.M. Tuesday through Sunday; closed most Mondays and Christmas Day

Fee: Grounds-only admission: adults, $10; children ages 2 to 12, $2; children under age 2, free. Free admission for all on Wednesdays and from 10 to 11 A.M. on Saturdays.

Contact: nybg.org; 718-817-8700

Bathrooms: Leon Levy Visitor Center

Water/Snacks: Full meals at the Garden Café; sandwiches, salads, and snacks at the Leon Levy Visitor Center Café

Map: USGS Central Park and Flushing; nybg.org/map

Directions by Car: Take I-87 South and merge onto I-278 East. Take Exit 51 and merge onto Bruckner Boulevard, then onto Bronx River Parkway. Take Exit 7W onto US 1 South and then take the exit for the New York Botanical Garden. Take a slight right onto Southern Boulevard and drive 0.3 mile to the entrance. *GPS coordinates:* 40° 51.690′ N, 73° 52.847′ W.

Directions by Subway: Take the B, D or 4 train to Bedford Park Boulevard. Take the Bx26 bus to the garden's Mosholu Gate entrance, or exit the subway station to your left and walk eight blocks downhill on Bedford Park Boulevard to Southern Boulevard; turn left, and Mosholu Gate will be on your right.

A National Historic Landmark, the New York Botanical Garden is the largest botanical garden in the United States and one of the most renowned in the world. This destination is devoted to breathtaking gardens, greenhouses, research facilities, a centuries-old forest, and rolling lawns. You may be surprised at how quiet and spacious the gardens feel when you arrive, and your kids will be wowed by the explosion of colors. Visit from late November through early January, and you can catch the Holiday Train Show in the Conservatory.

The four-season Everett Children's Adventure Garden is true to its name, and is a terrific stop for children ages 2 to 12. With hands-on activities, huge flowers, a boulder maze, a touch tank, and more, the garden will keep your

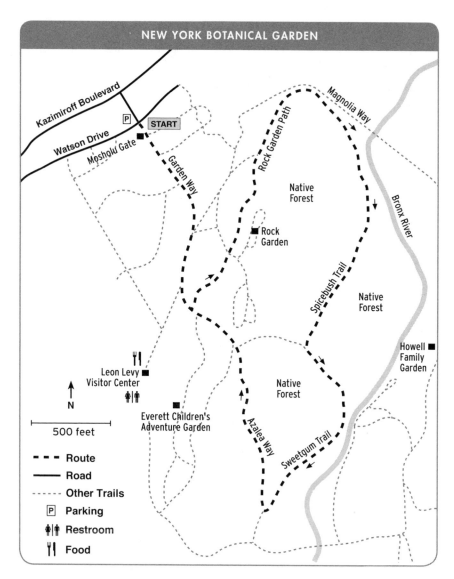

Kazimiroff Boulevard

P

START

Watson Drive

Mosholu Gate

Garden Way

Rock Garden Path

Magnolia Way

Bronx River

Native
Forest

Rock
Garden

Spicebush Trail

Native
Forest

Howell
Family
Garden

Leon Levy
Visitor Center

N

500 feet

Native
Forest

Everett Children's
Adventure Garden

Azalea Way

Native
Forest

Sweetgum Trail

- - - Route
—— Road
- - - - Other Trails
P   Parking
👫 Restroom
🍴 Food

kids engaged and excited. At the Howell Family Garden, on the eastern side of the grounds, children are encouraged to "dig in" to activities such as planting seeds and searching for worms in the dirt.

If you have time, allow two hours to explore the enormous oaks and maples of the 50-acre Native Forest, where mulch trails travel into the depths of the forest. From the main entrance at Mosholu Gate, take Garden Way (the trails are clearly marked) to the visitor center on your right. You will be at an intersection; turn left at Rock Garden Path and follow it north until it bends right and ultimately takes you to Spicebush Trail. You will pass a short path that leads onto Magnolia Way on the left. Keep an eye out, and you may spot raptors and hawks, which use the forest as part of their hunting grounds.

Spicebush Trail heads back south and, at a T intersection, connects to Bridge Trail. After soaking in this environment—and sometimes soaking your feet, as the path can have muddy patches and puddles for days after a rain—follow Bridge Trail to the footbridge that spans the freshwater Bronx River. The waterfall is captivating. Return to Bridge Trail, and turn left onto Sweetgum Trail, which eventually connects to Azalea Way, where you will turn right to head back to the visitor center. *Remember:* To enter the greenhouses and some of the themed gardens, you must purchase an all-garden admission ticket. Also, bicycles and scooters are not permitted in the garden.

PLAN B: The botanical garden shares Bronx Park, in the borough's center, with the legendary Bronx Zoo at 2300 Southern Boulevard.

WHERE TO EAT NEARBY: A picnic area is near the Everett Children's Adventure Garden. Stores selling food and beverages are along Bedford Park Boulevard, northwest of the Native Forest.

Trip 63

Pelham Bay Park: Orchard Beach and Twin Islands

This deep-woods retreat can be folded into a day at the beach.

Address: Park Drive, Bronx, NY
Hours: Dawn to dusk daily
Fee: Free; $8 parking fee applies in summer
Contact: pelhambaypark.org; nycgovparks.org/sub_your_park/vt_pelham_bay_park/vt_pelham_08.html; call 311 or 718-430-1890
Bathrooms: Nature center; Pelican Playground; pavilion
Water/Snacks: Water fountains at the bathrooms; concessions at the pavilion
Map: USGS Flushing and Mount Vernon; nycgovparks.org/sub_your_park/vt_pelham_bay_park/images/Pelham%20map-rev2005.pdf
Directions by Car: Take I-287 East to merge onto I-95 North. Take Exit 9 onto Hutchinson River Parkway North, then take Exit 5 toward Orchard Beach. Continue to the traffic circle, and take the second exit onto Orchard Beach Road. At the end of the road, turn left onto Park Drive. The parking lot is ahead on the right. *GPS coordinates:* 40° 52.225′ N, 73° 47.914′ W.
Directions by Subway: Take the 6 train to the last stop, Pelham Bay Park, and transfer to the Bx12 bus to Orchard Beach.

The Bronx is the only New York City borough on mainland America, and in the 1930s, the continent grew by 115 acres when 3 million cubic yards of landfill were brought in to create Orchard Beach. It was an impressive engineering feat at the time, and the mile-long, crescent-shaped beach—featuring white sand imported from the Rockaways in Queens and Sandy Hook, New Jersey—was given the nickname "The Riviera of New York."

The beach is divided into 13 sections, designated by signs. This is handy when trying to remember where your blanket is on a hot summer day. The nature center, which is open from 10 A.M. to 4 P.M. on weekends, Memorial Day through Labor Day, is on Twin Islands, across the promenade at the north end of the beach, in section 2. (Twin Islands are no longer actual islands, because of the creation of the beach.)

The trail on Twin Islands, which is not stroller friendly, begins to the right of the nature center, behind an opening in the pipe fence. The wide gravel path

Packed in summer, Orchard Beach is a quiet getaway in the off-season.

gives way to a small dirt path as you enter the woods. The trail is unmarked but easy to follow. It traces the rim of the former island, bringing you up hillocks that overlook Long Island Sound.

After making this loop of about a mile, return to the stroller-friendly promenade and walk the mile-long path to visit the splendid art deco pavilion that looms large in the distance. Two excellent playgrounds are along the way, one at section 6 and the other at section 11. *Remember:* In May and June, horseshoe crabs come ashore to lay eggs. With their long, pointed tails and tough-looking shells, they can be frightening at first sight.

PLAN B: Bring a canoe or kayak and paddle around the lagoon, to the west of the main beach parking lot.

WHERE TO EAT NEARBY: It is best to pack a picnic.

Trip 64

Ages 9–12

Pelham Bay Park: Hunter Island

The wetlands along the Kazimiroff Nature Trail attract a variety of animals all year long.

Address: Park Drive, Bronx, NY
Hours: Dawn to dusk daily
Fee: Free; $8 parking fee applies in summer
Contact: pelhambaypark.org; nycgovparks.org/sub_your_park/vt_pelham_bay_park/vt_pelham_08.html; call 311 or 718-430-1890
Bathrooms: Nature center; Pelican Playground; pavilion
Water/Snacks: Water fountains at the bathrooms; concessions at the pavilion
Map: USGS Flushing and Mount Vernon; nycgovparks.org/sub_your_park/vt_pelham_bay_park/images/Pelham%20map-rev2005.pdf
Directions by Car: Take I-287 East to merge onto I-95 North. Take Exit 9 onto Hutchinson River Parkway North, then take Exit 5 toward Orchard Beach. Continue to the traffic circle, and take the second exit onto Orchard Beach Road. At the end of the road, turn left onto Park Drive. The parking lot is ahead on the right. *GPS coordinates*: 40° 52.225′ N, 73° 47.914′ W.
Directions by Subway: Take the 6 train to the last stop, Pelham Bay Park, and transfer to the Bx12 bus to Orchard Beach.

Kazimiroff Nature Trail, located on Hunter Island (now connected to the mainland), can provide a much-needed respite from a crowded day on Orchard Beach. This destination, however, is attractive in any season—especially if trying to spot great-horned owls in winter is your fancy. You may also see deer, osprey, ducks, and raccoons in these woods.

The trail is named for Dr. Theodore Kazimiroff, a Bronx-born dentist who also served as the borough's official historian from 1953 until his death in 1980. An amateur zoologist, archeologist, and botanist, Kazimiroff was a consultant to the Bronx Zoo, the New York Botanical Garden (Trip 62), and the American Museum of Natural History. The outdoors was his passion, and preserving its delicate ecosystems his mission.

Two well-marked trails, red- and blue-blazed, take you through wetlands, around the bedrock cliffs that form the coast, and into deep coastal forest. From the Orchard Beach promenade (Trip 63), enter at section 3, to the left of the nature center. Keeping the vast picnic area to your left, you will see

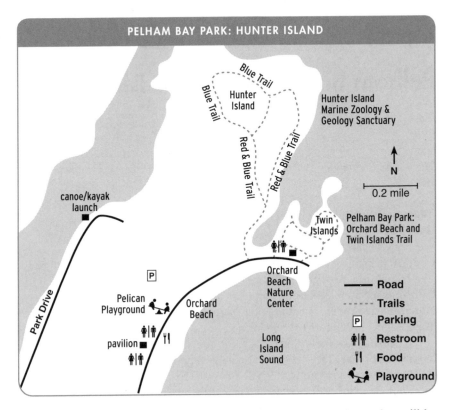

Map labels:

Blue Trail

Blue Trail

Hunter Island

Hunter Island Marine Zoology & Geology Sanctuary

Red & Blue Trail

Red & Blue Trail

N

0.2 mile

canoe/kayak launch

Twin Islands

Pelham Bay Park: Orchard Beach and Twin Islands Trail

P

Orchard Beach Nature Center

Pelican Playground

Orchard Beach

Park Drive

pavilion

Long Island Sound

Road

Trails

P   Parking

Restroom

Food

Playground

---

the trailhead in the woods in the distance. Upon entering the trail, you'll be among thick trees. The narrow path has short detours onto the bedrock bluffs that overlook the Hunter Island Marine Zoology and Geology Sanctuary. In summer, when the tide moves out, the pools left among the rocks are ad hoc aquariums, with baby fish and crabs swimming about. In fall, the foliage over Long Island Sound is spectacular.

Both the red and blue trails lead to a loop at the preserve's northern edge. Shortly after the loop, the red trail turns off to the left. The blue trail, which we recommend, is about 2.0 miles in total. It takes you through a deeply wooded area and then joins the red trail back to the trailhead. If you want to take to the water, you can head to the canoe and kayak launch, which is southwest of Hunter Island, near the parking lot. *Remember:* The trail can be muddy and marked by small puddles after it has rained, so wear boots.

PLAN B: The trail on Twin Islands (Trip 63) offers a shorter loop through similar terrain.

WHERE TO EAT NEARBY: It is best to pack a picnic.

Trip 65

Ages 5-8

Pelham Bay Park South

Walk along easy trails or begin a bike ride along the network of paths throughout New York City's largest park.

Address: Middletown Road and Stadium Avenue, Bronx, NY
Hours: Dawn to dusk daily
Fee: Free; $8 parking fee applies in summer
Contact: pelhambaypark.org or nycgovparks.org/sub_your_park/vt_pelham_
   bay_park/vt_pelham_08.html; call 311 or 718-430-1890
Bathrooms: At park headquarters and the Playground for All Children
Water/Snacks: Water fountains at the bathrooms; concessions at the pavilion
Map: USGS Flushing and Mount Vernon; nycgovparks.org/sub_your_park/
   vt_pelham_bay_park/images/Pelham%20map-rev2005.pdf
Directions by Car: Take I-287 East to merge onto I-95 North. Take Exit 7C and
   merge onto MacDonough Place. Turn right onto Middletown Road, then left
   onto Stadium Avenue. The parking lot is on the left. *GPS coordinates:*
   40° 50.935′ N, 73° 49.241′ W.
Directions by Subway: Take the 6 train to the last stop, Pelham Bay Park.

The southern section of Pelham Bay Park is home to hiking and biking trails, a dog run, ball fields and tennis courts, spray showers, and a universally accessible playground. The playground includes the Sensory Garden, which is designed to stimulate smell, sound, touch, and sight. The towering, 78-foot-tall Bronx Victory Column is set within a grove of more than 500 maple and linden trees that were relocated from the borough's Grand Concourse in 1928, when the storied boulevard was widened and the subway developed underneath it.

As you face the memorial, turn left to begin a hike (or snowshoeing circuit in winter) of about 1.5 miles around this verdant park and along the Eastchester Bay shore. An easy-to-follow path leads into the landscaped woods behind the memorial. This opens into a meadow where you will encounter a fork. Stay to the left, and when you come to a T intersection, turn right. This will take you to the bay, which you can walk along but not swim in. Stay on the well-worn dirt path past a right turn, take the second right, and then turn left onto a path that will lead you past a sports field. After the dog run, turn right and follow the path back to the Victory Column.

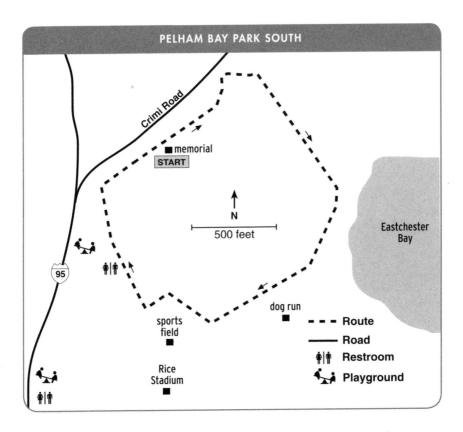

Crimi Road

■ memorial
START

N

500 feet

Eastchester
Bay

95

dog run
■

sports
field
■

Rice
Stadium
■

- - - Route
——— Road
Restroom
Playground

Pelham Bay Park is an endpoint on the North Bronx Greenway, beginning at Crimi Road in front of the memorial. The Greenway goes through Pelham Bay Park and City Island, then into the New York Botanical Garden (Trip 62) and the western terminus in Van Cortlandt Park (Trip 67). Visitors can bike along the Greenway, or stick to the paved paths in Pelham Bay Park. *Remember:* The paths along the bay are not stroller friendly.

PLAN B: Orchard Beach and the hiking trails throughout (Trips 63 and 64) are all-season alternatives. The Bronx Equestrian Center, at 9 Shore Road, offers trail and pony rides and riding lessons. Fees range from $5 to $35. For more information, call 718-885-0551.

WHERE TO EAT NEARBY: If you are driving or biking, head to Pelham Bay Split Rock golf course's small café. Nearby City Island has additional dining options.

Trip 66

Pelham Bay Park: Bartow-Pell Woods Hike

In summer, these thick, damp woods can feel like a rainforest.

Address: 895 Shore Road, Bronx, NY
Hours: 8:30 A.M. to dusk daily
Fee: Free
Contact: bartowpellmansionmuseum.org; call 311 or 718-885-1461
Water/Snacks: None
Bathrooms: Mansion museum
Map: USGS Flushing and Mount Vernon; nycgovparks.org/sub_your_park/
vt_pelham_bay_park/images/Pelham%20map-rev2005.pdf
Directions by Car: Take I-287 East to merge onto I-95 North. Take Exit 9 onto
Hutchinson River Parkway North, then take Exit 5 toward Orchard Beach.
Continue to the traffic circle, and take the third exit onto Shore Road. The
entrance is ahead on the right. *GPS coordinates*: 40° 52.425′ N, 73° 48.371′ W.
Directions by Subway: Take the 6 train to the last stop, Pelham Bay Park, and
then take the Bx45 bus to the Bartow-Pell Mansion stop.

A visit to the Bartow-Pell Woods and the mansion museum nestled within
will take you back to the time when the Bronx was a sought-after setting
for secluded homes and summer retreats. The woods are named for Thomas
Pell, a physician who bought this parcel of land in 1654, and Robert Bartow, a
publisher who later purchased it and built the mansion in 1842. The main trail
that runs through this area and beyond is named for the Siwanoy American
Indians who sold Pell the land.

To begin this thickly forested hike, stand in the parking lot with the mansion behind you and walk diagonally left across the lawn. A faded sign for
Siwanoy Trail is at the edge of the woods. The path is narrow, winding among
mature trees and a rich understory of shrubs and young saplings. You will encounter the main Siwanoy Trail at the same moment that Bartow Creek comes
into view through the tall reeds. Turn left, and follow the trail a short distance
until you come to another left that you should take to head back toward the
mansion and into the Bartow-Pell Woods.

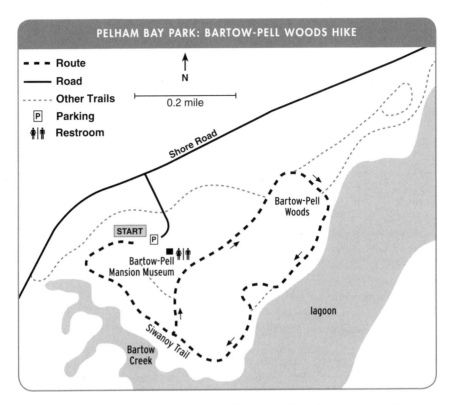

PELHAM BAY PARK: BARTOW-PELL WOODS HIKE

- - - Route
—— Road
······ Other Trails
P Parking
Restroom

N

0.2 mile

Shore Road

Bartow-Pell Woods

START

Bartow-Pell Mansion Museum

lagoon

Siwanoy Trail

Bartow Creek

You will periodically encounter a yellow blaze, but the narrow trail is easy to follow. When you come upon another junction, ignore the left turn and continue on an easterly bend toward the lagoon. Follow the beaten path around a U turn that will bring you southwest, through thick reeds and occasionally across a strip of beach. Depending on the tide, this stretch can have puddles. The path eventually connects with the link of Siwanoy Trail that you started on, and you can return to the mansion grounds the way you came.

The mansion grounds are well worth visiting, and kids might be particularly interested in the sundial that's to the right of the backyard. *Remember:* This trail can be soggy throughout, even if it hasn't rained recently.

PLAN B: Orchard Beach and the hiking trails throughout (Trips 63 and 64) are all-season alternatives. The Bronx Equestrian Center, at 9 Shore Road, offers trail and pony rides and riding lessons. Fees range from $5 to $35. For more information, call 718-885-0551.

WHERE TO EAT NEARBY: If you are driving or biking, head to Pelham Bay Split Rock golf course's small café. Nearby City Island has additional dining options.

Trip 67

Ages 5–8

Van Cortlandt Park: Greenway

An easy-to-follow network of bike paths within the southeastern corner of this vast park is a good place to learn the rules of the road.

Address: 115 Van Cortlandt Park South, Bronx, NY
Hours: Dawn to dusk daily
Fee: Free
Contact: vancortlandt.org; call 311 or 718-601-1553
Bathrooms: Pool complex; nature center; golf house; stadium; playgrounds on Cortlandt Avenue at West 239th Street and at Gouverneur Avenue
Water/Snacks: Golf house
Map: USGS Mount Vernon and Yonkers; vcpark.org/park/park_map.html
Directions by Car: Public parking is very limited in availability and duration, so driving is discouraged. *GPS coordinates*: 40° 53.371′ N, 73° 53.891′ W.
Directions by Subway: Take the 1 train to the last stop, Van Cortlandt Park; the park entrance will be on your right (east).

It may be hard to imagine that the Bronx was once a perfect location to build a rural farm or deep-woods retreat, but Van Cortlandt Park offers a glimpse of the region's past. The 1,100-acre tract is home to a series of hiking trails that wend through forests and wetlands. The park is named for Jacobus Van Cortlandt, who bought a swath of land in this area in 1694.

Van Cortlandt Park features a number of sporting fields and courts; a cross-country running course that is nearly a century old; a pool complex that has a large, 3.6-foot-deep intermediate pool and a small, foot-deep wading pool; and several large playgrounds. In short, there's something here for anyone who loves being outdoors.

The park is also the eastern launch for the North Bronx Greenway (a.k.a. the Mosholu-Pelham Greenway), which ultimately runs past the New York Botanical Garden (Trip 62) and onto Pelham Bay Park (Trips 63 to 66). Biking the paved path within Van Cortlandt's southeast corner will give new riders the chance to practice some steady slopes across varied landscapes. The path is also good for strollers.

For those who want to follow a walking or cycling route, enter the park at Broadway and West 242nd Street. At the fork, turn right at the pool complex.

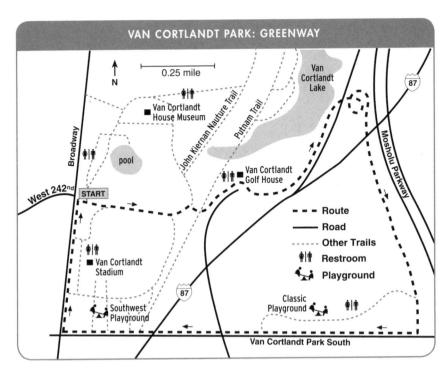

0.25 mile

N

Van Cortlandt Lake

87

Van Cortlandt House Museum

John Kiernan Nature Trail

Putnam Trail

Broadway

pool

Mosholu Parkway

West 242nd

START

Van Cortlandt Golf House

Route

Road

Other Trails

Restroom

Playground

Van Cortlandt Stadium

87

Classic Playground

Southwest Playground

Van Cortlandt Park South

The stadium will be on your right, and then, staying on the main trail, you will pass through wetlands just south of the John Kiernan Nature Trail (Trip 68). You will cross over Putnam Trail, which is a wide former rail bed, and pass the golf clubhouse on your left. The clearly marked Greenway continues north, heading uphill to a bridge that loops back over itself then runs south along the right side of Mosholu Parkway, which is separated by a wide concrete barrier. After a short distance, the trail descends back into the woods and ultimately meets Van Cortlandt Park South. Turn right, then right again at Broadway to return to the starting point. *Remember:* Bike riding is prohibited on all other trails. If you are planning to swim, observe city pool rules (see page 13).

PLAN B: Visit the Van Cortlandt Mansion and Museum, set in the borough's oldest house, located behind the pool complex.

WHERE TO EAT NEARBY: Shops are along Broadway.

Trip 68

Ages 5–8

Van Cortlandt Park (South)

If you're in the mood to swim, hike, or do both, head to this section of Van Cortlandt Park.

Address: West 242nd Street and Broadway, Bronx, NY
Hours: Dawn to dusk daily
Fee: Free
Contact: vancortlandt.org; call 311 or 718-601-1553
Bathrooms: Pool complex; nature center; stadium; playgrounds on Cortlandt
  Avenue at West 239th Street and at Gouverneur Avenue
Water/Snacks: None
Map: USGS Mount Vernon and Yonkers; vcpark.org/park/park_map.html
Directions by Car: Public parking is very limited in availability and duration, so
  driving is discouraged. *GPS coordinates:* 40° 53.371′ N, 73° 53.891′ W.
Directions by Subway: Take the 1 train to the last stop, Van Cortlandt Park. Exit
  the subway to your right (east) and enter the park.

Van Cortlandt Park prides itself on having a series of nature trails akin to those found in bigger woods like the Catskills and Adirondacks. John Kiernan Nature Trail combines both nature and history, with three outstanding historical artifacts hidden among the trees. This 1.25-mile jaunt offers quick access to woods and wetlands. The trail starts due east of the pool complex. This outdoor complex features a large intermediate pool and a smaller wading pool, very popular with swimmers of all ability levels in summer.

The trail is a fitting tribute to John Kiernan, a journalist who received the John Burroughs Medal in 1960 for his book *A Natural History of New York City*. He is among a group of amateur naturalists and preservation activists who were inspired by the natural beauty of the Bronx. Florence "Cass" Gallagher (1912–1983; Trip 69) and Dr. Theodore Kazimiroff (1914–1980; Trip 64) are two others.

At the park's West 242nd Street entrance, you will encounter a fork; go left and follow the paved route past the pool complex, Van Cortlandt House Museum, and Van Cortlandt Nature Center. On your left will be the vast parade ground. The path at the parade ground's eastern edge doubles as the John Kiernan Nature Trail. When you reach this, turn left and follow it a few hun-

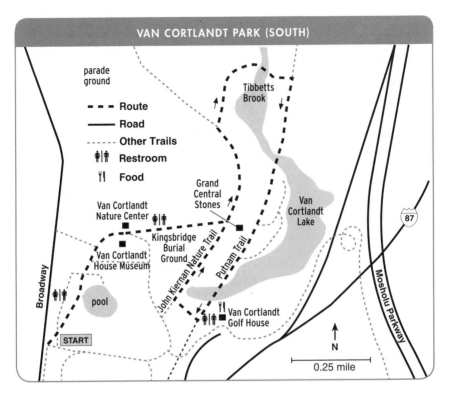

parade
ground

- - - Route

—— Road

······ Other Trails

🚻 Restroom

🍴 Food

Van Cortlandt
Nature Center

Grand
Central
Stones

Tibbetts
Brook

Van
Cortlandt
Lake

Kingsbridge
Burial
Ground

Van Cortlandt
House Museum

John Kiernan Nature Trail

Putnam Trail

Broadway

pool

Van Cortlandt
Golf House

START

N

0.25 mile

Mosholu Parkway

87

dred yards north to the trail entrance at the woods. From here on, you will be beneath a thick canopy of maple, oak, and ash trees. Once you are within the trees, the trail goes north before curving east to cross Tibbetts Brook. Shortly after this bridge, you will meet Putnam Trail, a former rail bed for the first train to run between New York and Boston. Deer seem to appreciate this soft, wide corridor.

Turn right and follow Kiernan-Putnam south, with Van Cortlandt Lake behind a chain-link fence on your left. Some narrow paths detour off the main trail, but stay on the wide route. In short order, the Grand Central Stones will loom large among the trees to your right. Cornelius Vanderbilt, of railroad fame and fortune, had the stones placed here to see which of the various types could best weather the elements before he built the massive Beaux Arts terminal in Manhattan. Continue south and turn right, just before you reach the steel girders of a long-gone train stop that protrude like ribs from the ground.

This path will lead you through wetlands and, as you curve right, past the eighteenth-century Kingsbridge Burial Ground, which is now absent of grave markers and enclosed by an iron fence. Follow this path up to the parade ground. *Remember:* Given the proximity to wetlands, portions of this walk are always slick and muddy.

PLAN B: Head south along Broadway to visit the popular Southwest Playground, at the corner of Van Cortlandt Park South (West 240th Street). It has two sections, a fenced-in one for children ages 2 to 5, and an open area for older kids up to age 12. It features several climbing structures, swing sets, and sprinklers in summer. Canine Court dog run is along the northwest side of the parade ground.

WHERE TO EAT NEARBY: Shops are along Broadway.

Van Cortlandt Park (North)

Within moments of leaving a busy intersection, you will be in forest primeval.

Address: Mosholu Avenue and Broadway, Bronx, NY
Hours: Dawn to dusk daily
Fee: Free
Contact: vancortlandt.org; call 311 or 718-601-1553
Bathrooms: Near the horse stables
Water/Snacks: At the golf house
Map: USGS Mount Vernon and Yonkers; vcpark.org/park/park_map.html
Directions by Car: Public parking is very limited in availability and duration, so driving is discouraged. *GPS coordinates:* 40° 53.271′ N, 73° 53.785′ W.
Directions by Subway: Take the 1 train to the last stop, Van Cortlandt Park, and walk north along Broadway until you pass the Henry Hudson Parkway.

Florence "Cass" Gallagher was one of the original "Friends of Van Cortlandt Park" in the mid-twentieth century, and today, a moderate, 1.4-mile hike through the Northwest Forest in Van Cortlandt Park bears her name. Enter the park at Broadway and Mosholu Avenue, and follow the paved path south to the horse stable. The trail begins across from the stables, and immediately takes you into the forest.

Follow the trail due north, staying to the left of the first two forks you encounter. Early on, you will be hiking parallel to a cross-country running route that has been a park feature since 1913. After the second fork, you will cross over the running route before looping back south near the park's northern border. At this curve, you will be near the park's—and the city's—northern border with Yonkers, in Westchester County. Follow the trail—which is rocky and steep at points—back south. It splits; stay left for the longer hike. Both paths will take you back to the starting point. Along the way, you may see rabbits, raccoons, or chipmunks.

If after this solid hike you haven't had enough, or you want to come back for more, follow John Muir Trail. Van Cortlandt's only east–west route, the trail opened in 1997 and was named for the Scottish-born American naturalist who founded the Sierra Club and advocated for preserving wilderness through national parks such as Yosemite. This moderately difficult but easy-

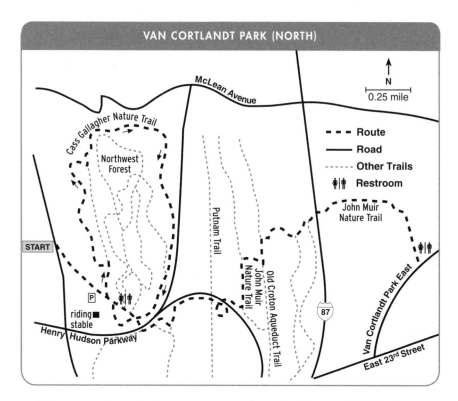

McLean Avenue

N
0.25 mile

- - - **Route**
——— **Road**
······ **Other Trails**
🛉🛉 **Restroom**

Cass Gallagher Nature Trail

Northwest
Forest

Putnam Trail

John Muir
Nature Trail

START

John Muir
Nature Trail

Old Croton Aqueduct Trail

P

riding ■
stable

Henry Hudson Parkway

87

Van Cortlandt Park East

East 23rd Street

to-follow 1.5-mile path also starts across from the horse stable. It takes you from the southern fringes of the Northwest Forest, under the Henry Hudson Parkway, over the nation's first municipal golf course (opened in 1895), up a steady incline through the Croton Woods, under the Major Deegan Expressway, and onto the Northeast Forest. *Remember:* Dogs are permitted off leash only in the three designated dog runs, and must be leashed in the woods.

PLAN B: The Riverdale Equestrian Centre in this section of Van Cortlandt Park provides lessons by appointment. For more information call 718-548-4848.

WHERE TO EAT NEARBY: Shops are along Broadway.

Section 6

The Islands of New York City

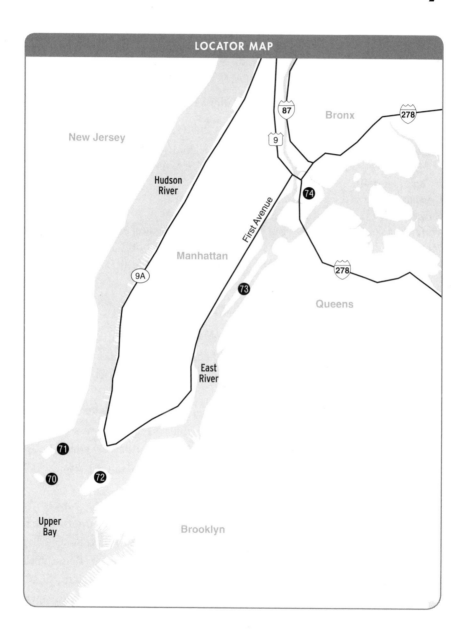

Trip 70

All Ages

Liberty Island

Lady Liberty's famous island is also a thought-provoking arboretum and a lovely place to walk and picnic.

Address: Battery Park, State Street and Battery Place, Manhattan, NY (ferry departure point)
Hours: 9:30 A.M. to 5 P.M. daily
Fee: Ferry: adults, $13; children ages 4 to 12, $5; children under age 4, free. Crown admission: $3 (request an additional free ticket to enter the statue museum and pedestal).
Contact: nps.gov/stli; 212-561-4588. Tickets: statuecruises.com; 877-LADYTIX
Bathrooms: In the monument; concession area
Water/Snacks: Water fountains at the restrooms; concession area
Map: USGS Jersey City; nps.gov/stli/planyourvisit/maps.htm
Directions by Car: Public parking is very limited; driving is discouraged.
GPS coordinates: 40° 41.403′ N, 74° 2.705′ W.
Directions by Subway: Take the 1 train to South Ferry, the 4 or 5 train to Bowling Green, or the R or W train to Whitehall Street Station.

The islands of Upper New York Bay have developed in ways that Henry Hudson couldn't have imagined upon his arrival in 1609. Today, hiking around the islands and considering the views from each direction will enrich your understanding of New York City's natural world.

New York Harbor is where the freshwater Hudson River meets the salty Atlantic Ocean and Long Island Sound. Back when the area was relatively untouched by humans, oysters thrived in the beds off the islands we now know as Liberty and Ellis, which were named the Oyster Islands by America's first Dutch settlers.

Liberty Island now receives an average of 15,000 visitors per day. Since only 3,000 people per day can enter the fabled statue—an 1886 gift of international friendship from the people of France to the people of the United States—the majority of visitors come to enjoy the island and its arboretum. Begin your half-mile walk at the ferry dock, on the southwest side of the 13-acre island. No native trees remain on Liberty Island, but the southern half is landscaped with about 400 trees that originated in Europe or Asia. Given the international significance of the island, this is apropos. Tree species are indicated by plaques,

An arboretum featuring trees from Asia and Europe is
an eloquent backdrop for Lady Liberty.

and include little-leaf linden, horse chestnut, Norway maple, Kwanzan cherry, and London plane.

From the ferry terminal with the statue on your left, New Jersey will be behind you, Brooklyn in front of you, and Staten Island to your right. The Verrazano Narrows separates Brooklyn and Staten Island and leads to Lower New York Bay. As you walk counterclockwise, the tree garden ends, giving the Statue of Liberty a clear stage. Governors Island (Trip 72) will come into view; farther north, you will see Manhattan's Battery Park coast (Trip 23).

As you pass the statue to your left, you are greeted by the cherry tree grove. This is a wonderful place to settle down and bask in the beauty of the statue, which is a World Heritage site and is on the National Register of Historic Places. *Remember:* Liberty Island is very popular on warm-weather weekends. Try to visit on a weekday or during late fall, winter, or early spring.

PLAN B: You might be able to fit in a trip to Ellis Island (Trip 71) on the same day. Alternatively, head back to mainland Manhattan to complete your appreciation of the harbor by traveling west up the Battery Park City Esplanade (Trip 24), or heading to East River Park (Trip 29).

Trip 71

Ellis Island

The American Immigrant Wall of Honor should not be missed, and a walk around the island offers terrific views of the Statue of Liberty, Battery Park, and Liberty State Park in New Jersey.

Address: Battery Park, State Street and Battery Place, Manhattan, NY (ferry departure point)
Hours: 9:30 A.M. to 5:15 P.M. daily
Fee: Ferry: adults $13; children ages 4 to 12, $5; children under age 4, free. Museum entrance: free.
Contact: nps.gov/elis/historyculture/index.htm; nyharborparks.org/visit/elis. html; 212-363-3200. Tickets: statuecruises.com; 877-LADYTIX
Bathrooms: Main building
Water/Snacks: Water fountains at the restrooms; concession area
Map: USGS Jersey City
Directions by Car: Public parking is very limited; driving is discouraged. *GPS coordinates:* 40° 42.022′ N, 74° 2.479′ W.
Directions by Subway: Take the 1 train to South Ferry, the 4 or 5 train to Bowling Green, or the R or W train to Whitehall Street.

It is estimated that 40 percent of Americans can trace their roots though Ellis Island. From 1892 to 1924, it was the nation's busiest immigration depot, processing more than 12 million individuals. After serving as a detention center, the island closed in 1954, and following almost four decades of disuse, the Immigration Museum opened on the northern part of the U-shaped island in 1990.

The museum is free and well worth visiting. The National Park Service offers the Junior Ranger program here (see page 129), and kids can complete an activity pack to earn a special badge. The activities take about an hour, and lead children all around the museum.

Touring the island itself is an equally moving experience. Behind the museum, the vast and continuously growing American Immigrant Wall of Honor displays more than 600,000 names of newcomers who passed through the island. It is an awesome exhibit to walk around, and a lawn nearby offers a wonderful view of Manhattan.

On the ferry ride to Ellis Island, passengers can see the island's Immigration Museum.

When walking the nearly half-mile perimeter of the northern section, you can't help but think about how such a stroll would have been an impossible luxury for the immigrants who were processed here. As they shuffled through the Great Hall, they would have seen Liberty Island to the south and Governors Island to the east—but their sights would have been set on Manhattan to the north.

The island's southern half—and the 28 buildings on it—remains closed despite periodic discussions about rehabilitating the area. *Remember:* Park rangers lead free, 45-minute museum tours, which depart from the main building.

PLAN B: You might be able to fit in a trip to Liberty Island (Trip 70) on the same day. Alternatively, head back to mainland Manhattan to tour Battery Park (Trip 23) after disembarking.

Trip 72

Governors Island

Just a quick ferry ride from Manhattan, this island offers car-free roads for biking, an open-air sculpture museum, and excellent picnic spots with terrific views.

Address: 10 South Street, Slip 7, Manhattan, NY (ferry departure point)
Hours: 10 A.M. to 5 P.M. Fridays; 10 A.M. to 7 P.M. Saturdays and Sundays,
    May 27 to September 25
Fee: Free (including ferry)
Contact: govisland.com; 212-440-2200
Bathrooms: Building 110 near the ferry landing; portable toilets throughout the
    island
Water/Snacks: Food vendors throughout the island
Map: USGS Jersey City; govisland.com/html/visit/map.shtml; govisland.com/
    downloads/pdf/map.pdf
Directions by Car: Public parking is very limited; driving is discouraged.
    GPS coordinates: 40° 41.566' N, 74° 0.927' W.
Directions by Subway: Take the 1 train to South Ferry, the 4 or 5 train to Bowling
    Green, or the R or W train to Whitehall Street Station.

A mere 800-yard trip from the southern tip of Manhattan, the ferry ride to Governors Island is over before you know it. Once reserved exclusively for use by New York's British colonial governors prior to the Declaration of Independence, the island was a U.S. military base for almost 200 years before becoming a national monument and park.

The island has a network of well-marked and easy-to-follow carless roads and paths that take you to the star-shaped Fort Jay and Castle Williams, both nineteenth-century fortifications. You can walk around the sprawling campus of former military facilities and residences that are eerily frozen in the mid-twentieth century. The island is also an open-air art museum, with a large and eclectic array of modern and industrial sculptures throughout.

The ferry brings you to the northern rim of the island, facing Fort Jay, and from here you can go right or left to circle the island—which is well worth doing. Given the lack of cars, this is an excellent bike ride, and bikes are available to rent near Castle Williams. Once you've completed the promenade loop—taking in vistas of the Statue of Liberty, New Jersey, and Manhattan—head inland to check out the art installations and any number of cultural events,

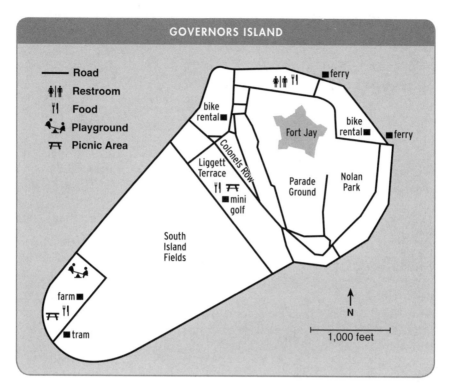

GOVERNORS ISLAND

- —— Road
- 🚹🚺 Restroom
- 🍴 Food
- 🛝 Playground
- 🪑 Picnic Area

ferry

🚹🚺 🍴

bike
rental

Fort Jay

bike
rental

ferry

Liggett
Terrace

Colonels Row

🍴 🪑

mini
golf

Parade
Ground

Nolan
Park

South
Island
Fields

farm

🪑 🍴

tram

N

1,000 feet

music festivals, or street fairs that might be taking place. *Remember:* Governors Island is in the process of extensive upgrades and renovations. For the latest information on these, visit govisland.com/html/future/future.shtml.

PLAN B: Battery Park (Trip 23) and Brooklyn Bridge Park (Trip 31) are both near the Manhattan and Brooklyn ferry landings for Governors Island.

Trip 73

All Ages

Roosevelt Island

Fascinating history, good trails, spectacular views, and recreational facilities can be found here.

Address: 59th Street and Second Avenue, Manhattan, NY (tram departure point)
Hours: All hours
Fee: Free
Contact: rioc.com; 212-832-4540. Tram information: 212-832-4543
Bathrooms: Lighthouse Park, on the northern tip of the island
Water/Snacks: Several cafés, as well as convenience and grocery stores, are within a short walk from the pedestrian walkway that circles the island.
Map: USGS Brooklyn and Central Park; nyc10044.com/wire/2722/map2722.pdf
Directions by Car: Public parking is very limited; driving is discouraged.
GPS coordinates: 40° 45.849′ N, 73° 56.855′ W.
Directions by Subway: Take the F train to Roosevelt Island, or take the F train to East 63rd Street in Manhattan, then walk three blocks east to take the aerial tramway to the island.

Roosevelt Island—2 miles long and 800 feet wide—is a residential island in the East River between Queens and Manhattan. Considered part of Manhattan, its history and geography make it a great destination for those wishing to explore a unique slice of New York City.

Children—and adults—will enjoy reaching the island by the Roosevelt Island Tramway, which you can board with a Metrocard. The tram affords breathtaking views of the skylines all around. Arriving by tram or subway (you can bring bikes on both) leaves you on the southern half of the island. Nearby Blackwell House Park and Playground is one of the few remaining farmhouses in the United States that date to the American Revolution.

Heading north up the western bank, the pedestrian promenade offers a stroll or bike ride around the island's edge, with spectacular views of Manhattan's Upper East Side. As you near the top of the island, you will pass Octagon Park, which features the landmark Octagon Tower. The building was once the entrance hall of New York's first asylum for the mentally ill and is today an apartment complex. The park has picnic and barbecue areas as well as playing fields. Lighthouse Park, at the northern tip of the island, boasts a Gothic

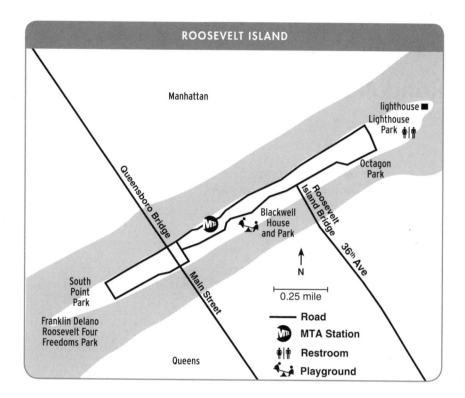

Manhattan

lighthouse ■
Lighthouse
Park

Octagon
Park

Queensboro Bridge

Roosevelt Island Bridge

36th Ave

Blackwell
House
and Park

↑
N

0.25 mile

South
Point
Park

Main Street

Franklin Delano
Roosevelt Four
Freedoms Park

Queens

Road

MTA Station

Restroom

Playground

lighthouse built in 1872 and is a terrific spot from which to view Manhattan, Queens, and the Bronx.

From here you will head south along the eastern bank, with Queens on your left. Just beyond the Roosevelt Island Bridge, you will encounter a stretch of sports fields and courts, as well as a good playground. After passing an apartment complex, you'll see another similar recreational area. Continue to the island's southern tip, past the hospital complex, to visit South Point Park, a rolling green space that surrounds a former smallpox hospital and laboratory. You won't be able to miss the construction site that is the Franklin Delano Roosevelt Four Freedoms Park. At the time of this writing, it was scheduled to open by fall 2012. *Remember:* You can walk or bike across the Roosevelt Island bridge to Astoria, Queens.

PLAN B: The East River Esplanade (Trip 14) and Carl Schurz Park (Trip 16) are just across the river in Manhattan.

WHERE TO EAT NEARBY: Main Street bisects the island north to south, and contains numerous eating establishments.

Trip 74

Randall's and Wards Islands

This destination offers abundant opportunities for all kinds of outdoor activities, with great views of three surrounding boroughs.

Address: East River Lane, Manhattan, NY
Hours: Dawn to midnight daily
Fee: Free
Contact: randallsisland.org; 212-830-7722
Bathrooms: Icahn Stadium, golf center, and tennis courts; portable toilets near some playing fields
Water/Snacks: Water fountains at the bathrooms
Map: USGS Central Park; randallsisland.org/maps-directions
Directions by Car: Take the Robert F. Kennedy Bridge toward Queens and take the exit for Wards and Randall's islands. Free parking is available on the island. *GPS coordinates*: 40° 47.641′ N, 73° 55.365′ W.
Directions by Bus: Take the M35 to Randall's Island.

Thanks to easy access from Manhattan and the RFK Bridge (for both bikes and cars), and to an array of headline summer concerts, performance arts, and professional sports that take place at Icahn Stadium, Randall's and Wards islands are becoming better known—and that's a wonderful thing.

Located at the confluence of the East and Harlem rivers, with commanding views of Manhattan, Queens, and the Bronx, these once-separate islands were joined by landfill in the 1930s and now span 500 acres. Despite the physical connection, Randall's and Wards still maintain distinct identities that are best appreciated on foot.

Begin your trip on the Upper East Side of Manhattan by walking across the East River on the 103rd Street pedestrian bridge. This will put you in Wards Island Park, which features more open space and gentle hills than its counterpart to the north. When you leave the bridge, follow the paved pedestrian path (suitable for strollers or kids on scooters and bikes) to your left and take it about a half-mile north. It will curve right and take you into the salt marsh and wetlands areas, and then onto Central Road. From here you can go left to visit Randall's Island, which is mostly filled with popular athletic fields and the awesome pillars for the RFK Bridge.

The view of Hell Gate Bridge is among the delightfully unusual vistas at this island getaway.

A walk through more open space can be had by turning right and continuing a loop around Wards Island Park. There are sports facilities, to be sure, but also many lawns and well-landscaped wooded areas. The islands' sole playground, Scylla Playground, is located near the fields just south of the Hell Gate Bridge. It has swings, slides, and brightly colored climbing equipment for children of different ages. *Remember:* Randall's and Wards islands are a work in progress, soon to feature more waterfront pathways and projects to restore the native environment.

PLAN B: Head back into across the East 103rd Street pedestrian bridge and walk down the East River Esplanade (Trip 14).

WHERE TO EAT NEARBY: Vendors selling snacks and drinks are sometimes on the island, but it's best to bring a picnic.

Section 7

Long Island

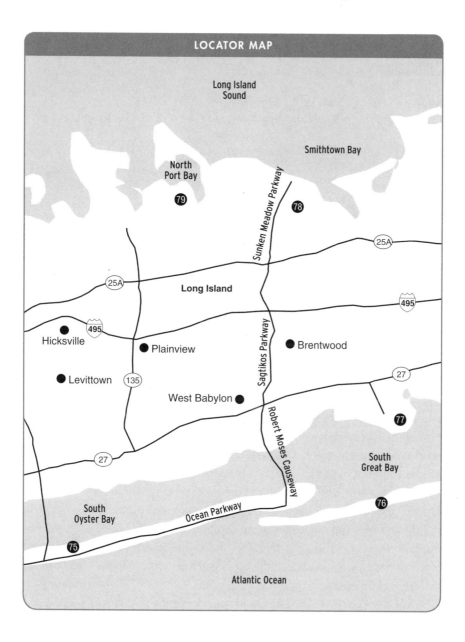

Trip 75

All Ages $ 🚶 🚴 🏊 🛶 🤿

Jones Beach State Park

Teach your kids about marine life and the ecosystem of a sand dune, then end the afternoon with a swim in the Atlantic Ocean.

Address: 1 Ocean Parkway, Wantagh, NY

Hours: Hours vary depending on activity and time of year. Check websites for details.

Fee: $10 per car June to September; $8 per car all other times; free with an Empire Passport

Contact: nysparks.com/environment/nature-centers/4/details.aspx; 516-780-3295; 516-679-7254

Bathrooms: Nature center; along the boardwalk

Water/Snacks: Concessions available at the boardwalk

Map: USGS Bay Shore West, Bay Shore West OE S, Jones Inlet, and West Gilgo Beach

Directions by Car: Take I-495 East to Exit 22A onto I-678 South. Drive for 5.9 miles, then take Exit 1 for NY 27 East. Merge onto the Belt Parkway/Southern State Parkway. Take Exit 23B onto NY 27 E/Sunrise Highway. Take the ramp to Jones Beach, then merge onto Meadowbrook State Parkway South. Follow the parkway to the beach. Five parking fields are in the park. Parking fields 4 and 5 are nearest to the beach. The Theodore Roosevelt Nature Center has its own parking lot, where parking is free with an Empire Passport. *GPS coordinates:* 40° 35.629' N, 73° 31.841' W.

Jones Beach State Park is a legendary swimming destination featuring 6.5 miles of Atlantic Ocean beach, another half-mile of beach along Zach's Bay, and an art deco swimming pool. The park is also home to the Theodore Roosevelt Nature Center, a fantastic resource for teaching kids about marine ecology.

Start your trip with a visit to the nature center, located at the west end of Ocean Parkway. The highlight of the nature center is a quarter-mile boardwalk leading out over the dunes, featuring exhibits that explain dune ecology. The displays range from the types of grasses and shrubs found on different sections of the dunes to scale models of the birds (such as white owls and bald eagles) that frequent the area.

After a walk around the boardwalk, check out the permanent whale-bone exhibit on the east side of the center. It is stunning to see the ribs tower over

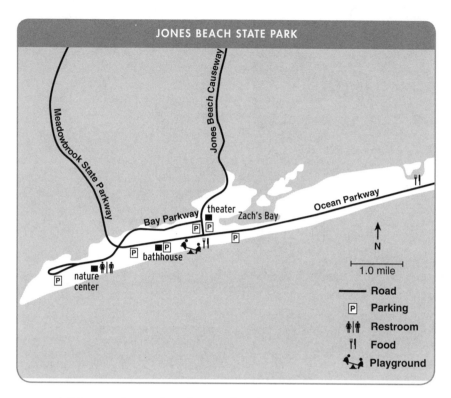

JONES BEACH STATE PARK

Meadowbrook State Parkway

Jones Beach Causeway

Bay Parkway

theater

Zach's Bay

Ocean Parkway

P P

P

P P

bathhouse

P

nature
center

N

| 1.0 mile |

—— Road
P Parking
Restroom
Food
Playground

young children, with vertebrae bigger than basketballs. Inside the center are interactive displays covering topics ranging from the geography of the ocean floor to the tracks different animals make in the sand. Throughout the year, the center also runs science, art, and outdoors programs for children and families.

During summer, after visiting the nature center, go swimming! The outdoor West Bathhouse pool is between parking fields 3 and 4. Parking field 5, just past the landmark water tower, has both ocean and bay beach access. You can also head to parking field 10, where you can launch your kayak next to the pier on the east side of the picnic area. A small playground is near Zach's Bay, and a larger one is west of the main pavilion on the ocean side. *Remember:* Don't miss the art deco beach signs along the boardwalk, where children can ride bikes from October through March.

PLAN B: Governor Alfred E. Smith/Sunken Meadow State Park (Trip 78) is a good alternative for hiking, and also offers a calm beach on Long Island Sound.

WHERE TO EAT NEARBY: Several food concessions are on the boardwalk fronting the swimming area.

Trip 76

Fire Island

Hike along boardwalks, take a bike ride, explore the Sunken Forest, or swim, paddle, or sail the Atlantic.

Address: 99 Maple Avenue, Bay Shore, NY (ferry departure)
Hours: Ferry hours vary. Call ahead for details.
Fee: Parking fees and ferry ticket prices vary. Visit fireislandferries.com for more information.
Contact: nps.gov/fiis; 631-687-4750; Sailors Haven Visitor Center, 631-597-6183
Bathrooms: Ferry dock
Water/Snacks: Grocery stores are at Fair Harbor and Ocean Beach
Map: USGS Long Island East; USGS Long Island West; nps.gov/fiis/planyourvisit/maps.htm
Directions by Car (to ferry terminal): Take I-495 East to the Southern State Parkway. Take Exit 42 South onto Fifth Avenue South. Take this to Montauk Highway. At the second traffic light, take a right onto Maple Avenue. The Ocean Beach ferry terminal is on the left. Parking lots are at 99 and 104 Maple Avenue. *GPS coordinates: 40° 42.991′ N, 73° 14.478′ W.*

Fire Island is wild. Only service and emergency vehicles are allowed on the island, so the sand and cement paths and boardwalks must be navigated on foot or by bicycle. This gives the hamlets and villages on Fire Island a rustic, frontier feel. Thirty-two miles long with more than 100 miles of coastline, the

Panoramic views from the lighthouse include miles of Fire Island's pristine coastline.

island is mostly protected land that will remain undeveloped, and the options for outdoor adventure are numerous. You can swim, sail, paddle, or surf the waters, bike along boardwalks, or hike through salt marshes and forest, all within a short trek of the ferry.

Start with a visit to the Sunken Forest, a maritime woodland located on the western side of the island just past the Sailors Haven Visitor Center. This rare habitat covers 40 acres and is a magnet for hikers and bird-watchers. The holly, bayberry, shadblow, blueberry, and sassafras trees here are more than 200 years old. You can join a guided tour during summer.

Other opportunities for outdoor recreation include fishing and bird-watching. You can view egrets, herons, red-winged blackbirds, and waterfowl at the Tidal Marsh at Great South Bay, and migrating warblers and eastern towhees at Sunken Forest. From September to mid-November, hawk migration is monitored from the Fire Island Lighthouse, and the William Floyd Estate provides good opportunities for catching sight of other birds. *Remember:* The Watch Hill campground is a half-mile from the Davis Park Ferry. The 26 sites each include a picnic table and a grill. Leashed dogs are allowed. Appalachian Mountain Club members and their guests can stay at the Fire Island Cabin in Atlantique. The cabin features two 12-person bunkrooms and a communal kitchen. Sailboats, kayaks, and canoes are available for guests, as well as boogie boards and other types of flotation devices for kids.

PLAN B: Visit Fair Harbor, somewhat larger and more developed than Ocean Beach, or the historic Fire Island Lighthouse, which is now an observatory and museum.

WHERE TO EAT NEARBY: Several restaurants are in Ocean Beach and Fair Harbor.

Trip 77

Heckscher State Park

This enormous park features a tranquil beach on the Great South Bay and 20 miles of paths for biking, hiking, cross-country skiing, and snowshoeing.

Address: Heckscher State Parkway, East Islip, NY
Hours: 7 A.M. to sunset daily
Fee: $10 per car June to September; $8 per car October to May; free with an Empire Passport
Contact: nysparks.com; 631-581-2100
Bathrooms: Comfort stations throughout the park
Water/Snacks: Refreshment stand at the bathhouse comfort station near the West Bathing Area
Map: USGS Bay Shore East
Directions by Car: Take I-495 East to Exit 22A East onto I-678 South. Take Exit 1 onto the Belt Parkway, and continue onto the Southern State Parkway East. Drive for 33.5 miles, then continue onto Heckscher State Parkway. Follow this road to the traffic circle. Eight numbered parking lots are available along the parkway. *GPS coordinates:* 40° 42.528′ N, 73° 10.023′ W.

Heckscher State Park is the southern endpoint of the Long Island Greenbelt Trail (Trip 78) and a multifaceted outdoor recreation area. It boasts a tranquil bay beach with a view of Fire Island in the distance, a range of hiking trails, boat launches, and paved paths for cyclists and pedestrians. In winter, this largely flat park is good for snowshoeing and beginning cross-country skiing.

Start your visit by following signs to the park office police station, where you can pick up a map to orient yourself. There are 4.5 miles of paved pedestrian paths to choose from, as well as dirt trails throughout the park. You can also connect to the Long Island Greenbelt Trail on the east edge of parking field 7 for more hiking.

The south end of the park features the West Bathing Area on Great South Bay. The bay surf is relatively mild, with small waves that are exciting for young children. Just north of the bathing area is a large, shady picnic area with dozens of benches and tables. The boat ramp, where you can launch a canoe

Young swimmers can learn how to ride the surf in Heckscher State Park's shallow waters.

or kayak if you've brought one, is northwest of this. *Remember:* Dogs are allowed in undeveloped areas only and must be leashed. As of 2011, the pool and campground were closed indefinitely. Check with park officials for updates.

PLAN B: Governor Alfred E. Smith/Sunken Meadow State Park (Trip 78) is due north on Long Island Sound.

WHERE TO EAT NEARBY: It is best to bring a picnic.

Trip 78

Governor Alfred E. Smith/Sunken Meadow State Park

Swim in tranquil Long Island Sound, hike on the Long Island Greenbelt Trail, and learn about the flora, fauna, and marine life of the sound.

Address: Sunken Meadow Parkway and Naples Avenue, Kings Park, NY
Hours: Hours vary depending on activity and time of year. Call ahead for details.
Fee: Fees vary between $8 and $10 throughout the year (free with an Empire Passport)
Contact: nysparks.com; 631-269-4333
Bathrooms: Gazebo in front of the beach
Water/Snacks: Vending machines and water fountains in the gazebo; snack bar on the boardwalk
Map: USGS Northport and St. James
Directions by Car: Take I-495 East to Exit 42 and merge onto the Northern State Parkway East. Take Exit 45 onto Sunken Meadow Parkway and drive for about 7.0 miles to the parking lot. *GPS coordinates:* 40° 54.670′ N, 73° 15.489′ W.

Governor Alfred E. Smith/Sunken Meadow State Park has a 3-mile beach along Long Island Sound, abruptly interrupted by glacier-formed bluffs. With this in mind, the park was developed as a nature sanctuary and recreation area to teach children about local flora, fauna, and marine life. It is also an access point to the northern terminus of the Long Island Greenbelt Trail, which begins 33 miles south in Heckscher State Park (Trip 77) and offers excellent hiking through the woods on mostly flat dirt trails near the coast. Heading farther inland, trail elevation gain can be moderate at points.

Begin your trip with a visit to the park office in the gazebo north of parking lots 1 and 2, in front of the bathing beach on Long Island Sound. The office has maps of the park, and displays in the gazebo provide information about the types of birds that migrate through the meadow, as well as marine life on the beach. These displays are educational—"Horseshoe Crab (*Limulus polyphemus*). Really not a crab at all, the horseshoe crab is more closely related to spiders..."—and up-to-date; for example, a notice displays how many species

Calm waves lap the sand along Long Island Sound.

of birds have been spotted in the park so far that year. Kids and adults alike are bound to learn something.

The waves at the beach are manageable (those at Heckscher State Park are even more mild) and the three-quarter-mile boardwalk is a lovely place to stroll. Large playgrounds are located near parking lots 1 and 2.

Hiking opportunities abound year round. Whether or not you plan to go the entire 33 miles to Heckscher, the outset of the trail makes for a rigorous out-and-back. To begin your hike, head back south and take your first left toward parking lot 4. You will pass picnic tables and a comfort station as the paved road rises up to where two stone benches mark the start of the trail. The path is slightly rugged, but suitable for young hikers. You can follow it as far as you like, then return the way you came to cool off with a swim at the beach. *Remember:* Dogs are not allowed in the bathing or picnic areas. Contact the park office for details.

PLAN B: For more rollicking waves and a well-done nature center, visit Jones Beach State Park (Trip 75).

WHERE TO EAT NEARBY: It is best to bring a picnic.

Long Island's fabled Gold Coast inspires thoughts of the bygone era of great mansions and dynastic wealth that will live forever in F. Scott Fitzgerald's *The Great Gatsby*. The stock market crash of 1929, tax hikes, and new zoning laws forced many of the land barons to shutter their estates—mostly summer homes—along the North Shore. The estates were sold off, appropriated by the government, or otherwise lay fallow in family hands for decades.

Today, thanks to a tremendous effort to revitalize and open these estates, visitors can see how the rich once lived. These estates are magical not only because of the grandeur of the homes, but also because those who have worked to restore and open the grounds share the original owners' love for beautiful landscapes. The restoration effort includes detailed site maps, public events for people of all ages, and guided tours.

Oheka Castle was the estate of the Gilded Age financier and philanthropist Otto Hermann Kahn, whose image, in cartoon form, kids may recognize from the board game Monopoly. Its expansive, Versailles-like gardens have been painstakingly restored based on archival blueprints and include 500 red cedars, 44 London plane trees, more than 2,500 boxwoods, and more.

At the Eagle's Nest Mansion and Vanderbilt Museum (Trip 79), children likely will be fascinated by the hundreds of jars containing preserved marine life that William K. Vanderbilt II collected on his voyages around the world. The massive back lawn features an artificially constructed hill that is great for rolling down, and the walk along the property's northern rim, overlooking Long Island Sound, is captivating.

Planting Fields Arboretum State Historic Park was once home of William Robertson Coe, who made his fortune in insurance and railroads. It is exquisitely landscaped to include 5 miles of woodland trails through 200 acres of native forest, flowering gardens, and greenhouses teeming with exotic plants. The 5-acre Synoptic Garden is a synopsis, or overview, of more than 1,000 types of plants that thrive on Long Island.

Sands Point Preserve, once a Guggenheim estate, has two massive mansions and the impressive Castle Gould stable. Six nature trails crisscross constructed and natural landscapes, including forests, meadows, beaches, cliff walks, and sculpted lawns and gardens. In a relatively small preserve (216 acres), visitors can see a wide variety of environments and the birds and animals attracted to them.

For more information on eight estates, visit historiclongisland.com or call 631-659-1360.

Trip 79

Vanderbilt Museum

This mansion and its grounds offer a glimpse of the Gilded Age, while also providing an outdoor park and museums to inspire young imaginations.

Address: 180 Little Neck Road, Centerport, NY
Hours: 10 A.M. to 5 P.M. Tuesdays through Saturdays; noon to 5 P.M. Sundays
Fee: Adults, $7; seniors and students, $6; children under age 12, $3. Mansion tour: add $5 per ticket.
Contact: vanderbiltmuseum.org; 631-854-5555
Bathrooms: Parking lot
Water/Snacks: Vending machines at the parking lot
Map: USGS Northport
Directions by Car: Take I-495 East to Exit 40E and merge onto NY 25 East. Turn left onto Broadway and follow to Little Neck Road; the Vanderbilt Museum is 1.5 miles up on the right. Free parking is available. *GPS coordinates:* 40° 54.264′ N, 73° 22.152′ W.

Of all the old mansions still glittering along the Gold Coast of Long Island, the Vanderbilt offers among the most dramatic seascape vistas when you're strolling about the grounds, along with a fantastic museum displaying the ambitions of someone who truly wanted to have it all. Visitors can also take a guided tour through the mansion itself—a stunning example of an architectural style, Spanish Colonial Revival, that became popular as the United States asserted itself as an imperial power at the start of the twentieth century. A visit to the Vanderbilt feels like a trip back to when the world seemed much larger and more mysterious, and exploring its mysteries was a rich man's adventure.

Follow the cobbled drive north between the two stone eagles that loom on either side, toward the six Corinthian columns lined in front of a stunning view of Northport Bay. Continue northwest down through the front gates of the Vanderbilt Mansion. In the courtyard to your left is a small museum containing numerous artifacts—both curious and bizarre—that William K. Vanderbilt II collected on his travels around the world. After you exit the museum, continue north, exiting the courtyard, to the landscape beyond. The lawns surrounding the Vanderbilt Mansion constitute a giant playground for energetic youngsters—an activity encouraged by museum staff. Head up and

Rolling grounds and incredible marine museums take visitors
back to the Gilded Age at the Vanderbilt Museum.

down the hills, tending southwest around the mansion back toward the Marine Museum, a two-story structure also built in the Spanish Colonial style. The museum contains countless specimens of the fish, frogs, eels, jellyfish, and crabs that Vanderbilt collected on his voyages. There are few places more likely to inspire a young child to continue exploring the great outdoors. *Remember:* Check the museum website for information on summer programs and workshops for children.

PLAN B: Governor Alfred E. Smith/Sunken Meadow State Park (Trip 78) is a great spot for hiking and swimming in Long Island Sound.

WHERE TO EAT NEARBY: Restaurants and shops are along County Road 86.

Section 8

Catskills and Hudson Valley

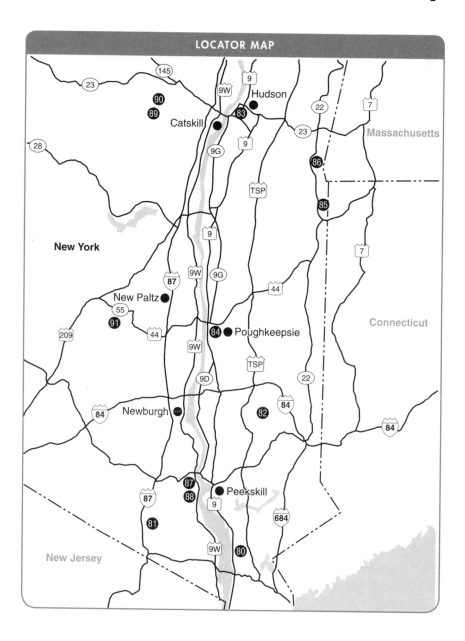

LOCATOR MAP

Trip 80

Rockefeller State Park Preserve

At Rockefeller State Park Preserve you can enjoy a quiet, pristine walk on a path encircling a looking-glass lake, or try fishing, horseback riding, or cross-country skiing.

Address: 125 Phelps Way, Pleasantville, NY
Hours: Hours are subject to change. Call ahead for details.
Fee: $6 per vehicle (free with an Empire Passport)
Contact: nysparks.state.ny.us/parks/59/details.aspx; 914-631-1470
Bathrooms: Parking lot
Water/Snacks: Water fountains at the bathrooms in the parking lot
Map: USGS Bridgeport; nysparks.state.ny.us/parks/59/maps.aspx
Directions by Car: Take I-87 North to Exit 9. Turn left onto NY 119, then right onto US 9 North. Drive 1.6 miles, then turn left onto North Broadway. Follow it for 1.7 miles and turn right onto NY 117/Phelps Way. The park is ahead on the right. *GPS coordinates:* 41° 6.704' N, 73° 50.199' W.

"Bucolic," "manicured," "austere," "inviting"—the mind reels at the variety of appealing adjectives one might use to describe the Rockefeller State Park Preserve. The land—topography formed 10,000 years ago by retreating glaciers—was purchased by the Rockefeller family and donated for the creation of a public park in 1983. Visitors can explore a network of trails for hiking, snowshoeing, and cross-country skiing, enjoy garden walks, or go sledding. The National Audubon Society has designated the park an Important Bird Area because of the more than 180 different species—including blue and yellow-winged warblers, wood thrushes, Baltimore orioles, eastern towhees, and red-bellied woodpeckers—that can be found here.

A walk around Swan Lake is an ideal way to get a feel for the park. The distance is about 2 miles. The sand and graveled paths make easy pushing for strollers, and the landscape is flat enough that kids ages 5 and up will have no problem. Enter the trail behind the visitor center and head south counterclockwise around the lake. In summer your kids will spot lily pads. The steepness of the shore leading from the path down to the lake is relatively mild and manageable.

A walk around Swan Lake is a pleasant way to enjoy the tranquil setting at Rockefeller State Park.

A longer (3-mile) and more rustic option is to follow Overlook Trail west, just before you arrive at Swan Lake following the path from the visitor center. After just more than a mile, you will encounter Ash Tree Loop connecting from the north. Follow the loop about a quarter-mile to Farm Meadow Trail. Follow Farm Meadow Trail back northeast to the southern end of Swan Lake. Visitors can also fish for bass on Swan Lake and brown trout in the Pocantico River, or go horseback riding (permits are required for both). *Remember:* Dogs must be leashed at all times.

PLAN B: Thirteen Bridges Trail and Pocantico Trail, just farther south along NY 117, are great spots for hiking. The latter is also popular for horseback riding.

WHERE TO EAT NEARBY: Numerous shops and restaurants are in Sleepy Hollow, which you'll drive through on your way to the park.

Trip 81

Ages 5–8

Harriman State Park: Lake Sebago

A hike along Lake Sebago is relatively easy, as is paddling its calm waters.

Address: Seven Lakes Drive, Harriman, NY
Hours: Lake: open seasonally, July 2 to August 7, 7:30 A.M. to 8 P.M. Other parts of Harriman State Park are open throughout the year.
Fee: $8 per vehicle (free with an Empire Passport)
Contact: nysparks.state.ny.us/parks/60/details.aspx; 845-351-2583
Bathrooms: Comfort station
Water/Snacks: Vending machines in the comfort station
Map: USGS Sloatsburg
Directions by Car: Take I-95 South to Exit 74 onto the Palisades Interstate Parkway North and drive for 27.2 miles. Take Exit 14 onto Willow Grove Road. Continue onto Kanawauke Road. At a traffic circle, take the third exit onto Seven Lakes Drive. Parking is located at the entrance of the trail up to Lake Sebago. *GPS coordinates:* 41° 12.981′ N, 74° 7.712′ W.

Harriman State Park, the second-largest in the New York State park system, has 31 lakes and reservoirs. Covering 310 acres, Lake Sebago is the largest lake in the park (*sebago* is Algonquian for "big water"). The lake is fronted by a brick comfort station with a first-aid clinic, bathrooms, and vending machines. Beyond this is a guarded beach with a swimming area designated by roped buoys. The campground, including tentsites, 40 popular rustic cabins, and two full-service cottages, covers a large area north and west of the beach. The campground is an easy hike from the beach, and has a playground.

Campers or visitors on day trips can experience the backwoods beauty of Harriman on a moderately easy walk around part of the lake. As you enter the beach area, head right (counterclockwise, or southwest) along the sandy beach. After about 100 yards you will encounter a footpath leading into the forest surrounding the lake. The rock-studded path includes slight inclines and exposed roots. While strollers are not an option, the hike is suitable for kids ages 5 and above. The path leads around the edge of the lake, and the views across and above to the surrounding woods are delightful. After about a mile, the path veers right (northwest) over to nearby Lake Skenon. Return the

Lake Sebago has many quiet coves for paddlers.

way you came and enjoy the beach. You can also head left (clockwise) around Lake Sebago, but the path is very rocky and less clear.

Three large and mostly shaded barbecue and picnic areas are between the parking lot and the beach, and boat launches are at designated areas on the beach for nonmotorized craft. After a few paddle strokes away from the busy beachfront, you will find yourself in the soul of quiet waters. *Remember:* No dogs are allowed.

PLAN B: The Appalachian Trail (AT) runs through Harriman State Park. At the intersection of the AT and Arden-Surebridge Trail, near the base of Island Pond Mountain, look for the "Lemon Squeezer," a large rock formation that requires hikers to "squeeze" through a nearly 10-foot-long opening—a favorite with kids.

WHERE TO EAT NEARBY: It is best to pack a picnic.

Trip 82

Clarence Fahenstock Memorial State Park: Pelton Pond

Deeply wooded and picturesque Pelton Pond offers a nature trail over rugged terrain, and is next door to swimming, camping, and paddling at Canopus Lake. The park is also a great place for skiing, snowshoeing, and sledding in winter.

Address: Cold Spring Turnpike, Kent, NY
Hours: Sunrise to sunset daily
Fee: $7 per vehicle (free with an Empire Passport); Winter Park admission: $9 for
    adults, $6 for children under age 17
Contact: nysparks.state.ny.us/parks/133/details.aspx; 845-225-7207
Bathrooms: Pelton Pond; Canopus Beach
Water/Snacks: Water fountains and concessions at Canopus Beach
Map: USGS Oscawana Lake; fofhh.org/files/ClarenceFahnestockTrailMap.pdf
Directions by Car: Take I-87 North to Exit 7A onto Saw Mill Parkway North for
    15.7 miles. Merge onto Taconic State Parkway for 27.3 miles, then take the NY
    301 East exit. Turn left onto NY 301 West, and the pond is ahead on the left.
    GPS coordinates: 41° 28.575′ N, 73° 48.205′ W.

With more than 50 miles of hiking trails (including 10 miles of the Appalachian Trail), 79 campsites, year-round fishing and birding, a beach at Canopus Lake in summer, and 15 miles of groomed cross-country trails and snowshoeing in winter, Clarence Fahenstock Memorial State Park offers outdoors activities for every season.

Many of the hiking trails are long and advanced, but Pelton Pond Nature Trail offers a beautiful setting and a good place for children to learn how to maneuver over tricky terrain. Much of the route is studded with rocks and exposed roots, and lined with thick, verdant moss.

Pelton Pond is just across NY 301 from Canopus Lake. From the parking lot, go left up a small hill to the restrooms. Just beyond the restrooms to the right, look for the wide, yellow-blaze trail and follow it until you come upon a narrow path that makes a sharp right. Take that right; the yellow blazes will appear again farther on. When you come to a T intersection in the path, follow the Pelton Pond sign. Heading clockwise, this will lead you around the south-

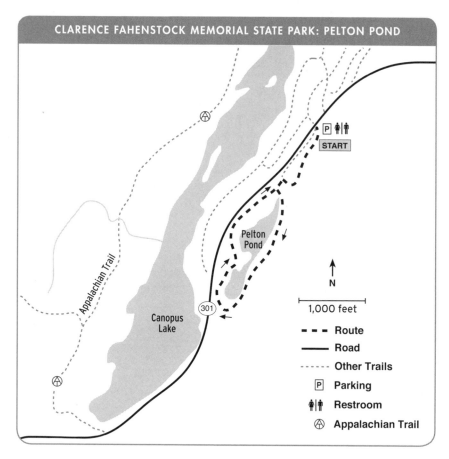

Pelton Pond

Canopus Lake

Appalachian Trail

301

↑
N

1,000 feet

- - - Route

———— Road

------ Other Trails

P   Parking

👫   Restroom

Ⓐ   Appalachian Trail

ern rim of the long, slender pond, and put you on the western bank heading north.

When you cross a wooden footbridge, you are about halfway along this bank. Around the top (northern) rim of the pond, there is a concrete wall with a rusted pull-wheel structure. It is jarring amid the tranquility, and it reveals that the pond is a flooded iron mine. The iron industry thrived in this region until just after the American Revolution. Continue following the periodic yellow blazes along the eastern bank of the pond back to the parking lot. This is a much gentler walk along well-delineated dirt paths.

A few hundred yards up NY 301 is Canopus Beach, a wide, sandy expanse where you can rent rowboats in summer. Winter Park, situated northwest of the lake at an elevation of 1,100 feet, offers a range of groomed tracks and mapped woods trails for cross-country skiing, snowshoeing, and sledding. Equipment, including tubes and baby sleds, is available to rent at the lodge, which is also the perfect place to warm up with hot chocolate after a brisk day on the slopes. *Remember:* All-season fishing for bass, pickerel, perch, and brook or rainbow trout is available on Canopus and Stillwater lakes, and on Fahenstock's four ponds (New York fishing license required).

PLAN B: Continue north to Taconic State Park to visit Rudd Pond (Trip 85) or Copake Falls Area and Bash Bish Falls (Trip 86).

WHERE TO EAT NEARBY: Restaurants and stores selling food and beverages are along NY 301, Cold Spring Turnpike.

Trip 83

Olana State Historic Site

Carriage paths wind through the grounds and woods of a landmark antebellum residence that has captivating views of the Catskill Mountains and Hudson River Valley.

Address: 5720 NY Route 9G, Hudson, NY
Hours: 8 A.M. to sunset daily
Fee: $5 per car on weekends and holiday Mondays, April through October (free with an Empire Passport); free all other times. House tours: adults, $9; children under age 12, free
Contact: olana.org; nysparks.com/historic-sites/23/details.aspx; 518-828-0135
Bathrooms: Visitor center
Water/Snacks: Water fountain near the restrooms; snacks and beverages in the gift shop
Map: USGS Hudson South; nysparks.state.ny.us/historic-sites/attachments/OlanaOlanaLandscapeMapandBrochure.pdf
Directions by Car: Take I-87 North to Exit 21 toward NY 23. Take NY 23 over the Rip Van Winkle Bridge, and bear right onto NY 9G south. The destination is 1.0 mile ahead on the left. *GPS coordinates:* 42° 12.590′ N, 73° 50.110′ W.

For artist Frederic Edwin Church, the hilltop where he built his Moorish-style home was both the inspiration for his painting, and a canvas itself. He first visited the property in 1845, as an 18-year-old protégé of Thomas Cole, a founding artist among the Hudson River School painters. In 1860, he bought an unprepossessing farm plot that he turned into a bucolic paradise, and in 1867, he acquired the hilltop.

Over these 250 acres, Church developed orchards, gardens, a 10-acre lake, stretches of woods, and a network of carriage roads thoughtfully laid out to capitalize on the landscapes and views throughout. The 1.5-mile Ridge Road loop will take you through the vistas that inspired Church's art, as well as the walks and views that he designed to captivate his well-heeled guests.

From the visitor center, follow the wide gravel path a short distance to the main paved road. Cross the road and enter the carriage trail just behind the wooden barricade and fire lane sign. Follow the woodsy path to a Y intersection and go left onto Ridge Road. This route soon opens out onto a panorama

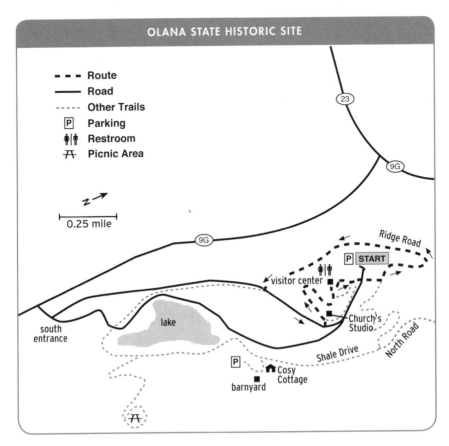

Route
Road
Other Trails
P **Parking**
Restroom
Picnic Area

0.25 mile

23

9G

9G

Ridge Road

P START

visitor center

Church's Studio

south entrance

lake

North Road

Shale Drive

P

Cosy Cottage

barnyard

of the Hudson River Valley, with the Rip Van Winkle Bridge at its center. It is easy to see how views like this inspired the Hudson River School artists.

A little farther on, the path curves to the left, into a heavily shaded stretch. A hairpin turn breaks off to the right; pass this and stay on the main path, which soon leads out to the paved road. Turn left and walk along the grassy bank until you come to a path with a bench where Church's studio once stood. You could follow the paved road back up to the parking lot, but take the gravel garden path up to the left. In a short distance, the path curves right, and before you emerges a view of the house that makes you stop in your tracks. This is the effect that Church was striving for. *Remember:* Bicycles are not permitted on the paths.

PLAN B: If the views of the Hudson River make you want to walk over it, head south to Walkway Over the Hudson (Trip 84).

WHERE TO EAT NEARBY: Olana is a perfect setting for a picnic, and bringing one is encouraged.

Trip 84

Ages 9–12

Walkway Over the Hudson

Walkway Over the Hudson is a 1.28-mile pedestrian bridge offering stunning views of the Hudson River, and is connected to the Hudson Valley Rail Trail.

Address: 87 Haviland Road, Highland, NY, to 61 Parker Avenue, Poughkeepsie, NY

Hours: 7 A.M. to sunset daily

Fee: Free

Contact: nysparks.state.ny.us/parks/178/details.aspx; walkway.org/dynamic. php?id=aboutthepark; 845-834-2867

Bathrooms: Both endpoints of the walkway

Water/Snacks: Vendors at both endpoints of the walkway

Map: USGS Poughkeepsie; walkway.org

Directions by Car (Poughkeepsie side): Take NY 9A North and continue onto the Henry Hudson Parkway, then onto the Saw Mill Parkway North for 15.7 miles. Take the ramp onto the Taconic State Parkway. Exit onto NY 55 West after 43.4 miles. After 8.3 miles, turn right onto Columbus Drive, which turns into Washington Street. Free parking is available on Brookside, Taylor, and Washington streets, and free lots are on Washington Street and Parker Avenue. (On the Highland side, free parking is along Haviland Road. A metered parking lot is located at the entrance to the walkway.) *GPS coordinates:* 41° 42.701′ N, 73° 55.749′ W.

Directions by Public Transit: By train, take Metro North to Poughkeepsie station, and walk four blocks north.

Walkway Over the Hudson State Historic Park, a pedestrian thoroughfare that stretches 212 feet above the Hudson River, invites biking, strolling, walking, and horizon gazing.

The site was created from the Poughkeepsie-Highland Railroad Bridge, an engineering marvel that, when it opened in 1888, was the longest railroad bridge in the world. The structure was severely damaged by a fire in 1974 and fell into disuse. Thanks to the efforts of the Walkway Over the Hudson non-profit organization, the bridge reopened in 2009 and returned to the record books as the world's longest elevated pedestrian park.

Start your hike on the Highland side and cross the walkway heading east, or on the Poughkeepsie side and head west. As you walk across, you will ex-

This former railroad bridge across the Hudson River is now a popular, paved path for pedestrians.

perience picturesque views of a river that played a central role in the westward expansion and economic development of the United States. The walkway features signs along the way detailing the site's history, as well as information about the Hudson itself. The walkway is also suitable for bikes and strollers.

If you continue heading west from the Highland side, the walkway can be part of a longer hike along the Hudson Valley Rail Trail. On the eastern side, it connects to the Dutchess Rail Trail. Another option is to integrate the walkway into a roughly 3.5-mile loop that, from the Poughkeepsie side, leads from Parker Avenue to Verrazano Boulevard and continues west along Rinaldi Boulevard and Gerald Drive to the Franklin D. Roosevelt Mid-Hudson Bridge. After crossing that bridge, follow Haviland Road back up to the western, or Highland, side of the walkway. *Remember:* Dogs are welcome but must be leashed at all times.

PLAN B: Several paths for biking and hiking are near the walkway. Visit walkway.org for details.

WHERE TO EAT NEARBY: Restaurants and shops are in the city of Poughkeepsie and the town of Lloyd.

Trip 85

All Ages $ 🚶   🏊   🛶   ⛷   ⛺

Taconic State Park: Rudd Pond

Rudd Pond is a good site for introducing kids to camping, with opportunities for hiking, boating, and swimming.

Address: 59 Rudd Pond Road, Millerton, NY
Hours: Subject to change, so call ahead. Beach: 11 A.M. to 7 P.M. weekends and holidays, late May to mid-August
Fee: $7 per vehicle (free with an Empire Passport)
Contact: nysparks.com/parks/141/hours-of-operation.aspx; 518-789-3059
Bathrooms: In front of the pond near the parking lot
Water/Snacks: None
Map: USGS Millerton
Directions by Car: Take NY 9A North and continue onto Henry Hudson Parkway, then onto Saw Mill Parkway North. Merge onto Cross County Parkway, and then onto Hutchinson River Parkway North. Take a slight left onto I-684 North. Continue onto NY 22 North and drive for almost 43 miles. Turn right onto Main Street, then left onto Rudd Pond Road, and drive for 2.3 miles to the pond. The parking lot is located at the entrance. *GPS coordinates:* 41° 58.805′ N, 73° 30.297′ W.

Taconic State Park is part of the Taconic Mountain Range, which runs all the way up to New England and is home to sections of the Appalachian Trail. The park covers 16 miles of this range along the Connecticut and Massachusetts borders, and offers an extensive trail network with varying terrain and stunning views.

Rudd Pond, in the southern section of the park, has a long history as an ideal fishing spot, and is now well suited for introducing kids to camping, or for boating and swimming in calm waters. The wide, sandy beach also has a large playground. Rudd Pond has fewer visitors than Copake Falls (Trip 86), its sister park to the north.

The campground features 15 tentsites and 26 tent platform sites, each with a picnic bench, a fire ring, and a grill. Restrooms and a hot-water shower house help ease families into the tent-camping experience. The sites are situated between the Taconic ridge and the pond, where anglers can try their luck at catching bass, sunfish, and pickerel (New York fishing license required). A rustic but easy hiking path leads around Iron Mine Pond, which is south of

*Family-friendly camping, fishing, paddling, and swimming
are popular activities at Rudd Pond.*

the tent platforms. In winter, the pond is a popular spot for ice fishing and ice skating. *Remember:* Quiet hours from 10 P.M. to 7 A.M. are strictly enforced at the campsites, contributing to its being a good fit for families.

PLAN B: Copake Falls (Trip 86) is an easy excursion and beautiful hike from Rudd Pond.

WHERE TO EAT NEARBY: Nearby Millerton village is home to many restaurants and cafés.

Trip 86

Copake Falls Area and Bash Bish Falls

This is a cool and lovely walk to a dramatic view, and best of all, it's all downhill on the way back! The area is great for camping and winter visits, too.

Address: NY Route 344, Copake Falls, NY
Hours: Sunrise to sunset daily
Fee: $7 per car (free with an Empire Passport)
Contact: nysparks.com/parks/83/details.aspx; 518-329-3993
Bathrooms: Portable toilets at the parking lot and at the falls
Water/Snacks: None
Map: USGS Bash Bish Falls and Copake
Directions by Car: Take NY 9A North and continue onto Henry Hudson Parkway, then onto Saw Mill Parkway North. Merge onto Cross County Parkway, and then onto Hutchinson River Parkway North. Take a slight left onto I-684 North. Continue onto NY 22 North and drive for almost 55 miles, then turn right onto NY 344. Take NY 344 to Taconic State Park and continue a short distance past the park entrance on your left to the Bash Bish Area parking lot on the right. Cross the creek on the cabin access road.
GPS coordinates: 42° 7.053′ N, 73° 30.500′ W.

With 16 cabins and more than 100 tent and trailer sites, Copake Falls Area offers a lively camping experience for families. A few cabins are available year-round, giving visitors a launching pad for (and resting place from) snowshoe and cross-country ski excursions on the miles of trails throughout the area.

A wonderful all-season hike is the steady trek up to Bash Bish Falls, which is just over the Massachusetts border. Like Kaaterskill in the Catskills (Trip 89), Bash Bish was among the most fashionable wilderness getaways of the nineteenth century. Today, it attracts a steady flow of visitors from both the New York and Massachusetts sides. With water falling 60 feet into a crystal-clear deep pool, Bash Bish is the highest single-drop cascade in Massachusetts. The water originates from a spring in Mount Washington, Massachusetts, and, after passing through the Roeliff-Jansen Kill, it ultimately joins the Hudson River.

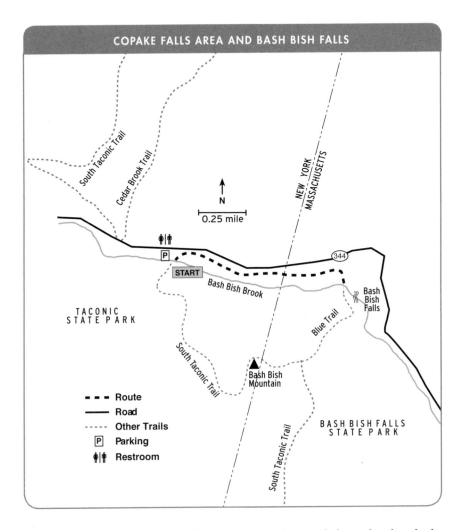

COPAKE FALLS AREA AND BASH BISH FALLS

South Taconic Trail

Cedar Brook Trail

N
0.25 mile

NEW YORK
MASSACHUSETTS

P

START

Bash Bish Brook

344

Bash
Bish
Falls

TACONIC
STATE PARK

Blue Trail

South Taconic Trail

Bash Bish
Mountain

- - - Route
—— Road
----- Other Trails
P Parking
Restroom

BASH BISH FALLS
STATE PARK

South Taconic Trail

From the parking lot, go left and take the dirt road through a hemlock-hardwood ravine forest. With the shade and the cool air emanating from Bash Bish Brook, the temperature is pleasant even on a hot day. Soon a gentle, steady incline begins, and remains for the duration of the hike. For about the first half of the 0.75-mile trek to the falls, there are benches along the way. When you come to a path forking off to the left, ignore it. You are almost to the well-marked New York State–Massachusetts border—as a geography lesson, this crossing makes an impression—and the falls are just beyond that.

You can take in the grandeur of the falls from the viewing platform, or you can descend a steep stone staircase with a center railing that leads to the base of the cascade. Return the way you came to complete the 1.5-mile hike. This is also a spectacular fall-foliage destination, and excellent for snowshoeing and cross-country skiing in winter. *Remember:* Swimming is prohibited.

PLAN B: For a rugged 3-mile loop, you could cross Bash Bish Brook via the bridge on the right side of the parking lot and, with the brook to your left, follow the South Taconic Trail and then the blue trail path up to the falls. Ore Pitt Pond, a short drive west on NY 344, has a swimming beach, a wading pool for toddlers, and a playground.

WHERE TO EAT NEARBY: The town of Copake has restaurants, diners, and shops. Take NY 344 to NY 22, and turn right onto East Main Street. Follow this (do not turn left onto Farm Road) to Main Street in the town's center.

Journaling can be a wonderful part of a family outing. Writing and drawing foster a connection with the natural world around you, while creating a lasting memento. With a flexible interpretation of what journaling is, children of all ages can participate. A plain, unlined notebook works well, especially one with a blank cover that children can decorate themselves. Each piece of paper is a clean slate for rendering and doodling, and it liberates writers from the need to use perfect penmanship. Journaling is a personal experience and an expression of creativity, not an assignment that needs to have all i's dotted and t's crossed.

When traveling on day trips or overnights, bring the journals and a plastic bag with markers, pencils, and crayons. Older children may like using watercolors. Before or after mealtime, or whenever there's a lull in activity, pull out the materials and allow children to express themselves on paper however they want. Perhaps ask them if they can sketch a landscape or detail that they saw during the day, or draw a scene of what they loved or found challenging.

A family journal can take this process to the next level. Parents might describe an entire day's excursion, or everyone can participate, round-robin style. One person has the power of the pen, and everyone offers an impression or memory from the day. Each description is jotted down next to the person's name.

Maps also make terrific ad hoc journals. If your destination provides paper maps, record notes on what you see at various places, or scribble down who made a poignant observation at a particular point. Such personalized maps can become keepsakes that just might inspire a passion for cartography. Maps mounted on bulletin boards at home also allow you to mark destinations with different-colored pins for everyone who made a trip.

Flip through the journals weeks and months later, and the trips truly come alive. We can feel our son Riley's energy as he leads us up a mountain where "you get to see the highest waterfalls" (Kaaterskill Falls, Trip 89). And it is recorded for posterity that we stayed in cabin 5 at Brookside Campground (while traveling in the Catskills and Hudson Valley) because, as our daughter Halina noted, "that's my age."

All Ages

Trip 87

Bear Mountain State Park: Hessian Lake

For nearly a century, millions of visitors have loved swimming, hiking, walking, biking, and ice skating at Bear Mountain.

Address: Seven Lakes Drive, Bear Mountain, NY
Hours: 8 A.M. to sunset daily
Fee: $8 per vehicle (free with an Empire Passport). Pool: adults, $2; children ages 6 to 12, $1; children 5 and under, free. Ice rink: adults and children over age 12, $4; children ages 4 to 11, $3; children age 3 and under, free
Contact: nysparks.state.ny.us/parks/13/details.aspx; 845-786-2701
Bathrooms: Near entrance to pedestrian underpass; merry-go-round, picnic area; pool; trailside museum
Water/Snacks: Concessions near the picnic area; restaurant at Bear Mountain Inn
Map: USGS Peekskill and Popolopen Lake; nysparks.state.ny.us/parks/attachments/BearMountainTrailMap.pdf
Directions by Car: Take I-95 South to Exit 74 onto the Palisades Interstate Parkway North and drive for 34.3 miles. Continue onto US 6 East. At the traffic circle, take the first exit onto US 9W South. Bear right, and the parking area is on the right. *GPS coordinates*: 41° 18.792′ N, 73° 59.311′ W.

A park of enduring legend and popularity, Bear Mountain State Park was designed as a system of lakes, trails, and scenic drives. In addition to trails coursing through natural beauty, Bear Mountain's signature attractions include large picnic and barbecue areas, an enormous outdoor, art deco swimming pool, an outdoor ice rink, boat and canoe rentals, and a landmark merry-go-round whose seats are hand-carved renditions of black bears, wild turkeys, deer, raccoons, skunks, and other local animals.

The park's idyllic Hessian Lake is a terrific spot for a kid-friendly, 1.25-mile hike. With the historic Bear Mountain Inn behind you, walk clockwise along the paved path around the southern rim of the lake. Shortly after the boat-

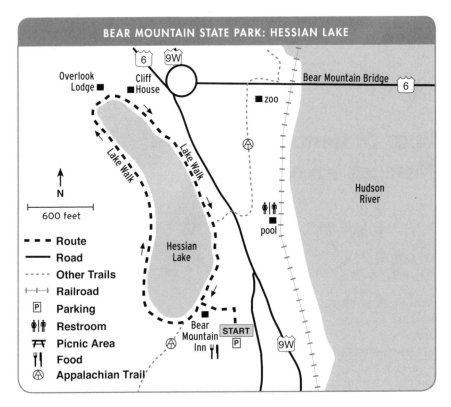

BEAR MOUNTAIN STATE PARK: HESSIAN LAKE

house the trail, which is blazed with red dots with white borders, gets quite wooded and covers some gentle hills. At a number of spots you can walk out onto boulders overlooking the lake. A rugged cliff is along the northern rim of the walk. (No official trail leads up the cliff and you should not attempt to climb it.) The route flattens out as you approach the lake's western bank. Most of this side is flanked by the shady picnic and barbecue area that slopes gently toward the lake. This route is also excellent for bicyclists of all ages. *Remember:* You cannot swim in Hessian Lake, but you can cast a line in for trout, black bass, or pickerel (New York fishing license required).

PLAN B: Paddle or pedal-boat around Hessian Lake. Boat rentals are $5 per person per hour. You can also hike the first-completed link of the Appalachian Trail (Trip 88).

WHERE TO EAT NEARBY: Restaurants, diners, and convenience stores are in nearby Highland Falls.

Trip 88

Ages 9–12

Bear Mountain State Park: Appalachian Trail

There's something special about saying you've hiked on the Appalachian Trail, and this easy link is perfect for beginner hikers.

Address: Seven Lakes Drive, Bear Mountain, NY
Hours: 8 A.M. to sunset daily
Fee: $8 per vehicle (free with an Empire Passport)
Contact: nysparks.state.ny.us/parks/13/details.aspx; 845-786-2701
Bathrooms: Near entrance to pedestrian underpass; merry-go-round, picnic area, pool; trailside museum
Water/Snacks: Concessions near the picnic area; restaurant at Bear Mountain Inn
Map: USGS Peekskill and Popolopen Lake; nysparks.state.ny.us/parks/attachments/BearMountainTrailMap.pdf
Directions by Car: Take I-95 South to Exit 74 onto the Palisades Interstate Parkway North and drive for 34.3 miles, then continue onto US 6 East. At the traffic circle, take the first exit onto US 9W South. Bear right, and the parking area is on the right. *GPS coordinates*: 41° 18.792′ N, 73° 59.311′ W.

The Appalachian Trail (AT) stretches from Maine to Georgia, but its "beginning" is in Bear Mountain. On October 7, 1923, the first, 16-mile section of the AT, from Bear Mountain through Harriman State Park, was opened here.

Although much of the AT through here is a traditional mountain hike, a stretch that's suitable for children and strollers starts along the eastern shore of Hessian Lake. With the historic Bear Mountain Inn behind you, walk counterclockwise around the lake until you see the restroom building in the picnic area to your right. Take the pedestrian underpass past the pool on your right. This will put you on a shady stretch of the AT, marked with the trail's signature white triangular blazes, that will take you through the Trailside Zoo. The zoo is an animal rehabilitation center for injured mammals, reptiles, amphibians, and birds.

You reach the lowest point on the AT—120 feet above seal level—across from the bear den. Go right and follow the short path past the amphitheater to an overlook that brings you to an outstanding view of the Hudson River. Returning to the AT, follow the well-marked trail north, to the campus of small

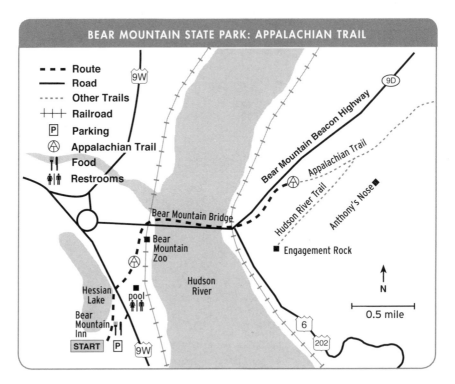

Legend:
- - - Route
—— Road
- - - - Other Trails
+++ Railroad
P Parking
Ⓐ Appalachian Trail
🍴 Food
🚻 Restrooms

9W

9D

Bear Mountain Beacon Highway

Appalachian Trail

Hudson River Trail

Anthony's Nose ■

Bear Mountain Bridge

Bear
Mountain
Zoo

■ Engagement Rock

Hessian
Lake

■ pool 🚻

Hudson
River

N

0.5 mile

Bear
Mountain
Inn

START P 9W

6

202

museums that explain the geology and human history—from early American Indians through the American Revolution—of the area.

From the museum area, the AT heads over the Bear Mountain Bridge, with the Hudson River flowing 360 feet below. Walk across the bridge on its southern sidewalk, which is separated from the traffic lanes by a barricade. When you reach the eastern side of the Hudson, you can return the way you came (recommended if you are with young children or if you are pushing a stroller), or watch for traffic and cross NY 9D. Turn left, and after a walk of about 600 uphill yards (the shoulder is narrow), you will see an AT blaze on your right. This rugged climb is not suitable for strollers or young children. Return the way you came. *Remember:* For a more traditional AT hike, take the stairs to the west of the inn (behind the playground) and look for the signature white blazes.

PLAN B: If it's summer, head to the pool. The vast shallow area gradually reaches 3 feet, and the large deep area has a series of diving boards. You can also enjoy an easy hike around Hessian Lake (Trip 87) or launch a boat from its southwest shore.

WHERE TO EAT NEARBY: Restaurants, diners, and convenience stores are in nearby Highland Falls.

Trip 89

Kaaterskill Falls

This easy hike leads to a waterfall that was once the most popular tourist destination in the United States.

Address: NY Route 23A, Hunter, NY
Hours: Dawn to dusk daily
Fee: Free
Contact: nynjtc.org/park/kaaterskill-wild-forest?gclid=CPuJlKPPk6wCFYSo4A
odG1k6lg
Bathrooms: None
Water/Snacks: None
Map: USGS Kaaterskill Clove
Directions by Car: Take I-95 South to NJ 4 West. Exit onto NJ 17 North, then merge onto I-287 North. Keep left at the fork and merge onto I-87 North and drive for 71 miles. Take Exit 20, then turn left onto NY 212. Turn right onto NY 32 North. Continue onto NY 32A North, then NY 23A West. The trailhead is at the crest of a hairpin turn on 23A, on the right. The parking lot is farther up the hill, on the left. *GPS coordinates:* 42° 11.476′ N, 74° 4.240′ W.

The Catskill Forest Preserve has long fueled a passion for wilderness travel. Today the Catskills endure as a premier and pristine place to hike, camp, snowshoe, cross-country ski, and, of course, swim, fish, and paddle on stunning lakes, ponds, and rivers.

Among the most famous hikes in the area is the trek up to Kaaterskill Falls. The cascade is the highest in New York State and in the late 1800s was the most-visited tourist destination in the United States. As you and your children stare up to the point where the water flows over the ridge and pours into the pool below, you will have no problem imagining how this object of natural wonder inspired legions of poets, artists, and writers.

Though the falls are past their heyday as a tourist draw, the path leading up and down remains busy. From the parking lot, cross NY 23A, climb behind the guardrail, and backtrack to the trailhead, which is marked by a large sign. This hike is not stroller friendly, but on the trail we saw two families with babies in packs.

The half-mile trail is steep but clear and well maintained. You'll climb over large boulders, hopscotch across flat stones, and walk up a few sets of log steps.

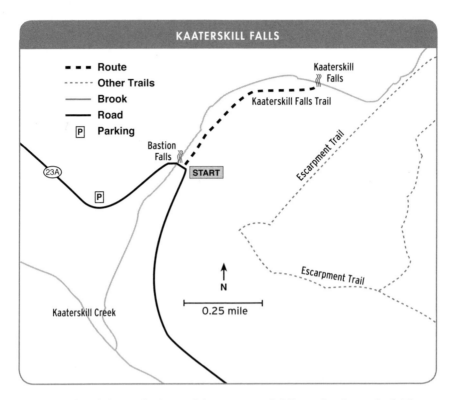

The end of the hike, at the base of the two-tiered falls, is clearly marked. This is an excellent site for a picnic. *Remember*: Going from the parking lot to the start of the trail requires walking along a winding, busy road. Use caution.

PLAN B: Visit North-South Lake (Trip 90) to swim, rent canoes or kayaks, or camp.

WHERE TO EAT NEARBY: Head to Haines Falls along NY 23A for restaurants, a general store, and seasonal produce markets.

All Ages

Trip 90

North-South Lake: Catskill Mountain House

Visit this popular campground for hiking, biking, paddling, and other games, as well as camping in tents.

Address: County Road 18, Haines Falls, NY
Hours: Dawn to dusk daily
Fee: $8 per vehicle (free with an Empire Passport)
Contact: dec.ny.gov/outdoor/24487.html; 518-357-2289
Bathrooms: Parking lot fronting North-South Lake
Water/Snacks: Vending machines near the parking lot
Map: USGS Kaaterskill Clove
Directions by Car: Take I-95 South to NJ 4 West. Exit onto NJ 17 North, then merge onto I-287 North. Keep left at the fork and merge onto I-87 North and drive for 71 miles. Take Exit 20, then turn left onto NY 212. Turn right onto NY 32 North. Continue onto NY 32A North, then NY 23A West. Turn right onto Country Road 18 and drive 1.9 miles to the entrance. *GPS coordinates:* 42° 12.133′ N, 74° 3.729′ W.

North-South Lake was once among the most fashionable mountain destinations in America, and today it remains the most popular public campground in the Catskill Forest Preserve. With miles of trails covering terrain as varied as brookside walks and 2,250-foot mountain passes, North-South Lake has hikes for everyone. The campground, with more than 200 tent and trailer sites, two picnic areas, two swimming beaches, and restrooms with showers, also has a playground and facilities for volleyball, horseshoes, and other recreational activities.

For day-use and overnight visitors alike, the easy hike to the remains of the Catskill Mountain House, an inn that once lodged presidents and other luminaries, is a must-do from the beach. The hike begins at the far end of the parking lot, where pavement turns into gravel. Walk uphill to catch the blue-blazed trail along a moderately steep path that, while rocky, is easily navigable

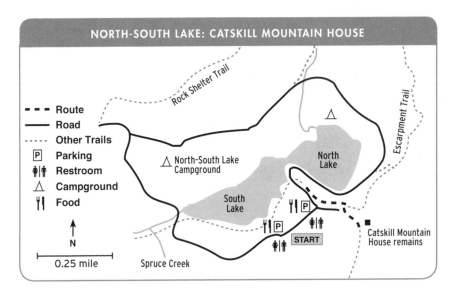

Legend:
- - - Route
— Road
- - - - Other Trails
P Parking
♦♦ Restroom
△ Campground
♦♦ Food

↑
N

0.25 mile

Rock Shelter Trail

Escarpment Trail

△ North-South Lake Campground

North Lake

South Lake

START

Catskill Mountain House remains

Spruce Creek

for young hikers and parents pushing a sturdy stroller. After half a mile you find the stone remains of the entrance gate to what once was a luxury hotel. As you continue along, the horizon over the Hudson Valley opens wide before you. On this high plateau, the stone outlines of this once-grand hotel present a surreal vista. To your right, an informational sign grippingly describes the rise and fall of the hotel.

Return the way you came, and if you want to extend your excursion, take the path to the left of the beach to begin a longer walk around North Lake. *Remember:* Motorized boats are not permitted on the lake. A paved boat ramp is located near the beach, and you can rent rowboats, kayaks, canoes, and paddleboats at the campground.

PLAN B: A hike up Kaaterskill Falls (Trip 89) will add to your appreciation of the area's natural beauty.

WHERE TO EAT NEARBY: Visit Haines Falls along NY 23A for restaurants, a general store, and seasonal produce markets.

Trip 91

Ages 5–8

Minnewaska State Park

Minnewaska State Park features a short hike to a picturesque waterfall and a challenging hike to a scenic mountaintop lake.

Address: Main Street, Kerhonkson, NY
Hours: Park: 9 A.M. to 9 P.M. daily; Beach: 11:15 A.M. to 6:45 P.M. seasonally
Fee: Free
Contact: lakeminnewaska.org/contact.php; 845-255-0752
Bathrooms: Parking lot at trailhead; near Minnewaska Beach
Water/Snacks: None
Map: USGS Gardiner, Kerhonkson, Mohonk Lake, and Napanoch; lakeminnewaska.org/hiking.html
Directions by Car: Take I-95 South to NJ 4 West. Exit onto NJ 17 North, then merge onto I-287 North. Keep left at the fork and merge onto I-87 North and drive for 30.0 miles. Take Exit 17 onto NY 300 North and follow it for about 3.0 miles. Continue onto NY 32 North and drive for 9.2 miles, then turn left onto NY 55 and follow it for almost 12.0 miles. The park entrance will be on the left. *GPS coordinates: 41° 44.106′ N, 74° 14.499′ W.*

Minnewaska State Park Preserve, covering 18 square miles of forest on the Shawangunk Ridge, was originally developed as a resort area in a rustic setting. Today, like much of the surrounding Catskill Forest Preserve, it is a breathtakingly beautiful day-use park, featuring three lakes and miles of wide gravel pathways (former carriage paths) that ascend at a steady incline.

Before you begin the 1.2-mile hike to Lake Minnewaska, treat yourself to a quick detour to Awosting Falls, set in a river valley that is incredibly verdant. To get there from the park entrance, follow the red-blazed trail to your left, heading downhill 0.2 mile on a wide, rutted gravel path. You will pass by the orange trail entrance on your right. The falls will be calling you all the while, and in short order, will appear on your left. It's worth the trip.

Head back up to the orange trail to begin the hike through a dense and soaring hardwood forest to Lake Minnewaska, which is cradled amid the peaks at the top of the preserve. The path is not suitable for standard strollers and is not recommended for children under age 5. The trail is popular with mountain bikers interested in a challenging ascent, followed by a hair-raising ride down.

Well-groomed, scenic carriage trails lead to this pristine mountaintop lake.

At the top you will find a mountaintop lake that owes its clarity to its acidic water, and a rocky shoreline that is inhospitable to aquatic vegetation and marine life. Like North-South Lake (Trip 90), Minnewaska was once home to popular resort hotels that catered to the well-heeled and influential. The hotels, dating to 1879, were ultimately abandoned and later burned to the ground.

Take a short walk down to the gravel beach for a swim, or continue along the red-blazed trail around the lake. The beach is guarded and features bathrooms and a changing room. *Remember:* Diving off the dock is not allowed.

PLAN B: North-South Lake (Trip 90) is another formerly famous hotel site-turned-wonderful state park.

WHERE TO EAT NEARBY: Trendy shops and restaurants are in nearby New Paltz.

Section 9

New Jersey

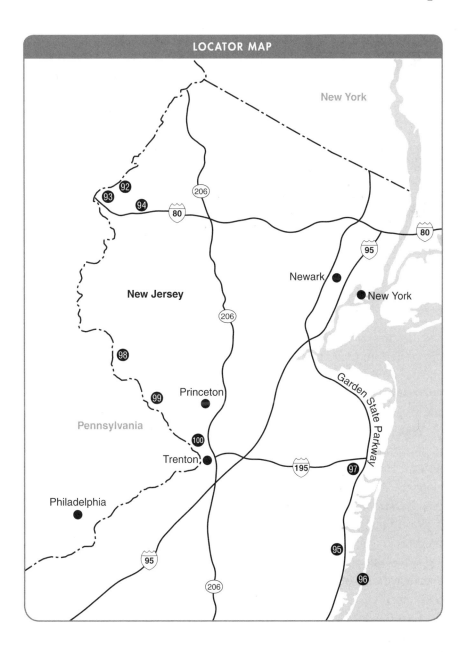

New York

92
93
94
206
80

80

95

Newark

New York

New Jersey

206

98

99   Princeton

Pennsylvania

100

Trenton

195   97

Garden State Parkway

Philadelphia

95

95

206

96

Ages
9–12

Van Campens Glen

Start with a leisurely walk from historic Millbrook Village to enjoy a moderately difficult hike up to a waterfall.

Address: Old Mine Road and Millbrook Road, Blairstown, NJ
Hours: Dawn to dusk daily
Fee: Free
Contact: nps.gov/dewa; 603-466-2721
Bathrooms: Entrance to Watergate Recreation Site
Water/Snacks: Water fountain at the bathrooms
Map: USGS Bushkill and Flatbrockville; millbrooknj.com/millbrook_interactive_
    building_m.htm
Directions by Car: Take I-95 South to I-280 West. After 18.0 miles, merge onto
    I-80 West for 33.6 miles. Take Exit 15 onto Country Road 521 and continue
    onto Hope Road. Turn left onto NJ 94, then take the first right onto Bridge
    Street. Quickly turn right onto Hope Road and continue onto Millbrook Road
    for about 7.0 miles. The parking lot is at Millbrook Village.
    GPS coordinates: 41° 03.504′ N, 74° 59.950′ W.

Outstanding rock-climbing cliffs, more than 100 miles of hiking trails covering diverse terrain (including 27 miles of the Appalachian Trail), campgrounds, and one mighty river are what you'll find in the Delaware Water Gap National Recreation Area. The area spans more than 100 square miles in New Jersey and Pennsylvania and is home to several state parks and forest preserves.

Within this, Worthington State Forest has a number of New Jersey's most popular trails and birding sites, as well as the only public campsites in the water gap. The campground, with 69 tent and trailer sites, stretches for 2 miles along the Delaware River, and includes playgrounds and an interpretative area, as well restrooms and showers.

Worthington's Van Campens Glen is one relatively challenging hike that prepares kids for more rugged trails and longer distances. The trailhead lies a quarter-mile from Millbrook Village, an outdoor museum where you can experience what life in New Jersey was like during the nineteenth century.

From the parking lot in Millbrook Village, follow the footpath leading between the hotel and the general store. Turn right across Millbrook Road, continuing past the church on your left and Sylvester Hill House on the right.

Van Campens Glen offers vigorous walks in a stunning ravine.

After about a quarter-mile you will arrive at Millbrook School. Continue along the path past two ponds. You will arrive at a third, larger pond, at the Watergate Recreation Site picnic area, where the trail begins.

Take the wooden bridge across the stream and follow the trail. After 1.4 miles you will cross an asphalt road, and at 1.8 miles you will arrive at the starting point for the yellow-blazed trail. Follow the trail off to the right. The path is rocky, intersected by tree roots, and at points requires easy climbing where the trail is somewhat steep. (It is not suitable for strollers, and would be awkward for parents wearing a baby carrier.) After 0.2 mile you will arrive at Van Campens Brook. Follow the trail left along the stream to the falls. After 2.5 miles you will cross another footbridge. Turn left past another set of falls at 2.75 miles before you arrive back in the Van Campens Glen parking lot. *Remember:* The trail can be slippery after rainfall.

PLAN B: If you would prefer a more challenging hike, try the Rattlesnake Swamp Trail (Trip 94). A less challenging hike is Dunnfield Creek Falls (Trip 93).

WHERE TO EAT NEARBY: It's best to pack a picnic, and the Watergate Recreation Site is a good spot to enjoy it.

Trip 93

Ages
5–8

Dunnfield Creek Natural Area

In a forest of chestnut, oak, and hemlock, you'll find an easy hike or snowshoe trek, 1.5 miles round-trip on a smooth trail, along with camping and paddling opportunities.

Address: Old Mine Road, Hardwick Township, NJ
Hours: Dawn to dusk daily
Fee: Free
Contact: nps.gov/dewa; 603-466-2721
Bathrooms: Portable toilets at the trailhead
Water/Snacks: None
Map: USGS Bushkill and Flatbrockville; outdoors.org/lodging/mohican/hiking-guide/dunnfield-creek-falls.cfm
Directions by Car: Take I-95 South to Exit 15 W onto I-280 West and drive for 17.5 miles. Merge onto I-80 West and follow for it for 44.9 miles and take the exit. The parking lot is ahead. *GPS coordinates:* 40° 58.307′ N, 75° 07.355′ W.

Within Worthington State Forest, the Dunnfield Creek Natural Area is a beautiful, forested ravine along Dunnfield Creek, a designated Wild Trout Stream (meaning it is home to native, wild trout, New Jersey's state fish). Worthington State Forest campground features 69 tent and trailer sites with picnic tables and fire rings, as well as showers and restrooms. The quiet setting and river access is ideal for families. You can also launch canoes and kayaks here.

The area also contains a gorgeous waterfall, and the trek to it is a great way to get kids started on hiking. The trail is relatively flat, well trod, and easy to follow, and reaching the falls is a nice reward for the effort. It's also great for snowshoeing in winter.

To start the hike, cross a wooden footbridge at the edge of the parking lot over to the east side of Dunnfield Creek. Follow the white-blazed Appalachian Trail, which, after about a half-mile, will intersect with the green-blazed Dunnfield Hollow Trail on the right. You will be deep in the hemlock ravine, a signature feature of the Delaware Water Gap. Take Dunnfield Hollow Trail another quarter-mile to Dunnfield Creek Falls, which you will find at the end of a short trail on your left. If you reach the Blue Dot trail you have gone too far. The rocks around the fall attract many young climbers and are relatively

This easy wooded hike leads to a beautiful waterfall and perfect picnic spots.

easy to navigate. You can explore a number of good outcroppings to view the falls from different angles.

For a different view of the falls, continue along the trail another quarter-mile. You can then retrace your route by following the Appalachian Trail back to the parking lot. *Remember:* The waterfall area makes an excellent spot for a picnic.

PLAN B: Rattlesnake Swamp Trail (Trip 94) is a much more challenging hike that is still suitable for kids. Van Campens Glen (Trip 92) is also a good hike that is only a bit more challenging than Dunnfield Creek Falls.

WHERE TO EAT NEARBY: It's best to pack a picnic.

Trip 94

Ages 9–12

Rattlesnake Swamp Trail

Swim, paddle, or fish on Catfish Pond, or enjoy a challenging hike up a steep trail that rewards you with fantastic views of the landscape below.

Address: 50 Camp Road, Blairstown, NJ
Hours: Dawn to dusk daily
Fee: Free
Contact: nps.gov/dewa; 908-362-5670
Bathrooms: Mohican Outdoor Center
Water/Snacks: A store with snacks at the Mohican Outdoor Center
Map: USGS Blairstown; outdoors.org/lodging/mohican/hiking-guide/
  rattlesnake-swamp-trail-short-west-loop.cfm
Directions by Car: Take I-95 South to I-280 West. After 18.0 miles, merge onto
  I-80 West and drive for 33.6 miles. Take Exit 15 onto Country Road 521 and
  continue onto Hope Road. Turn left onto NJ 94, and follow for it 1.2 miles.
  Turn left onto Mohican Road. After 3.2 miles, turn left onto Gaisler Road,
  then right onto Camp Road, which becomes dirt. The visitor center is ahead
  on the left. *GPS coordinates:* 41° 2.052′ N, 75° 0.134′ W.

The Mohican Outdoor Center (see page 232) is a wonderful launching point
for a variety of hikes and day trips: You can cross-country ski or rock-climb at
Blue Mountain Lakes, swim, paddle, or fish on Catfish Pond (New Jersey fishing license required), look for wildlife in the wetlands, or embark on a variety
of hikes. The west loop of Rattlesnake Swamp Trail is a challenging option,
but the route is short enough that it is a good way to prepare young hikers for
longer trips.

The start of the trail is just a quick walk from the visitor center. As you
leave the center, turn right down Camp Road to where it is bisected by the
Appalachian Trail (AT). Turn left at the sign marking the AT and follow the
white-blazed path up a very steep hill. The hike gets steeper as you ascend, and
at points it will feel like you are climbing high stairs. After hiking up over a
series of ridges, you will reach the top, where a stunning vista awaits.

After about 0.3 mile along the ridge, you emerge from the thick canopy of
trees facing southeast. When you look down you will see Gaisler Road and the
Upper Yards Creek Reservoir. As you continue along the ridge, you will find
several points where it is worth pausing to gaze out over the landscape below.

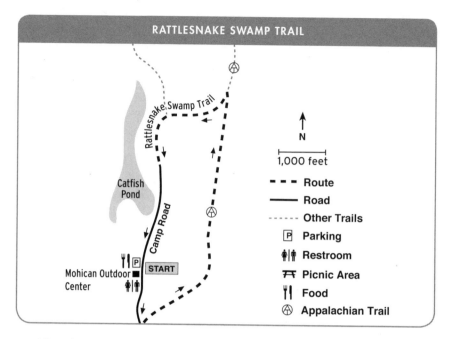

Catfish
Pond

Rattlesnake Swamp Trail

Camp Road

Mohican Outdoor ■
Center

START

N

1,000 feet

- - - **Route**
——— **Road**
- - - - - **Other Trails**
🅿 **Parking**
🚻 **Restroom**
⛉ **Picnic Area**
🍴 **Food**
Ⓐ **Appalachian Trail**

After about 1.5 miles, the orange-blazed trail will intersect to the left. Follow the orange-blazed trail back down the ridge (the blazes are painted on rocks along the path, so be sure to look down). After about a mile, Rattlesnake Swamp Trail will intersect on the right. The trail will lead you back to the Trails End Lodge section of the Mohican Outdoor Center. Follow Camp Road left back to the visitor center, or turn right and head to the Catfish Pond to swim or paddle. You can rent canoes, kayaks, and paddles at the Mohican Outdoor Center. *Remember:* Keep an eye out for bears and rattlesnakes—we met both.

PLAN B: Dunnfield Creek Natural Area (Trip 93) and Van Campens Glen (Trip 92) both offer less challenging hikes than Rattlesnake Swamp Trail.

WHERE TO EAT NEARBY: It's best to bring a picnic. Or stay at the Mohican Outdoor Center (see page 232) and have meals provided during summer.

Whether you're an experienced tent camper or new to the idea of sleeping deep in the woods, AMC's Mohican Outdoor Center (MOC) makes the wilderness accessible for all families. Set high in the Delaware Water Gap National Recreation Area, between two ridges of the Appalachian Mountains, MOC is the southernmost AMC lodge.

Lodging accommodations here include small and large group cabins, walk-in campsites, group campsites, and tent platforms. The facilities are open to AMC members and nonmembers. Some cabins are equipped with full-service kitchens and bathrooms; outhouses are near some smaller cabins. You can also barbecue outside the cabins and at the tentsites, and volunteers run hikes and programs throughout the year. During summer, breakfast, a trail lunch, and dinner are available for purchase in the main lodge.

MOC is both a destination unto itself and a well-positioned launch point for dozens of hikes through the area's vast wilderness (see Trips 92 to 94). Catfish Pond, a 60-acre glacial lake whose shores are blanketed with lily pads, is MOC's centerpiece. Paddling around it is the quintessence of serenity. Canoes, kayaks, and life preservers are stored at the large stone boathouse on the pond's eastern shore, and are available to rent across from the visitor center. The pond's southern shoreline is shaped like a Y, and as you paddle toward the left branch, you can see the chimney park barbecue area. Go all the way down the right branch, and you will see the interpretive center.

The overland route to the interpretive center is a flat though sometimes rocky path through thick woods dotted with tentsites. The center has informational posters on animal tracks, butterflies, snakes, birds, and more. There is also a simple display with animal riddles and fur samples for moose, deer, and beavers, and an array of books covering the natural world. It is a place for independent study to complement the range of guided programs that MOC offers. These include seasonal hikes, canoe and kayak excursions, and rock-climbing courses, as well as classes on topics such as digital photography and sketching.

MOC is about 90 minutes west of New York City. See Trip 94 for directions. The center will also assist with arranging public transportation. Reservations for overnight stays are required. For more information, visit outdoors.org/lodging/Mohican or call 908-362-5670.

Trip 95

Ages 5–8

Double Trouble State Park

Double Trouble State Park introduces visitors to the New Jersey Pine Barrens and the region's ecological history.

Address: 581 Pinewald Keswick Road, Bayville, NJ
Hours: 8 A.M. to dusk daily
Fee: Free
Contact: state.nj.us/dep/parksandforests/parks/double.html; 732-341-6662
Bathrooms: Interpretive center
Water/Snacks: None
Map: USGS Brookville, Forked River, Keswick Grove, and Toms River
Directions by Car: Take I-95 South to Exit 11 onto US 9. Merge onto the Garden State Parkway and drive for about 50.0 miles, then take exit 77. Turn left off the ramp and drive 0.5 mile south on Double Trouble Road to a traffic signal. The park entrance and parking lot are straight ahead across Pinewald Keswick Road. *GPS coordinates:* 39° 53.879' N, 74° 13.263' W.

Double Trouble State Park, situated within the eastern edge of the Pine Barrens, is part of a historic district encompassing more than 200 acres. Double Trouble Village dates to the 1860s, when it was developed as a company town for seasonal workers helping with the cranberry harvest. The town is named for this company, though the origin of the company name itself is up for debate. The town's preserved buildings—dormitories, a one-room school, a saw mill, and a general store among them—are just beyond the entrance to the park. Guided tours of Double Trouble Village can be arranged ahead of time.

The area's natural environment—a cedar-pine forest with a rapidly flowing stream—made it an ideal place for the lumber industry. The cutting of the forest from the eigtheenth to the twentieth centuries opened up swampland, creating a bog that proved perfect for growing cranberries. Double Trouble Village was purchased by the state of New Jersey in 1964 to protect the Cedar Creek watershed.

A 1.5-mile nature trail loop punctuated with informational signs begins behind the packing house, taking walkers around bogs. Lower Hooper Bog is the farthest afield, and beyond that lies another 2.25-mile hike that takes visitors

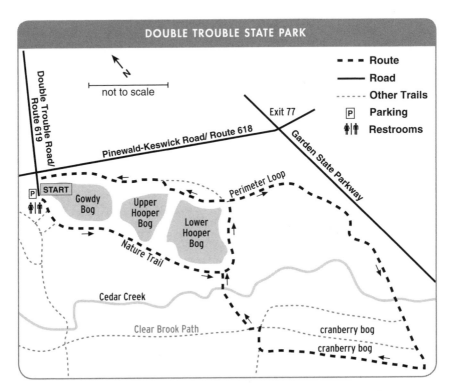

DOUBLE TROUBLE STATE PARK

Legend:
- – – – Route
- ——— Road
- ········· Other Trails
- P Parking
- 🚻 Restrooms

not to scale

Double Trouble Road/ Route 619

Pinewald-Keswick Road/ Route 618

Exit 77

Garden State Parkway

START

Gowdy Bog

Upper Hooper Bog

Lower Hooper Bog

Perimeter Loop

Nature Trail

Cedar Creek

Clear Brook Path

cranberry bog

cranberry bog

deeper into the pine forest, looping around two more bogs after crossing over Cedar Creek to the south. This trail eventually loops back up to Lower Hooper.

Much of Double Trouble consists of miles of unmarked sandy trails that also serve as service roads, which are very much worth exploring on follow-up trips. Young mountain bikers will enjoy the sandy roads. *Remember:* The sandy paths in the park are unsuitable for strollers. Canoes and kayaks are not available to rent on Cedar Creek, but boaters can drive through the village to a launch point. Tubing, rafting, and swimming are prohibited. No picnic tables are in the park, but there are benches, and several other nice spots for picnicking.

PLAN B: Island Beach State Park (Trip 96) and Allaire State Park (Trip 97) are both relatively close by. The latter offers forested trails, and the former provides scenic walks along the coast.

WHERE TO EAT NEARBY: Remember to pack a picnic, as no shops or restaurants are nearby.

Trip 96

All Ages

Island Beach State Park

Explore short, easy trails through well-preserved coastal habitats that attract a wide array of birds year round.

Address: Central Avenue, Berkeley, NJ
Hours: 8 A.M. to dusk daily; 7 A.M. to dusk during summer
Fee: From Memorial Day through Labor Day, $6 per vehicle on weekdays and $10 per vehicle on weekends. Free all other times.
Contact: nj.gov/dep/parksandforests/parks/island.html#recarea; 732-793-0506
Bathrooms: Park entrance; swimming areas 1 and 2; Fisherman's Walkway; Forked River Interpretive Center; near mobile sportfishing vehicle access
Water/Snacks: Water fountains at the restrooms
Map: USGS Barnegat Light and Seaside Park
Directions by Car: Take I-95 South to Exit 11 onto US 9. Merge onto the Garden State Parkway and drive for about 50.0 miles, then take exit 82. Merge onto NJ 37 East and drive for 6.8 miles, then merge onto NJ 35 South. Turn right onto Northwest Central Ave and follow it for about 6.0 miles to the park entrance. *GPS coordinates:* 39° 54.265′ N, 74° 4.899′ W.

The Jersey Shore has much to offer, and a lot of it is tranquil, family friendly, and, in parts, untouched since Henry Hudson came ashore from his ship the *Half Moon* in 1609. Located just south of Seaside Heights, Island Beach State Park is one of the last barrier island ecosystems remaining in New Jersey. This thin strip of white sand buffers Barnegat Bay from the Atlantic Ocean. Osprey, falcons, long-legged wading birds, migrating songbirds, and the ubiquitous seagull all thrive in well-preserved primary dunes, freshwater wetlands, tidal marshes, and maritime forests.

In summer, visiting the beach is a must. There is guarded swimming only on the ocean side. Year round, eight short trails take you through the various habitats, and many have interpretative signs. You can bike along the paved roadway, or park in any of the seven designated lots that are evenly spaced along the island.

Johnny Allen's cove, located 7.1 miles from the main entrance, has both ocean and bay trails. The oceanside trail takes you through a break in the primary dunes and onto a nonswimming beach. Across the road, the bayside trail goes through freshwater wetlands that lead to the bay. The nearby Forked

Combine nature walks in a barrier island ecosystem with a day at the beach at Island Beach State Park.

River Interpretive Center, marked by giant whale bones at its parking lot, is packed with information on local flora, fauna, birds, and marine life.

A walk along A13 Trail, 6.3 miles from the main entrance on the ocean side, will lead you on a boardwalk through a small freshwater wetland cranberry bog, and onto a stunning landscape of dunes. *Remember:* Be on the lookout for poison ivy in vine and shrub form. Also, always check for ticks after walking the trails.

PLAN B: Head to Point Pleasant Beach, 21 miles north on NJ 35, to enjoy a mile-long family-friendly boardwalk that is lovely to walk year round.

WHERE TO EAT NEARBY: Shops and restaurants are along NJ 35.

Trip 97

Allaire State Park

Renowned for its preserved nineteenth-century village, Allaire State Park is also a terrific place to hike, paddle, camp, and fish.

Address: 4265 Atlantic Avenue, Wall Township, NJ
Hours: 8 A.M. to 4:30 P.M. daily
Fee: $5 per vehicle on weekends from Memorial Day through Labor Day
Contact: state.nj.us/dep/parksandforests/parks/allaire.html; 732-938-2371
Bathrooms: Historical village; campsite
Water/Snacks: Concession stands near the historical village
Map: USGS Asbury Park and Farmingdale; state.nj.us/dep/parksandforests/
  parks/maps/Allairehighmap.PDF
Directions by Car: Take I-95 South to Exit 11 onto US 9. Merge onto the Garden
  State Parkway and drive for about 30.0 miles. Take Exit 98 onto NJ 34 South.
  After 0.8 mile, turn right onto Allenwood Road, then turn right onto Atlantic
  Avenue. Allaire State Park is on the left. *GPS coordinates:* 40° 9.447′ N,
  74° 7.181′ W.

At Allaire State Park, families can camp, explore easy trails within the Manasquan River flood plain, and visit the Historic Village at Allaire, a well-preserved nineteenth-century neighborhood. The park is part of the 300-mile New Jersey Coastal Heritage Trail Route, which seeks to preserve a diverse range of historical and natural sites.

Hiking, mountain biking, and horseback riding trails wind throughout the more than 3,000 acres. River Trail, accessible from the northeast corner of the Allaire Village parking lot, is a comfortable hike for families, with some hills and a section that follows along the river's edge. Manasquan River is stocked annually with trout, increasing the likelihood of success for young anglers (New Jersey fishing license required). Other well-maintained paths around the village take day-hikers short or longer distances into the woods. At 16.5 miles, the orange trail is the longest and most rigorous. The yellow, red, and green trails are easy walks, at 0.5, 1.5, and 4.5 miles respectively.

The campsite has 45 tent and trailer sites, four yurts, fire rings, restrooms with showers, and many picnic tables. It is open all year. A playground for all park visitors is near the campground and the main parking lot. The park does

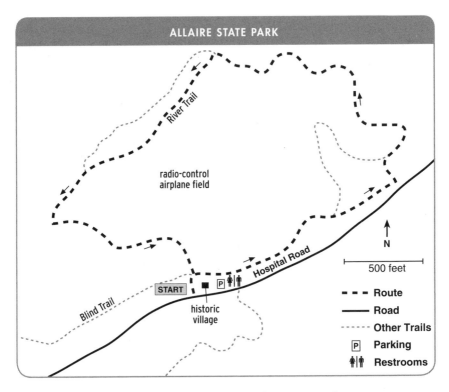

ALLAIRE STATE PARK

River Trail

radio-control
airplane field

Blind Trail

START

historic
village

Hospital Road

N

500 feet

- - - Route
—— Road
······ Other Trails
P Parking
Restrooms

not rent canoes, but rentals are available nearby. Contact the visitor center or visit funnj.com/water/fboat/index.htm for possibilities.

The Historic Village at Allaire includes well-preserved homes and trade shops, such as a bakery and an ironworks that still periodically operate, and offers lessons in activities such as gardening and sewing. Check the website or call in advance for hours and programming (allairevillage.org; 732-919-3500).

To the west of the village, families can visit the Pine Creek Railroad to board eighteenth-century train cars that make a slow, half-mile journey around farmland. Even for city kids who are accustomed to subways and interstate railways, this little train is a treat. *Remember:* As this area is a low-lying river basin, trails can be muddy and slippery for a few days after a rainfall. Younger children may want to use a walking stick for balance.

PLAN B: Double Trouble State Park (Trip 95) is another preserved village with easy hikes through cranberry bogs, though without programming, and Island Beach State Park (Trip 96) is a year-round hiking and fishing destination, as well as a great beach in summer.

WHERE TO EAT NEARBY: Atlantic Avenue is fairly rural, so it is best to bring your own food and beverages.

Trip 98

All Ages

Delaware and Raritan Canal State Park

The scenic Delaware and Raritan Canal is a perfect spot for strollers and for the youngest hikers.

Address: Bridge Street, Lambertville, NJ
Hours: Sunrise to sunset daily
Fee: Free
Contact: nj.gov/dep/parksandforests/parks/drcanal.html
Bathrooms: None
Water/Snacks: None
Map: USGS Lambertville and Stockton; nj.gov/dep/parksandforests/parks/ images/d-r_canal_map-4-11-08.pdf; newhopepa.com/Directions/maps_3z_ lg.gif
Directions by Car: Take I-95 South to Exit 14 onto I-78 West. Take Exit 29 to US 202 South. Merge onto NJ 179 South to Lambertville. Free public parking is available in Lambertville at the end of Mount Hope Street, next to the playground. *GPS coordinates: 40° 21.742′ N, 74° 56.656′ W.*

The Delaware and Raritan Canal State Park comprises one half of a network of trails stretching 60 miles north and south on the Pennsylvania and New Jersey coasts of the Delaware River. Five connecting bridges along the trail allow you to go back and forth across the river for pristine views in all directions. In its heyday during the nineteenth century, the canal was a site of bustling industry. Some evidence of the canal's former life, such as locks, remains today. The towns at the 15-mile point on each side of the canal—Lambertville (in New Jersey) and New Hope (in Pennsylvania)—have retained much of their Victorian charm. They are quiet, attractive spots to begin and end your journey with a picnic or a restaurant meal.

Pick up the trail in Lambertville and follow it either north or south. If you feel up to a long trek or are on bicycles, you should consider heading 7.0 miles south to Washington Crossing State Park (Trip 99). At this point you can take the bridge across the river to Washington Crossing Historic Park on the Pennsylvania side, and head back north (passing Bowman's Hill Tower and Wildflower Preserve) to cross back into Lambertville at New Hope. Alterna-

Tubing down the Delaware River is a wonderful treat on a hot summer day.

tively, you can head 4.0 miles north to Stockton and take the bridge across the river to the town of Centre Bridge, and return south on the Pennsylvania side. *Remember:* Rafting trips down the river are available on both the Pennsylvania and New Jersey sides of the river. You can also rent boats for paddling.

PLAN B: Tubing, rafting, and paddling are good outdoor activities you could substitute for a hike, or you could visit Grounds For Sculpture (Trip 100), a wonderful, kid-friendly outdoor sculpture garden nearby.

WHERE TO EAT NEARBY: Both Lambertville and New Hope have many restaurants and shops.

Trip 99

All Ages $ 🐕 🚶 🚴 ⛺

Washington Crossing State Park

From fishing to snowshoeing to camping, the activities at Washington Crossing State Park make it a great year-round destination.

Address: 355 Washington Crossing-Pennington Road, Titusville, NJ
Hours: 8 A.M. to 6 P.M. daily
Fee: $5 per vehicle, Memorial Day to Labor Day
Contact: state.nj.us/dep/parksandforests/parks/washcros.html; 609-737-0623;
　　Nature Center, 609-737-0609
Bathrooms: Visitor Center Museum; Nature Center; various other locations
　　throughout park
Water/Snacks: Water fountain in Visitor Center Museum
Map: USGS Pennington
Directions by Car: Take I-95 South to Exit 9 and merge onto US 1 South and
　　follow it for 20.0 miles. Merge onto I-95 South, then take the exit to merge
　　onto Scotch Road. Turn left onto Washington Crossing-Pennington Road and
　　follow the signs to the park. Free public parking is available. *GPS coordinates:*
　　40° 18.550′ N, 74° 50.783′ W.

As school-age children know, on December 25, 1776—when morale was low and the Continental Army was badly in need of a boost—George Washington led his troops across the Delaware River on a successful surprise attack on Hessian soldiers who had been hired by Great Britain to help quash the revolt in its colonies. The rest, as they say, is history. Today, Washington Crossing State Park is a 3,100-acre destination popular for hiking, biking, horseback riding, camping, fishing, snowshoeing and cross-country skiing, and picnicking.

The Visitor Center Museum, where you can find a map of the park, is a good place to begin your visit. After you leave the visitor center, head southwest down the shady paved path toward the Delaware River. You can pick up either Red Trail or Green Trail off this path, or follow the Pedestrian Overpass across Daniel Bray Highway and cross the Delaware on the loop trail bridge to visit Washington Crossing Historic Park on the Pennsylvania side. Fishing is also allowed in the Delaware River, so bring your pole if you'd like to catch bass, shad, catfish, panfish, and trout (New Jersey fishing license required).

Another option is to begin your visit at the Nature Center and Amateur Astronomers of Princeton Observatory toward the northern edge of the park.

Tree-lined, paved paths along the Delaware River make for great bike rides.

In addition to 13 miles of hiking trails, this area contains biking trails (5 miles) and horseback riding trails (2 miles), as well as a camping area. The hiking trails are popular during winter for snowshoeing and cross-country skiing. *Remember:* The Nature Center offers a year-round program of nature education events. For further information, call the number listed above.

PLAN B: The park is connected to the Delaware and Raritan Canal (Trip 98).

WHERE TO EAT NEARBY: Numerous shops and restaurants are in nearby Lambertville.

Trip 100

Ages 5–8

Grounds For Sculpture

This outdoor museum invites kids to explore artwork and nature at the same time.

Address: 126 Sculptors Way, Hamilton, NJ

Hours: 10 A.M. to 6 P.M. Tuesday through Sunday

Fee: Adults, $12; children ages 6 to 17, $5; children under age 5, free

Contact: groundsforsculpture.org; 609-586-0616

Bathrooms: Museum Building; Domestic Arts Building; Motor Exhibits Building; Seward Johnson Center for the Arts; Gazebo

Water/Snacks: Water fountains at the restrooms; snacks and sandwiches at the Gazebo Café and the Peacock Café; fine dining at Rat's Restaurant

Map: USGS Trenton East; groundsforsculpture.org/map.htm

Directions by Car: Take I-95 South to Exit 9 onto NJ 18 North, then merge onto US 1 South. Take the ramp onto I-295 South to Exit 63 and merge onto Nottingham Way. Drive for 1.3 miles, then turn sharply right onto Scultptors Way. *GPS coordinates:* 40° 14.027′ N, 74° 43.288′ W.

Directions by New Jersey Transit: Take New Jersey Transit to the Hamilton stop. Exit the parking lot heading southwest (toward the right with the platform behind you). Cross Sloan Avenue and go right on Klockner Road. At East State Street Extension, turn right, and take the second left onto Sculptors Way. Turn left, and left again into the main entrance. The walk is 1.7 miles, but the streets are not busy. Alternatively, you can take a taxi.

"Please touch" is not a sign that often accompanies statues, but many of the 258 works at the Grounds For Sculpture (GFS) have that invitation, making this an excellent place for children to explore art and the outdoors. This 42-acre public sculpture park, located on the former New Jersey State Fairgrounds, is equal parts arboretum and outdoor art exhibit. Prides of peacocks wander freely about, adding an element of intrigue and grandeur to the place.

GFS is best approached with no specific route or goal in mind. Indeed, in the short film that you can watch in the Museum Building before entering the grounds, the curators encourage adults and children to do just that: go where a sculpture or garden draws you. It is a great place to let kids take the lead.

From the Museum Building parking lot, head toward the piece that inspires the most intrigue—the willowy metal butterfly to your left, for example, or the steel and granite cuckoo's nest to your right. Circle around to the back of

*At Grounds For Sculpture, children can explore art
in a beautifully landscaped arboretum.*

the building. There are clear paths to follow, but you can also walk across well-kept lawns to get up close and personal with King Lear or a granite interpretation of the Garden State. Most of this terrain is good for strollers. Kids can also stretch out on the grass near the sculpture of a young girl who is lying down writing in a notebook, or step into a lifesize re-creation of Claude Monet's painting *Terrace at Sainte-Adresse*. From any one cluster of artworks, you will catch a glimpse of something else that might lure your group into a hedgerow tunnel, through a pine forest, or to the banks of a pond that has a thick fringe of ornamental grasses.

There is also a self-guided tree tour of the more than 100 species that now cover the plot. When landscape construction began in 1989, there were only 15 decrepit maple trees on the site. Now there are more than 2,000 trees, along with carefully cultivated botanical gardens. Several buildings from the fair era, which lasted from the 1920s to the 1970s, have been turned into a greenhouse, water garden, and the Museum Building visitor center. *Remember:* Running through the grounds and climbing on the sculptures are not allowed.

PLAN B: If you are driving, Delaware and Raritan Canal State Park (Trip 98) and Washington Crossing State Park (Trip 99) are nearby alternatives for hikes, history, and riverfront activity.

WHERE TO EAT NEARBY: Restaurants and shops are along Nottingham Way, which is south of GFS. Turn left on Sculptors Way, and then right or left on Nottingham Way.

ADDITIONAL RESOURCES

City, State, and National Agencies

New York City Department of Parks and Recreation: nycgovparks.org or call 311

New York State Office of Parks, Recreation and Historic Preservation: nysparks.state. ny.us; 518-474-0456

New York State Department of Environmental Preservation: dec.ny.gov, 518-402-8044

New Jersey Division of Environmental Protection, Division of Parks and Forestry: state.nj.us/dep/parksandforests; 866-DEP-KNOW

Gateway National Recreation Area: nps.gov/gate; 718-338-3799 for Jamaica Bay or 718-354-4500 for Staten Island

National Park Service: nps.gov

Delaware Water Gap National Recreation Area: nps.gov/dewa; 570-828-2253 or 908-496-4458

Recommended Reading

Case, Daniel. *AMC's Best Day Hikes Near New York City*. Boston: Appalachian Mountain Club Books, 2010.

Day, Leslie. *Field Guide to the Natural World of New York City*. Baltimore, MD: Johns Hopkins University Press, 2007.

Kick, Peter W. *AMC's Best Day Hikes in the Catskills & Hudson Valley, 2nd edition*. Boston: Appalachian Mountain Club Books, 2011.

Kirkland, Jane. *Take a Tree Walk: Your Adventure Guide to Exploring, Identifying, and Understanding Trees in Any Season*. Lionville, PA: Stillwater Publishing, 2006.

Kroodsma, Donald. *The Backyard Birdsong Guide: A Guide to Listening*. San Francisco: Chronicle Books, 2008.

Louv, Richard. *Last Child in the Woods: Saving Our Children from Nature-Deficit Disorder*. Chapel Hill, NC: Algonquin Books of Chapel Hill, 2008.

McCully, Betsy. *City at the Water's Edge: A Natural History of New York*. Piscataway, NJ: Rutgers University Press, 2007.

Sanderson, Eric W. *Mannahatta: A Natural History of New York City*. New York: Harry N. Abrams, Inc., 2005.

Recommended Reading for Kids

Hansen, Judith. *Seashells in My Pocket: AMC's Family Guide to Exploring the Coast from Maine to Florida*. Boston: Appalachian Mountain Club Books, 2008.

Lumry, Amanda. *Adventures of Riley* (series). New York: Scholastic Press.

Morrison, Gordon. *Nature in the Neighborhood*. New York: Houghton Mifflin, 2004.

O'Connor, Jane. *Fancy Nancy Explorer Extraordinaire*. New York: Harper Collins Children's Books, 2009.

OUTDOOR EVENTS
THROUGHOUT THE YEAR

BIKE NEW YORK
Each May, the TD Bank Five Boro Bike Tour (a.k.a. Bike New York) gives some 32,000 cyclists (and young enthusiasts in bike carts or safety seats attached to an adult's bike) access to 42 miles of car-free roadways in the five boroughs. For more information, visit bikenewyork.org.

SUMMER STREETS
Since 2008, sections of the city have been closed to vehicular traffic (some of them permanently, see page 21) so thousands of pedestrians, joggers, cyclists, and skateboarders can enjoy the roads. Food, beverage, and merchandise vendors abound. To find out where Summer Streets is happening, visit nyc.gov/html/dot/summerstreets.

SHAKESPEARE IN THE PARK
Camping out for tickets is half the fun; free Shakespeare performances in Delacorte Theatre in Central Park (Central) is the other half. Launched in 1954, Shakespeare in the Park is one of the city's most beloved summertime events, and as you take turns waiting for tickets, there is no shortage of great places to go in Central Park (see Trips 1–5).

FEAST OF ST. FRANCIS
You can always go to the zoo or circus to see elephants, camels, snakes, goats, and more, but each October you can see them up close, uncaged, and walking down Amsterdam Avenue for the annual Blessing of the Animals at the Cathedral Church of Saint John the Divine in Morningside Heights. This storied event takes place inside the world's largest Gothic cathedral, and afterward there is a petting zoo and open-air festival in the churchyard. For more information, visit stjohndivine.org/SaintFrancis.html.

EVENTS THROUGHOUT THE YEAR
From pumpkin picking and Easter egg hunts to guided nature walks and arts-and-crafts events, the city's Department of Parks and Recreation maintains a robust calendar of activities for the five boroughs. For more information, visit nycgovparks.org/events/all or nycgovparks.org/highlights/festivals.

OTHER WAYS
TO SEE THE CITY

There are so many nooks and crannies to explore in New York City that sometimes you overlook the obvious excursions and experiences. To supplement your walking, hiking, biking, and paddling trips, enjoy some of the other ways to see the city.

BY BUS
Whether you live in New York or are visiting, a guided tour on an iconic double-decker bus is a great way to get the lay of the land, and learn a great deal along the way. During the day, you can hop on and off the bus at designated stops so you can explore a park, neighborhood, or historical building.

For more information, visit newyorksightseeing.com.

BY BOAT
Seeing the city from its rivers and harbor broadens your understanding of the geographic phenomenon that is New York City. For a 360-degree perspective, take a Circle Line Sightseeing Cruise around Manhattan and alongside Brooklyn, Queens, and the Bronx. The three-hour, full-island cruise is packed with well-delivered information.

For more information, visit circleline42.com/new-york-cruises.

FROM HIGH UP
After you've trekked through parks, paddled along shorelines, and circumnavigated the city on bike, take an elevator to the top of the Empire State Building or Rockefeller Center to get a full panorama of where you've been, what you've accomplished—and where you want to go next.

For more information on the Empire State Building, visit esbnyc.com/tourism. For more information on Rockefeller Center, visit topoftherocknyc.com.

FOLLOWING ON FOOT
If you want to explore a new park or neighborhood but don't know where to begin—or if you just had a great visit to a far-flung park and want to know more about it—let a guided tour lead you along. The Department of Parks and Recreation offers free walking tours in the five boroughs throughout the year.

For more information, visit nycgovparks.org/events/2011/10/25/free-guided-walking-tour.

BY CAR

If you have your heart set on exploring a particular park in a faraway borough but the subway you need is rerouted for maintenance, hop in a by-the-hour car and get yourself there. Cars can be picked up and dropped off at parking garages and rental agencies across the city, and they include gas and an EZPass for tolls.

INDEX

ABOUT THE AUTHORS

Cheryl and William de Jong-Lambert live with son, Riley, and daughter, Halina, in Morningside Heights in New York City. Cheryl is a writer at the Mount Sinai Medical Center and a longtime freelance journalist. William is an associate professor of history at Bronx Community College at the City University of New York, and affiliate faculty at the Harriman Institute at Columbia University. They were both Peace Corps volunteers in the 1990s.

APPALACHIAN MOUNTAIN CLUB

Founded in 1876, AMC is the nation's oldest outdoor recreation and conservation organization. AMC promotes the protection, enjoyment, and understanding of the mountains, forests, waters, and trails of the Northeast outdoors.

People

We are more than 100,000 members, advocates, and supporters, including 12 local chapters, more than 16,000 volunteers, and over 450 full-time and seasonal staff. Our chapters reach from Maine to Washington, D.C.

Outdoor Adventure and Fun

We offer more than 8,000 trips each year, from local chapter activities to adventure travel worldwide, for every ability level and outdoor interest—from hiking and climbing to paddling, snowshoeing, and skiing.

Great Places to Stay

We host more than 150,000 guests each year at our AMC lodges, huts, camps, shelters, and campgrounds. Each AMC destination is a model for environmental education and steward-ship.

Opportunities for Learning

We teach people skills to safely enjoy the outdoors and to care for the natu-ral world around us through programs for children, teens, and adults, as well as outdoor leadership training.

Caring for Trails

We maintain more than 1,500 miles of trails throughout the Northeast, including nearly 350 miles of the Appalachian Trail in five states.

Protecting Wild Places

We advocate for land and riverway conservation, monitor air quality, research climate change, and work to protect alpine and forest ecosystems throughout the Northern Forest and Mid-Atlantic Highlands regions.

Engaging the Public

We seek to educate and inform our own members and an additional 2 million people annually through the media, AMC Books, our website, our White Mountain visitor centers, and AMC destinations.

Join Us!

Members meet other like-minded people and support our mission while enjoying great AMC programs, our award-winning *AMC Outdoors* magazine, and special discounts. Visit outdoors.org or call 800-372-1758 for more information.

APPALACHIAN MOUNTAIN CLUB
Recreation • Education • Conservation
outdoors.org

AMC IN NEW YORK, NEW JERSEY, AND CONNECTICUT

AMC's New York–North Jersey Chapter offers more than 2,000 trips per year, ranging from canoeing and kayaking to sailing, hiking, backpacking, and social events. The chapter is also active in trail work and conservation projects and maintains a cabin at Fire Island. AMC's Mohawk Hudson Chapter serves residents of Albany, Columbia, Fulton, Greene, Montgomery, Rensselaer, Saratoga, Schenectady, Schoharie, Warren, and Washington counties. The chapter offers a variety of outdoor activities for all levels of ability. The Connecticut Chapter has 2,000 members, offers hiking, biking, paddling, ice climbing, and mountaineering trips, and is active in trail maintenance, including on sections of the Appalachian Trail.

To view a list of AMC activities in New York, New Jersey, Connecticut, and other parts of the Northeast, visit activities.outdoors.org.

AMC BOOK UPDATES

AMC Books strives to keep our guidebooks as up-to-date as possible to help you plan safe and enjoyable adventures. If after publishing a book we learn that trails have been relocated or route or contact information has changed, we will post the updated information online. Before you hit the trail, check for updates at outdoors.org/bookupdates.

While hiking, biking, or paddling, if you notice discrepancies with the trail description or map, or if you find any other errors in the book, please let us know by submitting them to amcbookupdates@outdoors.org or in writing to Books Editor, c/o AMC, 5 Joy Street, Boston, MA 02108. We will verify all submissions and post key updates each month.

AMC Books is dedicated to being a recognized leader in outdoor publishing. Thank you for your participation.

AMC Kids outdoors

This **free online community** offers parents, educators, and leaders of youth groups advice on getting kids outside in and around New York City, including:

- "How to" advice from experts
- Trip ideas from the Appalachian Mountain Club and the community
- Upcoming activities, deals, and discounts
- Discussions on gear, outdoor tips, and more

Join the discussion!
outdoors.org/nyckids

NOV 2012

AMC Books

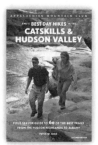

AMC's Best Day Hikes in the Catskills & Hudson Valley, 2nd edition

Peter W. Kick

With more than 600 miles of trails within just a few hours of New York City, the Catskills and Hudson Valley are a hiker's paradise, boasting varied and scenic terrain from Westchester County to Albany. The fully updated guide leads hikers of all ability levels along 60 of the region's most spectacular trails.

$18.95 • 978-1-934028-45-2

Quiet Water New York
2nd edition

John Hayes and Alex Wilson

From clear-flowing waterways to picturesque ponds, the trips in this guide allow paddlers to explore the great variety of water excursions New York has to offer. With 90 spectacular destinations to choose from, experts and beginners alike will enjoy this guide.

$19.95 • 978-1-929173-73-0

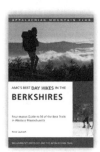

AMC's Best Day Hikes in the Berkshires

René Laubach

Discover 50 of the most impressive trails in the Berkshires, a region rich with waterfalls and mountains, serene ponds, and rocky cliffs. Each trip description includes a detailed map, trip time, distance, and difficulty rating.

$18.95 • 978-1-934028-21-6

Catskill Mountain Guide
2nd edition

Peter W. Kick

A must-have for every Catskills hiker, this revised and updated guide offers hikers comprehensive coverage of more than 300 miles of trails in the Catskill Mountains. Inside you'll find detailed descriptions of trails to suit every ability level — from an easy walk to Kaaterskill Falls to strenuous climbs in the Indian Head Wilderness Area, including Devil's Path.

$23.95 • 978-1-934028-19-3